Commonsense Vegetable Gardening for the South

William D. Adams

and

Thomas LeRoy

Photography by William D. Adams

TAYLOR PUBLISHING COMPANY
DALLAS, TEXAS

Book design and illustrations by **Deborah Jackson-Jones.**

Copyright © 1995 by William D. Adams and Thomas LeRoy.

Photographs © 1995 by William D. Adams.

Published by Taylor Publishing Company
1550 West Mockingbird Lane
Dallas, Texas 75235

Library of Congress Cataloging-in-Publication Data

Adams, William D.
   Commonsense vegetable gardening for the South / William D.
Adams & Thomas LeRoy : photography by William D. Adams.
      p.   cm.
   Includes index.
   ISBN 0-87833-876-4
   1. Vegetable gardening—Southern States.   2. Vegetables—
Varieties—Southern States.   I. LeRoy, Thomas R.   II. Title.
SB321.5.A29   1995
635'.0975—dc20   94–25304
                                                        CIP

Printed in the United States of America
10 9 8 7 6 5 4 3 2 1

I'd like to dedicate this book to my assistant, typist, and wife, Sandy, for all she's done to support me all along the way as the book was being written. The support of my family, daughters, Christie and Niki, son-in-law, Brent, and new grandson, Tyler, are also greatly appreciated.
—*Thomas R. LeRoy*

I would like to dedicate this book to my grandmother for giving me a chance to experience the taste of fresh garden peas. I appreciated her patience—the times we spent looking through seed catalogs, the garden we planted, and our last summer together. I would also like to dedicate this book to my mother for her encouragement and for giving me the freedom to pursue a career of my choice.
—*William D. Adams*

CONTENTS

Acknowledgments

First of all, we owe a big thanks to our wives—Debbi Adams and Sandy LeRoy. Without their understanding and help, this book wouldn't have been possible. Stephanie Gebhardt, our faithful associate, has been very supportive, too.

Tom Robb, Lois Sutton, David Parish, Kelly Shirley, John Twining, Jimmy Heeter, Roy Wood, Bob Frederick, Clyde Cannon and other Master Gardener volunteers helped us in many ways, from growing the vegetables we've written about to reading sections of the manuscript. Charlie Appleman and Dr. Dean McCraw also reviewed the manuscript.

George and Mary Stewart helped by growing some of the best gardens ever known in the South and sharing their experiences with us. They not only tested new varieties in result-demonstration programs, they have lectured extensively, sharing their experiences with the gardening public. Dr. Bob Randall and George McAfee conducted numerous variety trials through an extensive community garden system and they've been generous in sharing their results.

And finally, Dr. Sam Cotner, Dr. Bastian Drees, Dr. Jerral Johnson, and Frank Daniello, all extension specialists, have been most generous with their advice.

INTRODUCTION

Does the gardening world really need another vegetable book? We think so, if it's written especially for the Southern gardener and is a working manual that's handy and full of easy-to-find information that you can take out to the garden. For instance . . .

- How many times have you struggled to convert tons per acre to pounds per 100 square feet or pounds per 100 gallons to tablespoons per gallon? These conversions and many others are listed on pages 231–232.

- Topics that are universal, such as soil preparation, are discussed in the beginning of the book, so you don't have to sort through a lot of other information to get started. The vegetables' special requirements are covered in straightforward sections about each type of plant.

- Special gardening techniques and time-saving tips are featured throughout the book.

- If you come across a term you don't know, just refer to the glossary (page 264).

- The section on garden tools explains why it's wise to rent a tiller for a while before you spend $2,000 on the top-of-the-line super-duper, rear-tined tiller.

- If you've always wanted to grow your own tomato transplants, you'll discover how to get started in the chapter on starting with seed.

- Irritated by weeds, bugs, and fruit rot? We cover the basics of pest control and show you how to tell the good guys from the bad guys.

- Not being able to find a source for a vegetable that sounds interesting can be extremely frustrating. We've tried to solve this problem for you as best we can. Almost every variety mentioned in this book is referenced to a seed source by a number. The numbers in parentheses after variety listings indicates the catalog that stocks the variety; **WA** means that the variety is widely available. (See the Appendices for the list of seed catalogs.) This list is meant to be a helpful guide, not an endorsement of these seed sources. Be aware that sometimes a variety is available in a catalog one year and gone the next. Perhaps the seed wasn't available from growers or maybe the seed company got negative feedback from customers and the variety was dropped from their offerings. Some varieties are marketed primarily to commercial growers, and the big seed companies don't make small packets available for the backyard gardener. If we don't list a seed source for a variety, it's usually for this reason—either the variety is too new or is only sold to commercial growers and no dependable source exists. As new varieties become popular, they do become available for home gardeners. Finding new varieties can be difficult, but don't give up! There are always good substitutes and if you just must have a particular variety, check with your local county extension agent. Chances are he or she can help you find the seed you want.

Gardening should be enjoyable and good therapy. We believe this book will solve many of the problems that Southern gardeners come across and, consequently, hope it will enhance your gardening experience.

William D. Adams and Thomas LeRoy

Getting Started

PLANNING THE HOME GARDEN

Vegetable gardening is an exciting and enjoyable hobby that provides the home gardener with a chance to get outdoors, to learn about and enjoy nature, and produce a harvest of delicious homegrown vegetables.

Vegetable gardening is one of the few things that many of us (especially those of us who have spent our lives working behind a desk) will do in which we can actually see the result of labors materialize into something of real value. The enjoyment gained is difficult to understand until you experience it for yourself.

Planning next season's garden can be almost as much fun as growing or harvesting this season's crops. Planning your garden includes selecting a location, determining which crops to plant, poring through seed catalogs to pick out the newest and best varieties to grow, laying out the beds, and much more.

Spend some time planning your garden; it will help ensure a successful season and save you lots of time.

Selecting Your Garden Site

There are a number of things to consider when selecting a location for your garden. Some things you'll be able to control, others you may have to accept and work with.

Light is of primary concern. Select a location that receives a minimum of 6 hours of direct sunlight. With very few exceptions, vegetables perform best where they receive full sun all day long. There are a few vegetables that tolerate a little shade, but don't fool yourself into thinking they grow better or produce more under shaded conditions.

When possible, plant your garden where it will receive southern or southeastern exposure. It will warm up faster in the spring and receive the maximum amount of sunlight throughout the growing season.

Vegetables That Tolerate Some Shade					
Asparagus	•	Kale	•	Spinach	
Cabbage	•	Lettuce	•	Swiss chard	
Celery	•	Parsley	•	Turnips	
Carrots	•	Radishes			

Trees are one of the vegetable garden's enemies. Trees not only shade the plants, but their roots invade the beds, competing for valuable nutrients and moisture. The roots can overtake a garden soil in one season, making tilling and soil-improvement work difficult. We're not suggesting you cut down those valuable landscape trees, but try to plant as far away from the trees as possible.

One of the problems gardeners in the South must contend with is the change from swamplike to desertlike conditions in a matter of weeks. This phenomenon means a garden location should drain well and simultaneously be able to hold moisture well. Both of these can be accomplished by working your soil, adding the proper amendments, and raising the garden beds. (Soils and their care will be discussed later.)

Much of the South is plagued with strong seasonal winds that can damage tender plants and reduce yields. Shrubs, fences, and buildings can be used as windbreaks, but care should be taken to avoid shading. Fiber row cover offers the best answer to wind damage. Row cover also excludes insects and can provide a few degrees of frost protection.

Space and Time

When planning your garden, try to keep in mind that gardening done well requires time. Only plan and prepare enough space for the amount of time that you can devote to it. It is always easier to enlarge a garden's size (where space permits) than to reduce it once you realize it's too large to manage. Weeds are a good size indicator. If your weeds get larger than the vegetables, you've probably bitten off more than you can chew. Remember, a small, well-cared-for garden will give you more enjoyment and vegetables than a large, poorly cared-for garden.

Variety Selection

Plant breeders and seed companies have provided gardeners with a nearly endless supply of vegetable varieties to try, and each year seed catalogs are loaded with new ones. The best approach to variety selection is to rely on the experience of others. Your local county extension agent will be happy to

GUIDE TO VEGETABLE PRODUCTION

Crop	Average Yield Per 100 Feet of Row	How Much to Plant Per Person	
		Fresh	Fresh with Some Left Over for Storage
Asparagus	15 to 30 lbs.	10 to 15 plants	25 to 30 plants
Beans (Bush)	120 lbs.	15 to 20 feet	30 to 60 feet
Beans (Pole)	150 lbs.	5 to 10 feet	10 to 25 feet
Beans (Lima)	25 to 50 lbs.	5 to 10 feet	10 to 25 feet
Beets	50 to 125 lbs.	5 to 10 feet	10 to 20 feet
Broccoli	50 to 100 lbs.	3 to 5 plants	10 to 15 plants
Brussels Sprouts	25 to 75 lbs.	5 to 7 plants	10 to 20 plants
Cabbage	150 lbs.	2 to 3 plants	5 to 10 plants
Cabbage (Chinese)	80 head	3 to 5 plants	N/A
Carrots	50 to 100 lbs.	5 to 10 feet	10 to 25 feet
Cauliflower	50 to 100 lbs.	3 to 4 plants	10 to 20 plants
Celery	100 to 200 stalks	2 to 3 stalks	N/A
Chicory	50 to 75 lbs.	2 to 5 feet	5 to 10 feet
Collards	100 lbs.	5 to 10 feet	10 to 25 feet
Cucumbers	120 lbs.	1 to 2 hills	5 to 10 hills
Eggplant	100 to 200 lbs.	1 plant	2 to 4 plants
Endive	50 to 75 lbs.	3 to 5 plants	N/A
Garlic	40 to 50 lbs.	1 to 2 plants	1 to 5 feet
Kale	100 lbs.	3 to 5 plants	5 to 15 plants
Kohlrabi	75 to 100 lbs.	3 to 5 plants	5 to 15 plants
Leeks	50 to 100 lbs.	3 to 5 plants	5 to 15 plants
Lettuce (Leaf)	50 to 75 lbs.	10 feet	N/A
Lettuce (Head)	75 to 100 lbs.	10 feet	N/A
Melons (Honeydew)	75 fruit	3 to 5 hills	N/A
Muskmelons	100 fruit	3 to 5 hills	N/A
Mustard Greens	100 lbs.	5 to 10 feet	10 to 25 feet
Okra	100 to 150 lbs.	4 to 5 feet	8 to 10 feet
Onions	75 to 100 lbs.	3 to 5 feet	30 to 40 feet
Parsley	30 lbs.	1 to 3 feet	1 to 3 feet
Parsnips	50 to 100 lbs.	5 to 10 feet	10 to 20 feet
Peas (English)	20 lbs.	15 to 30 feet	50 to 100 feet
Peas (Edible Podded)	30 lbs.	15 to 30 feet	50 to 100 feet
Peas (Southern)	40 to 60 lbs.	10 to 15 feet	20 to 50 feet
Peppers	60 lbs.	1 to 2 plants	3 to 5 plants
Potatoes	100 to 200 lbs.	25 to 50 feet	N/A
Pumpkins	75 to 100 lbs.	1 to 2 hills	1 to 2 hills
Radishes	100 bunches	3 to 5 feet	N/A
Rhubarb	200 stalks	1 plant	2 to 3 plants
Rutabagas	50 to 75 lbs.	1 plant	2 to 3 plants
Spinach	40 to 50 lbs.	5 to 10 feet	10 to 15 feet
Squash (Summer)	150 to 200 lbs.	1 to 2 hills	2 to 5 hills
Squash (Winter)	100 lbs.	1 to 2 hills	2 to 3 hills
Sweet Corn	10 dozen	10 to 25 feet	30 to 50 feet
Sweet Potatoes	100 lbs.	2 to 5 plants	10 to 15 plants
Swiss Chard	50 to 75 lbs.	1 to 3 plants	5 to 10 plants
Tomatoes	100 to 200 lbs.	1 plant	3 to 10 plants
Turnips	75 to 100 lbs.	5 to 10 feet	5 to 10 feet
Watermelons	40 to 60 fruit	2 to 3 hills	N/A

VEGETABLE PLANTING GUIDE

Crop	Seeds Per Ounce	Vegetables Planted from Seed	Vegetables Planted from Transplant	Seed to Transplant	Planting to Harvest	Flowering to Harvest
Asparagus	1,200		•	1–2 years	1–2 years	N/A
Beans (Bush)	100–125	•			45–60 days	7–10 days
Beans (Pole)	100–125	•			60–70 days	7–10 days
Beans (Lima)	25–75	•			65–90 days	14–21 days
Beets	1,600	•			55–70 days	N/A
Broccoli	9,000		•	6–8 weeks	55–80 days	N/A
Brussels Sprouts	9,000		•	6–8 weeks	90–120 days	N/A
Cabbage	9,000		•	6–8 weeks	60–120 days	N/A
Cabbage (Chinese)	9,000	•	•	4–6 weeks	65–80 days	N/A
Carrots	23,000	•			50–95 days	N/A
Cauliflower	9,000		•	6–8 weeks	55–90 days	N/A
Celery	72,000		•	10–12 weeks	90–120 days	N/A
Chicory	27,000	•	•	4–6 weeks	65–90 days	N/A
Collards	9,000	•	•	4–6 weeks	65–80 days	N/A
Cucumbers	1,100	•			50–70 days	4–5, pickle 15–20, slice
Eggplant	6,500		•	6–8 weeks	50–80 days	25–40 days
Endive	27,000	•	•	6–8 weeks	85–100 days	N/A
Garlic	N/A		•	Planted from Cloves	180–220 days	N/A
Kale	9,000	•	•	4–6 weeks	45–55 days	N/A
Kohlrabi	9,000	•	•	4–6 weeks	50–80 days	N/A
Leeks	11,000	•	•	10–12 weeks	150 days	N/A
Lettuce (Leaf)	25,000	•	•	4–6 weeks	45–65 days	N/A
Lettuce (Head)	25,000	•	•	4–6 weeks	70–80 days	N/A
Melons (Honeydew)	1,300	•			90–110 days	40–50 days
Muskmelons	1,300	•			90–110 days	40–50 days
Mustard Greens	15,000	•	•	4–6 weeks	35–45 days	N/A
Okra	500	•	•	2–4 weeks	50–60 days	2–5 days
Onions	8,500		•	10–12 weeks	90–150 days	N/A
Parsley	18,500	•	•	6–8 weeks	50–80 days	N/A
Parsnips	12,000	•			90–120 days	N/A
Peas (English)	90–175	•			55–80 days	20–30 days
Peas (Edible Podded)	90–175	•			60–70 days	10–14 days
Peas (Southern)	225	•			65–85 days	25–35 days
Peppers	4,500		•	6–8 weeks	65–90 days	45–55, green 60–70, fully ripe
Potatoes	N/A		• (seed potatoes)	Plant seed pieces	90–110 days	N/A
Pumpkins	100–300	•			100–120 days	70–110
Radishes	2,500	•			20–35 days	N/A
Rhubarb	N/A		•	Divide existing plant		N/A
Rutabagas	12,000	•			90 days	N/A
Spinach	2,800	•	•	4–6 weeks	40–55 days	N/A
Squash (Summer)	120–400	•			40–50 days	3–5 days
Squash (Winter)	120–400	•			85–110 days	60–90 days
Sweet Corn	120–180	•			65–90 days	20–27 days
Sweet Potatoes	N/A		• (slips)	Plant slips	120–150 days	N/A
Swiss Chard	1,600	•	•	4–6 weeks	50–60 days	N/A
Tomatoes	7,000		•	4–6 weeks	60–90 days	45–60 days
Turnips	15,000	•			35–60 days	N/A
Watermelons	300–600	•	• (some seedless)	2 weeks	75–95 days	42–50 days

provide you with a list of varieties adapted to your area. Local gardeners are one of the best sources of information. Rely on their personal experiences. And, of course, this book will prove invaluable; we've spent considerable time compiling lists of varieties adapted to the Southern climate.

When you first get started, select a few good reliable varieties, but don't be afraid to experiment. Each season we try a few new varieties just to see how they do. Sometimes you'll find a real winner.

As you pore through an endless sea of seed catalogs, you'll notice some vegetables listed as hybrids, others as open-pollinated varieties. Generally, the hybrid seeds are more expensive, but in most cases their increased yield, vigor, and disease resistance makes the added expense well worthwhile.

Speaking of disease resistance, we're working very hard to reduce the use of pesticides in the garden. One of the best solutions to this is the use of resistant varieties. These varieties were developed to be less susceptible to a particular problem. Right now, there are many varieties that are resistant to all sorts of common disease problems. Plant breeders are trying to produce plants that are resistant to a number of insect pests. If they are successful, we may someday find ourselves growing virtually pest-free vegetable plants.

Garden Tools

Most home gardeners don't need a tiller. If you must have one, wait until July and check the classifieds. By then, some less-determined beginner will be interested in selling his for a bargain. Unless you have a large garden, the tiller you will find most useful is the mini-type. (See photo on page 28.) Several brands are available now, and though they are mostly designed for cultivation, this is one of the chores you'll put off unless you have an easy-to-use little tiller to fire up. They will do shallow tilling, but for the heavy work you will need an industrial-strength spading fork.

Gardeners with 3,000 square feet of garden or more may want to invest in a rear-tined tiller. This is a big investment—a thousand dollars or more—so you may want to rent a tiller for a few years before you take this leap. Front-tined tillers will do the job, but even when set up right, they often work the gardener almost as much as they work the soil.

Beginning gardeners can get by with a few hand tools. If you are working with the existing soil, you'll need a spading fork or shovel to turn the soil and work in organic matter and fertilizer elements. If you decide on raised beds filled with the local dirt yard's "garden soil," then you will still need a shovel and a wheelbarrow, but the spading fork won't be necessary. Instead, invest in a good set of hand tools—a trowel, weeder, hand spade, and hoe. You will also need a rake, garden hose, and sprayer. The pressurized type is the most accurate, but a hose-on sprayer is inexpensive and handy to have, too. The first set of garden tools you'll need to care for a small garden should

SPRING PLANTING TIMES

Vegetables	Two Months Before Last Freeze	One Month Before Last Freeze	LAST FREEZE DATE	One Month After Last Freeze	Two Months After Last Freeze	Three Months After Last Freeze
Beans (Bush)			━━━━	━━━━	━	
Beans (Pole)			━━━━	━━━━	━	
Beans (Lima)			━━━━	━		
Beets	━━━━	━━━━				
Broccoli		••••	•			
Brussels Sprouts	•••					
Cabbage	━━━━	━━••	•			
Cabbage (Chinese)		━━━━				
Carrots	━━━━	━━━━				
Cucumbers				━━━	━━━━	━━━
Eggplant				━━	━━━━	━━━
Endive	━━━━	━━━━				
Kale		━━━━	━			
Kohlrabi		━━━━	━			
Lettuce (Leaf)		━━━━	━ ••	••		
Lettuce (Head)		━━━━	━			
Melons (Honeydew)					━━━	━━━
Muskmelons					━━━	━━━
Mustard Greens		━━━━	━━━	━		
Okra					━━━	━━━
Onions (Plants)	••••					
Parsley		••••	•••	••		
Parsnips		━━━━	━			
Peas (English)		━━━━	━			
Peas (Edible Podded)		━━━━	━			
Peas (Southern)					━━━	━━━
Peppers					━━━	━━━
Potatoes			━			
Pumpkins					━━━	━━━
Radishes		━━━━	━━━	━━		
Spinach		━━━━	••			
Squash (Summer)			━	━━━━	━━━━	━━━
Squash (Winter)			━	━━━━	━━━━	━━━
Sweet Corn			━━━	━━━	━	
Sweet Potatoes (Slips)				••••	••	
Swiss Chard		━━━━	━			
Tomatoes			••••	••		
Turnips		━━━━	━━━	━		
Watermelons					━━━	━━━

• • • • = *Transplants only*

FALL PLANTING TIMES

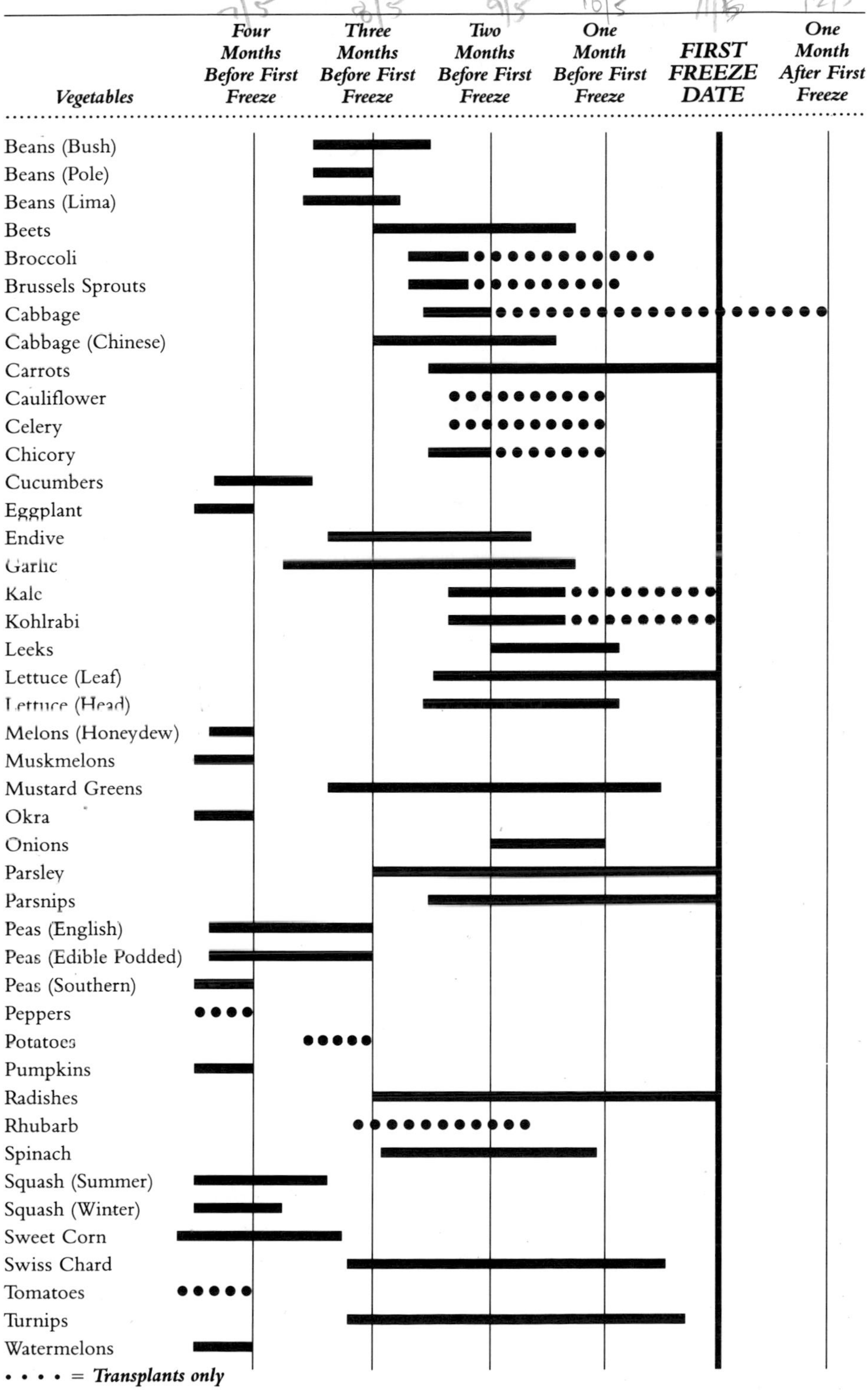
7/5 8/5 9/5 10/5 11/5 12/5
Vegetables
Four Months Before First Freeze
Three Months Before First Freeze
Two Months Before First Freeze
One Month Before First Freeze
FIRST FREEZE DATE
One Month After First Freeze
Beans (Bush)
Beans (Pole)
Beans (Lima)
Beets
Broccoli
Brussels Sprouts
Cabbage
Cabbage (Chinese)
Carrots
Cauliflower
Celery
Chicory
Cucumbers
Eggplant
Endive
Garlic
Kale
Kohlrabi
Leeks
Lettuce (Leaf)
Lettuce (Head)
Melons (Honeydew)
Muskmelons
Mustard Greens
Okra
Onions
Parsley
Parsnips
Peas (English)
Peas (Edible Podded)
Peas (Southern)
Peppers
Potatoes
Pumpkins
Radishes
Rhubarb
Spinach
Squash (Summer)
Squash (Winter)
Sweet Corn
Swiss Chard
Tomatoes
Turnips
Watermelons

• • • • = *Transplants only*

cost less than a hundred dollars. (This assumes you can borrow a shovel and wheelbarrow to move the soil.) Most gardeners don't garden to save money, though, and the hundred-dollar tomato is still pretty common. Consider it cheap therapy.

Garden Bed Systems

The way we garden has changed considerably in the past 20 years. The varieties, types of irrigation, our concern for the environment, and the cropping systems have evolved to include the best of science, tradition, and personal experience.

*T*RADITIONAL GARDEN ROWS Traditionally, all gardens were planted like small farms. More ambitious gardeners may use this technique today, as well. To do so, the garden is plowed and straight raised rows are built to plant the vegetables on. The height of these beds is dependent on the soil's type and drainage. Soils that hold moisture too long must be raised as high as possible and the plants must be planted on ridges, while beds in well-drained soils can be left almost flat. (See photo on page 28.)

Garden rows are generally spaced about 30 to 36 inches apart. This allows for easy cultivation using a push plow/cultivator or small tiller. The furrows between the rows are used as walks and make it easy for you to water. Water can be applied with flood irrigation, which allows the water to move slowly down the furrow until it saturates the soil in the beds. (See illustration on page 27.)

A traditional garden is best suited for those who want a large garden. It requires the minimum experience, is easy to work with a good tiller, and is excellent for vegetables that require lots of space, like corn, okra, watermelon, and Southern peas.

*W*IDE-BED PLANTING Like the traditional system, wide beds are usually laid out in straight rows with furrows between them. The tops of the wide beds are usually 20 to 48 inches across, upon which several rows of a given vegetable are planted.

The wide beds can be used in conjunction with the traditional system or exclusively. They increase the planting area and, thus, greatly increase the potential yield of a given area. (See illustration on page 27.)

Wide-bed planting is excellent for smaller vegetables like bush beans, broccoli, most greens, and root crops. You can use intensive-garden (I.G.) spacing with this system, which increases the production of smaller planting areas. Specific I.G. information is given in the planting charts for each individual vegetable.

RAISED-BED OR BOX GARDENING   The raised-bed or box garden has a number of advantages the more traditional systems don't have. It allows for higher yield in smaller areas because more of the garden space is used for growing plants. It also makes it easier to build a healthy soil that's high in organic matter. Where drainage is poor, this is probably the only sensible method to use.

With this technique, there is less soil compaction because walks are used instead of furrows. You'll be able to extend your garden season because raised beds warm earlier in the spring, drain well (so wet weather won't slow you down), and can be easily covered to protect plants from early fall frosts or late spring freezes.

Generally, the beds should be 3 to 4 feet wide and whatever length that fits your needs, but 25 to 30 feet long works very well. Keep in mind that a bed 4 feet by 25 feet is 100 square feet—a size that makes it easy to calculate the fertilizer applications. (See illustration on page 27.)

The beds or boxes should be spaced out so there is enough room to get in and out of the garden. Walks can range from 18 to 30 inches wide, or wider if special access is needed to accommodate a wheelchair or your favorite garden cart.

The height of the beds will vary according to soil type and your particular needs but should generally range from 6 inches to as much as 12 inches. Gardeners with special needs may want to install beds that allow for increased accessibility.

One of the greater advantages of a raised-bed system is that it can be built to cater to the needs of an individual gardener. (For additional information on modifying gardens for those with special needs, check out *The Enabling Garden* by Gene Rothert.)

A commercial soil mix can be used to fill the beds. These mixes usually consist of partially composted bark and sand. Additional washed bank sand or good sandy soil should be added at the rate of 50% soil mix to 50% sand. Don't expect great things the first season. It takes time to build a healthy soil that is balanced and productive.

For best light exposure, beds should be laid out in an east-to-west direction with the taller plants at the north end. A simple sketch of your yard can be used to lay out garden plots. When you're designing your garden, don't be afraid to mix garden beds in with your landscape; many vegetables can be very ornamental.

The beds can be built with a variety of materials: treated lumber, landscape timbers, railroad ties, brick, stone, concrete block, or any other suitable material. (See photo on page 29.)

Cropping Systems

There are a number of systems that can be used to help gardeners make the most of every inch of available garden space. This is especially important in small urban gardens, where space is always at a premium.

*I*NTERCROPPING Intercropping is used by many gardeners to maximize the use of available space. By mixing early maturing vegetables with long-season vegetables we can break up a planting, which will help reduce disease and insect problems and make efficient use of the space. For example, you can plant lettuce, spinach, onions, and radishes around tomatoes, squash, peppers, or cauliflower or plant radishes and turnips with potatoes. You'll begin harvesting the early maturing vegetables as the larger, later maturing plants grow, allowing them more space to grow and mature.

*S*UCCESSION PLANTING Succession planting is accomplished by planting a crop immediately following the removal of another. This requires a little planning on your part but means that the garden is used to its fullest. For example, potatoes planted in the spring can be followed by Southern peas and then broccoli in the fall. This will allow you to grow three or four crops per season in a single bed.

SUCCESSION PLANTING		
Early Spring	*Summer*	*Fall/Winter*
Onions	Okra	Carrots/Beets
Radishes and Turnips	Squashes	Cauliflower
Lettuces	Tomatoes	Beans
Potatoes	Cantaloupes and Watermelons	Lettuces
Broccoli	Southern Peas	Chard
Mustard and Collards	Corn	Edible Podded Peas

*S*TAGGER PLANTING Many vegetables, like tomatoes, broccoli, most greens, peppers, and okra, can be harvested over a long period of time. Because these vegetables are harvested continually for months, there is no need to stagger the planting. These vegetables should be all planted at once to take advantage of a long growing season.

Some vegetables, however, are best planted in small quantities several times over a long period of time. By staggering your planting, you can prolong the harvest over several weeks or even months. Vegetables like bush beans, corn, radishes, lettuces, carrots, and turnips all lend themselves to a stagger planting system.

Remember, one of the major reasons for vegetable gardening is to have *fresh* vegetables for the table. By staggering your planting, you can harvest your vegetables when they're at their peak and extend the harvest season.

VERTICAL GARDENING Many vegetables grow to very large sizes, which makes it difficult to grow them in a small garden. By using a trellis or cage to support the vine crops, tomatoes, and pole beans, you can grow these vegetables in small spaces.

Large-fruited vegetables like watermelons, cantaloupes, and some winter squashes can even be grown on trellises if the fruit is supported. Inventive gardeners build movable wire shelves to hold up fruit or place developing fruit in the stretchable legs of panty hose, which are tied to the trellis and support the fruit until harvest. (See photo on page 30.)

Garden Layout

Everyone has a slightly different idea about the way a garden should be laid out. Some use a garden diagram to plan next season's layout, some number beds and assign vegetables to specific beds, others go out to the garden and just start planting.

Regardless of the method, a little planning is necessary to ensure there will be room for the vegetables you want to grow, to maximize use of available space, and to plan succession and staggered plantings. It is also important to move related vegetables to new spots in the garden to avoid the buildup of diseases and insects. Some considerations are each vegetable's height, planting date, time needed to reach maturity, and space required. Taller vegetables should be planted along the northern end of the garden to avoid shading adjacent plants.

Many vegetables must be planted at a specific time to achieve a successful harvest. Keep this in mind during planning so you don't miss the planting time. Planting at the wrong time can reduce yield, decrease quality, increase disease or insect problems, or even doom the crop to failure.

Mixing quickly maturing vegetables with slower ones will help maximize space but can make soil work difficult. Try to plan on reworking each bed at least once per season, when you'll add soil amendments, clean up, mulch, and prepare for a new planting.

Always keep in mind the size of a healthy mature vegetable plant. Vegetables planted too close together become weeds, reducing yields and robbing each other of needed nutrients. Use your space wisely, but give them the room they require.

Vegetable Rotations for Gardening Success

Vegetable crop rotation is the key to long-term success in the vegetable garden. Experienced vegetable gardeners know that a proper crop-rotation program is a significant factor in maintaining a productive garden through the years. New gardeners soon learn that certain vegetables, planted year after year in the same plot, become diseased and decline in vigor.

Crop rotation is a planting system that involves the proper arrangement of vegetable plantings in sequence to assure maximum yield and quality from season to season. Some of the factors that reduce garden potential when rotation is not employed are: increased soil-borne diseases, nematodes, and soil insects; decreased organic matter; an increased chance of toxic chemical residue buildup, and an imbalance of essential mineral elements.

In a rotation system, vegetables are often arranged according to families so that individual vegetables from the same family do not follow each other in the rotation. The reason for this is that each family of vegetables has a unique effect on the factors that reduce a garden's potential. For instance, most vegetables within a given family fall prey to the same diseases and insects. Most of the vegetables planted in home gardens belong to ten distinct families. It is important to know that the **pea** or **legume family** includes peas and beans of all kinds. Beets, chard, and spinach belong to the **goose foot family.** The **mustard family** has many members: cabbage, collards, brussels sprouts, kale, cauliflower, broccoli, kohlrabi, rutabaga, turnips, cress, horseradish, and radishes. Carrots, parsley, celery, and parsnips all belong to the **parsley family.** The **nightshade family** encompasses potatoes, tomatoes, eggplants, and peppers. The **gourd family** claims the vine crops: summer squashes, winter squashes, pumpkins, watermelons, cantaloupes, and cucumbers. Chicory, endive, salsify, dandelions, lettuces, Jerusalem artichokes, and globe artichokes are all included in the **composite family.** The **lily family** includes onions, garlic, leeks, and chives. Sweet corn is a member of the **grass family.** Last is okra, which is claimed by the **mallow family.**

In a small garden, it is often impossible to rotate families of vegetables when only a few plants of each kind are planted. In these situations, different vegetables belonging to the same family (for example, tomatoes, peppers, eggplants, and potatoes) can be treated as a single unit in a rotation.

Common vegetable diseases that survive in soil and attack vegetables can be prevented by timely rotation. Fusarium root rot fungus infection will be severe in beans and peas unless there is a span of 2 to 3 years between plantings on the same plot of land. Cabbage club rot, once introduced into a garden, will infect many members of the mustard family for a period of 4 to 5 years. A planting of broccoli or cauliflower this year will easily contract the club root disease that infected last year's cabbage crop. Tomato bacterial canker will persist in a viable state for 3 years, once it is introduced into the soil.

Verticillim wilt fungus that infests a tomato crop this year will probably still linger in the soil for 2 years, and also will infect peppers, eggplants, and potatoes. There are vegetable varieties that can resist or tolerate being infected by certain fungi and bacterias. Today, a gardener who knows that his soil harbors verticillim wilt, fusarium wilt, and root-knot nematodes can select tomato varieties that are resistant to all three diseases.

With careful planning, you can avoid planting vegetables or combinations of vegetables that invite diseases and pests to the garden. Tomatoes, okra, potatoes, and carrots are very susceptible to injury from the root-knot nematode and encourage the buildup of this nematode in the soil, but corn and other grasses suppress this nematode. Nematodes do not usually infest onions, watermelons, or California #5 black-eyed peas. Study the information in the planting charts when planning your garden to help you make the best choices.

Wireworms and white grubs thrive in grass turf, and a new garden plot will usually contain many active soil insects. Therefore, sweet corn, watermelons, and winter squashes are better choices than root or tuber crops for planting in newly tilled soil.

It is wise to plant a crop that favors the decomposition of organic matter after one that produces a large amount of loose organic material. Sweet corn produces a coarse crop refuse that resists decomposition. Pumpkins, winter squashes, and watermelons accelerate the decay of crop refuse and grow well

Family Groups for Crop Rotation

Goosefoot Family:	Beets, Chard, Spinach
Legume Family:	Peas, Beans
Mustard Family:	Cabbage, Collards, Brussels Sprouts, Kale, Cauliflower, Broccoli, Kohlrabi, Rutabagas, Turnips, Cress, Horseradish, Radishes
Parsley Family:	Carrots, Parsley, Celery, Parsnips
Nightshade Family:	Potatoes, Tomatoes, Eggplants, Peppers
Gourd Family:	Squashes, Pumpkins, Watermelons, Cantaloupes, Cucumbers, and Gourds
Composite Family:	Chicory, Endive, Salify, Dandelions, Lettuces, Jerusalem Artichokes, Globe Artichokes
Lily Family:	Onions, Garlic, Leeks, Chives
Grass Family:	Sweet Corn
Mallow Family:	Okra

following corn. It is wise to precede shallow-rooted crops that require close cultivation, such as lettuce, beets, and other greens, with clean-culture crops, such as tomatoes, peppers, summer squashes, or melons, which extend roots deeply into the soil and discourage weed growth by shading the soil surface.

Some vegetables leave organic residues in the soil that are toxic to certain crops that may follow. Plant crops in a compatible sequence so that one that produces a toxic effect will not precede one that is susceptible to that toxin. Consider the relationship between corn and some other vegetables. The decomposition of sweet corn stubble liberates organic toxins that inhibit the early season root growth of lettuce, beets, and onions. Sunflowers, broccoli, and cabbage inhibit the growth of nearby plants.

Certain vegetables feed heavily on the available nutrients, thereby creating a shortage for subsequent vegetables that are less efficient feeders. For example, it is unwise to plant celery after heavy feeders like tomatoes because celery has a very shallow, limited root system.

Expert vegetable gardeners plan rotations several years ahead. A rotation is easy to plan and implement. First, think of your garden in the circular shape of a clock face. Then draw a large circle on paper. Divide the circle into sections as you would cut a pie. The number of sections you have will be the same as the number of vegetable families that you intend to plant. An example would be a garden with 4 vegetable families: (1) sweet corn (grass family); followed by (2) black-eyed peas and snap beans (pea family); followed by (3) cabbage, broccoli, and radishes (mustard family); followed by (4) tomatoes, peppers, and potatoes (nightshade family). To determine which family will occupy the four plots next year, simply rotate the plan clockwise one section. Next year, the black-eyed peas will be planted where the corn grew this year, and so on. More complicated plans can be worked out using the same procedure. Of course, you may not want the same size plot of every vegetable that you plant, but a well-designed rotation plan will help you avoid a helter-skelter arrangement that would cause trouble in the long run.

Garden Sanitation

Everything you can do to prevent problems will help make your gardening experience more enjoyable, reduce the use of chemicals, and increase the yield and quality of the vegetables you grow. One of the first steps toward reducing problems is good garden sanitation. This includes good weed control, cleaning up garden debris, and removing old, dead, and diseased plants.

Some common mistakes can increase the presence of disease and insects to the garden. Fruit allowed to rot on the plant and fall to the soil can greatly increase disease problems. Failure to remove old, dead plants can contribute to insect and disease problems. Weeds growing in and around the garden become a breeding ground for numerous pests and diseases.

Spend a few minutes each week cleaning up around the garden. Remove rotten fruit and diseased plants. When a crop is finished, clean the garden well and place debris in a compost bin. Anything you can do to keep the garden areas clean will make you a more successful gardener.

Beyond the Backyard

There's money to be made in vegetables, especially in the high-quality, homegrown sort. Exotic and new vegetables are catching on, too, and some commercial growers are even specializing in herbs. Granted, giving vegetables to your friends is fun, but paying off the mortgage is fun, too. If you've grown a successful large garden, maybe you have another income source of potential you're overlooking.

A move like this is a really big decision, so don't quit your day job today or even tomorrow. First you need a plan, which amounts to the usual pencil pushing, but this time you'll do it for your benefit.

First consider your potential clientele. If you plan to sell from a roadside stand, most of your customers will live within 20 to 30 miles of the retail outlet. If you're close to a city, that's ideal; if you live more than 50 miles from civilization you'll have to deliver. People will drive a considerable distance for pick-your-own (PYO) crops like peaches but not for the daily vegetables.

Even if you're in a somewhat remote location, you still have options. You can sell through a farmer's market in town or to brokers/grocery stores. Selling to gourmet restaurants or selling plants (especially herbs) to nurseries is also a potential outlet. Find out if there's a farmer's market you can participate in. Visit it and make notes. Can you deliver a better quality, more specialized product? Is the market successful? Check with vegetable buyers. Do they require a contract? How much volume will they need to be interested? Can you supply year round? Ask restauranteurs and nurserymen what they would buy and how much they will pay.

You can't just be a good grower, you've got to be a good business person, too. The countryside is full of good farmers who can't sell their products. Even if you're good at the business end, sometimes the weather wipes you out anyway. If you're successful in the beginning, then build a reserve to get you through the hard times. Better yet, consider being a broker for all sorts of gourmet vegetables, fruits, and herbs. This way you can cushion a local weather disaster with production from another area. (If interested, contact producers and offer to sell their produce for a percentage or buy on contract for resale.)

Based on your survey of local businesses and clientele, let's say you've decided that you will base your income on a roadside market with PYO sales of overages and some transplant sales to area nurseries with your extra greenhouse capacity. How many acres should you plant? How big is your greenhouse? A 30- × 100-foot greenhouse will produce a lot of starter plants, enough to plant the fields and cultivate in addition to producing extras to sell at a stand and to nurseries. After the transplant season has passed a greenhouse will yield hanging baskets for additional sales. As you can see, this isn't something you can manage casually.

Regarding acreage, we'll assume you're not a beginner. Otherwise an acre might be adequate to test whether you should become a gentleman farmer. Let's say you've got 15 acres of land adjacent to a busy two-lane highway and 5 acres of it is well-drained, prime growing space. Five acres should supply lots of produce to test your marketing potential.

Planning should begin months, or preferably a year, in advance. One of the best references to help you with this planning is *Sell What You Sow* by Eric

Garden Planning Tips

- Vegetables need lots of sun; locate the garden where it receives at least 6 hours of direct sunlight.
- Fruiting vegetables need the most sun.
- Root crops and leafy vegetables are somewhat shade tolerant.
- A good water source should be close by.
- Drainage is important, so pick a dry spot or plan on building a raised-bed garden.
- An enclosed area is a good idea. Two-legged varmints, in addition to the usual varmints, can really reduce your yield.
- Space is also a consideration. Consider how much is available, how much is needed, and how much you can realistically care for.
- Don't plant a larger garden than you can easily take care of. You can always enlarge the garden, if space allows.
- In areas that get strong winds, a windbreak should be used.
- Consider mature vegetable plant size and space requirements when planning the garden.
- A garden diagram will help you to plan for crop rotation, space limitations, and planting dates.
- Where possible, rows should run east to west.
- Plant tall plants on the north end of the garden to prevent them from shading adjacent rows.

Gibson (available from Wilhite Seed Co.—see appendices for address). It will help you line up resources, develop a financial plan (your banker will insist on one), determine how much to charge (40 percent to 50 percent over the cost of growing is a good starting point) and, most important, it will help you plan your marketing strategy.

Sound challenging? It should; you'd be putting your financial stability on the line. But don't forget you'd also have the fun and satisfaction of growing crops, being your own boss, and perhaps having more freedom. Late summer is a slow time. Why not shut down and spend your summers fishing in Canada, or just traveling?

What to grow? Warm-season crops should include tomatoes (lots of them, including the gourmet varieties), peppers (sweet and hot), snap beans, Southern peas, sweet corn, cucumbers, and possibly melons. You will want fruit in your stand, but you may not have to grow it if that doesn't appeal to you. Sell your neighbors' fruit or truck it in if necessary. Also try a few specialty items, such as Cucuzzi gourds, Asian eggplant, climbing okra, climbing or Malabar spinach, and bitter melons.

Cool-season crops should include broccoli, cauliflower, lettuces, onions, radishes, carrots, greens, and more. Cool-season specialty crops are especially plentiful. They include Chinese cabbage, bok choy, daikon, cilantro, arugula, garlic, kohlrabi, shallots, and snow peas.

Even moderate success should bring in a minimum gross income of $2,000 to $3,000 per acre (or possibly much more) from your growing operation. Just don't forget, you can't only grow it, you've got to sell it, too. You'll need a good location, good signage, all the editorial promotion you can garner, some paid advertising (especially in the newspaper), and if you can't make the experience fun—for you and for your customers try something else.

SOIL BUILDING

Soil is the heart of your garden. It's a mixture of minerals (clay, silt, sand), organic matter, air, nutrients, water, and a variety of bacteria, fungi, worms, insects, and roots. This mixture determines the soil texture, drainage, color, and structure. You don't have to become a soil scientist to be a good vegetable gardener, but understanding your soil and how to build it up properly will give you years of productive gardening pleasure.

The soil type is determined by its contents. Soils containing high levels of organic matter—20% to 65%—are called muck soils. Very few Southern soils have a level of organic matter this high, but they can be developed by adding humus (fully composted organic matter) in large amounts. Vegetables like celery, beets, and lettuce do especially well in this type of soil.

Soils containing less than 20% organic matter are called mineral soils. The mineral portion of soils are sand, silt, and clay. Sands are relatively large particles that help improve drainage and add air space. Clays are the smallest particles, which help hold moisture and nutrients and can be slow to drain. Mineral soils can be described as sands (less than 15% silt or clay), loams (20% clay, 30% to 50% sand, 30% to 50% silt), or clays (30% or more clay).

The perfect garden soil is a loam or sandy loam with a pH of 6.0 to 6.5 (slightly acid). It should contain 5% to 10% organic matter and be well drained with about 50% pore space, made up of air, water, and microorganisms. Some gardeners are blessed with near-perfect soil; the rest of us have to take what we have and improve it to make it balanced and productive.

One of the first steps is to determine what you are starting with. A soil sample, taken from the area you have selected for your garden, can be sent to a soil-testing lab. Most agricultural colleges have soil-testing labs that will analyze your soil.

The results will tell you the soil pH (acidity or alkalinity), the level of nutrients present, and make recommendations on how you might correct any nutritional needs. It is worth the money to have the soil checked every 2 to 3 years to make sure no imbalances have developed.

Soil pH has a tremendous effect on the availability of nutrients. Agricultural lime (calcium carbonate), which is used to make acid soils less acid, or sulfur, which is used to make alkaline soils more acid, may be added to achieve the proper pH.

LIMESTONE NEEDED TO CHANGE pH TO 6.5

pH Change Needed	Limestone Added Per 100 Square Feet		
	Sand	Loam	Clay
4.0 to 6.5	6 pounds	16 pounds	23 pounds
4.5 to 6.5	5 pounds	13 pounds	19 pounds
5.0 to 6.5	4 pounds	9½ pounds	15 pounds
5.5 to 6.5	2¾ pounds	8 pounds	9½ pounds
6.0 to 6.5	1½ pounds	4 pounds	5 pounds

SULFUR NEEDED TO CHANGE pH TO 6.5

pH Change Needed	Sulfur Added Per 100 Square Feet		
	Sand	Loam	Clay
8.5 to 6.5	5 pounds	6 pounds	7 pounds
8.0 to 6.5	3 pounds	3½ pounds	5 pounds
7.5 to 6.5	1 pound	1¾ pounds	2½ pounds
7.0 to 6.5	N/A	N/A	¾ pound

SOIL pH EFFECTS

Soil Type	Soil pH	Effect
Extremely Acid	below 4.5	Very few crops survive. Leads to manganese and aluminum toxicity.
Very Acid	4.5 to 5.0	Acid-tolerant plants like azaleas and blueberries should do well. Ideal for Irish potatoes.
Moderately Acid	5.5 to 6.0	Most vegetables will show no adverse effects. Tomatoes and peppers may show signs of calcium deficiency.
Slightly Acid	6.0 to 7.0	Ideal for most vegetables. Optimum nutrients available.
Slightly Alkaline	7.0 to 8.0	Micronutrients like iron, zinc, manganese, boron, and phosphorus will be unavailable at this level.
Alkaline	8.0+	Severe micronutrient deficiencies. Most vegetables do poorly.

Organic Matter or Materials

Many products that claim to cure all sorts of garden soil problems and ills have come and gone, but few can deliver like organic matter. The list of benefits is long and the disadvantages are few. Don't be afraid to add lots of organic matter, and to do it often.

Benefits of Organic Matter

- Source of energy for soil microorganisms and a source of nutrients for plants.
- Absorbs minerals and holds them until released by microorganisms.
- Soil microorganisms produce complex carbohydrates that help cement soil particles together into aggregates, creating air space and thus loosening tight soils and improving drainage.
- Acid produced in decomposition may help make micronutrients more available.
- Percolation and entrance of water are increased, thus helping to decrease erosion.
- Increased aeration helps plant roots penetrate the soil deeper and more easily.
- Sandy soils will hold more water with added organic matter.
- Constant decomposition and oxidation of organic matter means it must be constantly added to in order to maintain required levels.

Occasionally most gardeners, especially beginners, are forced to use organic materials that are less than perfect. Humus (completely decomposed organic matter) is the only perfect source we know of. But don't let this stop you from using what you have on hand or can get easily and inexpensively.

Be aware that most organic material, once added to the garden, will continue to break down or compost until it can be used by the plants. This decomposition process will ultimately release nutrients into the soil in a form the plant can use.

The bacteria and fungi involved in breaking down the organic matter need nitrogen to complete this process and compete with the plants for the nitrogen present. If you don't add extra nitrogen to newly prepared soil, or

ORGANIC MATERIALS FOR IMPROVING GARDEN SOILS

Material	Description
Animal Manure	Excellent source of organic matter. Investigate its source. Some manure can be full of weed seed. New pasture herbicides may pass through animals and damage sensitive plants like tomatoes.
Compost (humus)	This is the best source of organic matter. It's fully decomposed and ready to go to work. Many commercially available so-called composts are not fully decomposed. This doesn't mean they are bad, but you will need to add nitrogen to help complete the composting process.
Composted Bark	Works well to break up tight soils, but always add extra nitrogen to aid in microbial breakdown or plants will suffer.
Grass Clippings	Excellent source of organic matter that is high in nitrogen, but we suggest using it as a mulch or composting it first. Avoid grass that contains weed seed.
Hardwood Leaves and Pine Needles	Excellent sources of organic matter, but we prefer to use them as mulch or compost them first. Try to avoid excessive use of pecan or hickory leaves in the garden. They contain chemicals that act like a herbicide.
Mushroom Compost	Excellent material for improving garden soils, but high levels of salts can cause problems in tight soils.
Sawdust and Wood Chips	Helps break up tight soils, but a lot of nitrogen is needed to prevent severe yellowing and stunted plants due to microbial action.
Sewage Sludge or Tankage	An excellent source of nitrogen and phosphorus, but local health laws may prohibit their use and heavy metals can be a problem.
Others	There are lots of other acceptable sources of organic matter, but remember if they are not fully decomposed, you may have to add nitrogen to help with the decomposition process.

after the addition of large amounts of raw organic matter, your vegetable plants will suffer. Additional nitrogen (blood meal, cotton seed meal, poultry manure, ammonium nitrate, or ammonium sulfate) can be added at the same time you work in the organic matter.

Improving Drainage

Soil drainage is critical to good plant health. Poorly drained soils result in weak, diseased plants. Air must be present in the soil if the roots are to function properly. During periods of prolonged rain, water forces the air out of the soil, which causes the roots to stop functioning. This results in plant stress, wilting, and even plant death.

Correcting Poor Drainage

- Adding coarse sand (sharp sand or builder's sand) will help break up tight soils and add pore spaces. On heavy clay soils, always add organic matter with sand.
- A number of products containing fired clay particles are now available to help improve drainage. They do work, but the cost is often prohibitive.
- Organic matter does an excellent job of breaking up tight soils.
- Raised beds are always advisable in high rainfall areas where drainage can be a problem. Height of beds are determined by the type of soil and the drainage.
- Gypsum (calcium sulfate) will help break up some alkaline clays, but it is of no value with acid soils. It is particularly helpful on soils watered with high-sodium water.

Working the Soil

An important part of gardening is working the soil. (We're a bit reluctant to call it tilling, because some gardens will be hand dug, some plowed, and some mechanically tilled, while other gardeners may select a no-till or minimal-till program.) Working the soil involves the incorporation of nutrients, soil amendments, and organic matter. It also helps improve soil aeration. Tilling or digging to a depth of 8 to 12 inches is usually adequate.

Be careful when tilling the garden to the same depth several times each year. This can create a plow pan or hard pan. A plow pan is a thin layer of clay that accumulates just below the tilling depth and prevents the normal percolation of water. This can make an otherwise well-drained soil a poorly draining soil.

There has been a good bit of interest in no- or minimal-till gardening. This is an easy way to maintain a productive garden, but it requires that you have a good, balanced soil to begin with. The no-till approach works best on wide beds or box gardens, after the soil is well prepared, bedded up, and mulched. Avoid walking on or stepping in the beds, because this compacts the soil. Each season, you should top off the beds with a generous amount of compost and additional mulch. The idea behind this system is to create a healthy environment for worms and microorganisms. These good guys help out by working in the organic matter and aerating the soil. Every couple of years you will want to dig the beds to add lime or sulfur and other amendments, based on soil-test data.

Mulching

Mulching is an important part of successful vegetable gardening. Mulches help insulate the soil, keeping it warm in the winter and cooler in the summer. They also help control weeds, prevent compaction and erosion, conserve water, and prevent crusting. Pasture hay (Coastal Bermuda or Prairie) can release small amounts of herbicide that will damage sensitive plants like tomatoes.

CHARACTERISTICS OF TYPICAL MULCH MATERIALS

Material	Mulch Remains Loose and Dry	Grass and Weed Control	Last the Whole Season	Available Nutrients Present
Bark	Excellent	Good	Excellent	Poor
Black Polyethylene	Poor	Excellent	Excellent	Poor
Compost	Excellent	Good	Good	Excellent
Cotton Seed Hulls	Poor	Good	Good	Good
Hay—Coastal Bermuda	Excellent	Fair	Good	Good
Hay—Alfalfa	Excellent	Fair	Good	Excellent
Lawn Clippings	Poor	Fair	Fair	Good
Leaves	Fair	Fair	Good	Fair
Newspaper (3 to 4 Sheets)	Poor	Good	Fair	Poor
Pine Straw	Fair	Good	Good	Fair
Sawdust	Good	Good	Good	Poor
Shredded Newspaper	Poor	Fair	Fair	Poor
Straw	Excellent	Good	Good	Fair
Weed Fabric	Poor	Excellent	Excellent	Poor
Wood Chips	Excellent	Fair	Excellent	Poor

Large-seeded vegetables, like beans and squashes, or transplanted vegetables can be planted right through the mulch. Small-seeded vegetables, or those that are slow to come up, can be mulched after the plants are up and established.

The amount used will vary with the material. Coarse materials like hay or pine straw should be at least 3 to 4 inches deep. (See photo on page 32.) Materials like sawdust or grass clippings need only be an inch or so deep.

Laying down sheets of black plastic is an excellent spring mulch because the plastic absorbs heat, which warms the soil and gets the plants off to an early start. But once temperatures begin to rise, you have to be sure to cover the black plastic with a light-colored material, like hay or straw, before the summer heat cooks the plants' roots.

When using organic mulches, keep in mind that materials like sawdust, wood chips, bark, and shredded newspaper can rob the soil of needed nitrogen. (See photo on page 33.) When using these materials, always add a little extra nitrogen to prevent stunted plant growth.

Garden Irrigation

A well-prepared garden soil holds moisture well and the addition of mulch helps conserve that much-needed water. But even with all this preparation, you'll need additional water to help germinate seeds and keep vegetable plants healthy during periods of prolonged drought.

There are basically three methods of delivering water to the garden. Sprinkler irrigation is excellent for germinating seeds and for establishing transplants. Try to avoid using sprinklers during the rest of the season because their use promotes disease problems. Most diseases must have free moisture to infect the plant, so if you must use sprinkler irrigation, try to finish watering before 2:00 or 3:00 P.M. so that the foliage can dry off before dark.

Furrow irrigation is the oldest form of irrigating crops. In a more traditional garden, the furrows run slightly downhill, which allows the water to slowly travel down the field until the soil is saturated. On steep grades, small dams are built every few feet to slow down the water flow. This method of irrigating is simple to do, doesn't wet the foliage, and waters the soil thoroughly.

The newest addition to irrigation techniques is drip or microirrigation. With a growing concern for water conservation, more emphasis is being placed on the use of drip or microirrigation. As a result, numerous systems are becoming available to the home gardener. They are inexpensive and easy to set up. The biggest advantage of drip irrigation is the ability to add small but regular amounts of water to keep the soil moisture at a near-optimum level. (See photo on page 34.)

Building Fertile Soils

Maintaining proper soil fertility is important if you want consistent production and healthy plants. Most vegetables require moderate to high levels of nitrogen, phosphorus, and potash.

Nitrogen. Nitrogen is required in most plant-growth processes. Even though the atmosphere is about 80% nitrogen, it's not in a form that most plants can use. Nitrogen is also very volatile and leaches out readily. It is constantly being lost from the soil, so we must continually replenish the supply.

Organic forms of nitrogen are much more stable than chemical forms, but plants cannot use organic nitrogen. Soil microorganisms convert organic nitrogen into ammonium and nitrate, which can be used by the plants. But ammonium and nitrate can also be leached from the soil or lost through the air.

PLANT NUTRIENT-DEFICIENCY AND TOXICITY SYMPTOMS

Plant Nutrient	Deficiency Symptoms	Toxicity (Excess) Symptoms
Nitrogen	Slow, stunted growth, yellow-green leaves, and older leaves may burn on tips and margin.	Excess, weak growth susceptible to disease and insects.
Phosphorus	Slow growth with purplish color on leaves and leaf veins.	May cause nitrogen, zinc, iron, and copper deficiencies.
Potassium	Tip and marginal leaf burn, weak stems, and small fruit.	Interveinal yellowing.
Calcium	Weak stems, death of buds, and shedding of blossoms and buds.	Micronutrient deficiency due to high pH.
Magnesium	Yellowing between veins of older leaves. Leaf curling.	Micronutrient deficiency due to tie-up in soil.
Sulfur	Young leaves are yellow-green. Growth is weak.	Micronutrient deficiency due to low pH.
Iron	New leaves are yellow with darker veins.	Causes manganese deficiency.
Boron	Poor fruit or seed set. Soft spots on fruit or tubers.	N/A
Copper	Stunted plants with twig die-back.	N/A
Manganese	Yellowing of leaves.	N/A
Molybdenum	Stunting, cupping, or rolling of leaves or leaf burn.	N/A
Zinc	Short internodes with mottled leaves.	Causes iron and manganese deficiency.

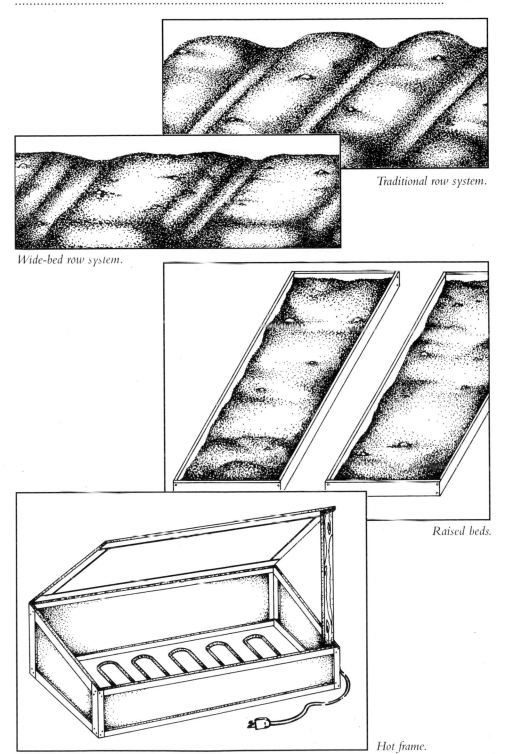

Traditional row system.

Wide-bed row system.

Raised beds.

Hot frame.

Small, or mini-, tiller.

*Soil worked up
into a ridge for planting.*

Trellis for peas and other low vining plants.

Raised beds created with railroad ties.

Trellis with pantyhose attached to support Charantais melon.

Welded-wire trellis.

*Lattice trellises
for a vegetable garden.*

Greenbeans with hay mulch.

A newspaper and hay mulch.

Buttercrunch lettuce with newspaper and leaf mulch.

Above: Water-saving irrigation tape used here to water okra.
Right: Drip irrigation.

Compost bins.

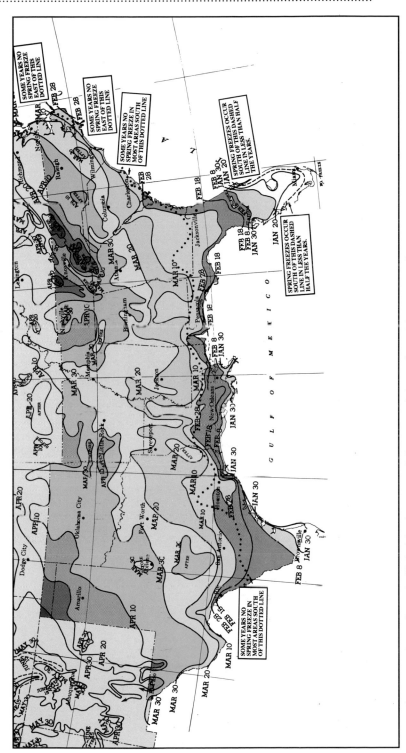

Average last spring freeze dates. (Published by the National Oceanic and Atmospheric Administration.)

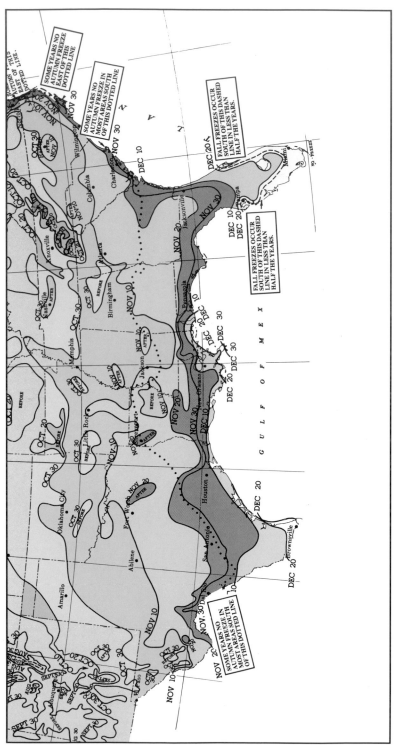

Average first fall freeze dates. (Published by the National Oceanic and Atmospheric Administration.)

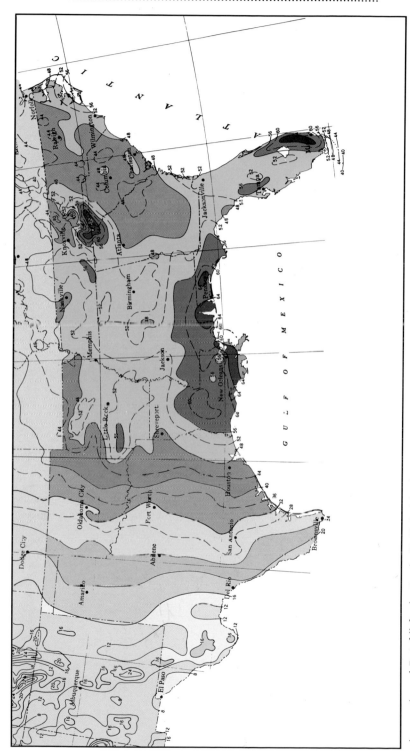

Average Annual Rainfall for the South. (Published by the National Oceanic and Atmospheric Administration.)

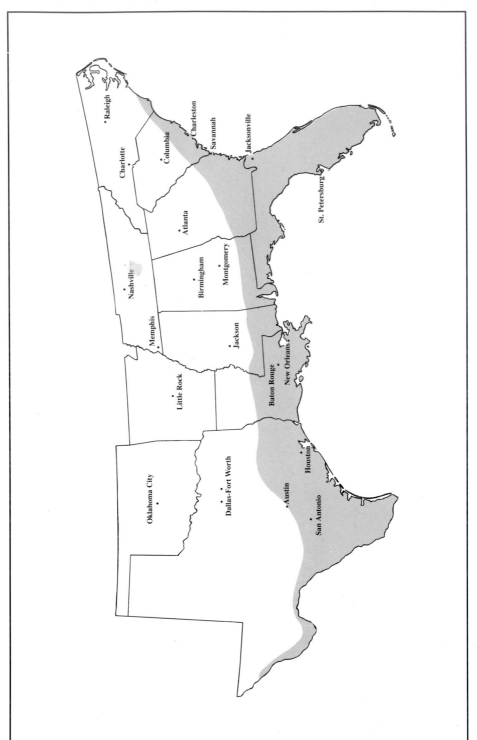

Planting zones for the South.

Broccoli starter plants under row cover.

Buttercrunch lettuce transplants.

Hearty tomato transplants.

Broccoli grown in a container.

Romaine lettuce also has a place in the container garden.

Lettuce thrives in a simple greenhouse, made with PVC pipe and sheets of plastic.

Nitrogen can also be added to the soil by growing beans, peas, and other legumes. Legumes, in association with symbiotic bacteria, have the ability to convert atmospheric nitrogen into a form the plants can use. When the plants are plowed under, the nitrogen remains and is rereleased into the soil. Atmospheric nitrogen can also be added to the soil by lightning and rainfall.

There's no question that vegetables can be grown with chemical fertilizers or organic fertilizers alone, but research has shown that a combination of the two improves the yield and quality of the vegetables produced.

Phosphorus. Phosphorus is probably the most misused nutrient. It is important for root development, flowering, and fruiting. Phosphorus is only available in acid soils. Because it does not leach readily, years of using high phosphorus fertilizers can cause a buildup that may become toxic to the plants. It will also cause nitrogen, zinc, and iron to become tied up and unavailable to the plants. Because it does not move in the soil it must be worked into the root zone in order for the roots to absorb it.

Be careful about overdoing the phosphorus. Many soils are naturally high in phosphorus. Past years of farming may have provided the soil with enough phosphorus to last for years of gardening, so always have the phosphorus level checked before you add more.

Potassium. Potassium is the last of the major nutrients needed for plant growth. Potassium is important in most plant functions. Most root crops require large amounts of potassium. Potassium is mobile in the soil, and can be leached out, but it is held by organic matter and clay particles, which makes it more stable than nitrogen.

Major Micronutrients

Magnesium, calcium, and sulfur, although needed in smaller quantities than the big three, can be lacking in some soils. Calcium is usually lacking in acid soils, but liming supplies the soil with this much-needed nutrient.

Magnesium is needed in chlorophyll formation, as well as in photosynthesis. It is usually only lacking in very sandy soils. If magnesium is needed, add dolomitic limestone instead of agricultural lime. KMag (potassium magnesium sulfate) is also an excellent source of magnesium.

Sulfur is available in most fertilizers, so there is no need to add more except for highly alkaline soils in which sulfur is used to lower the pH.

Other Micronutrients

Minor elements, like iron, manganese, zinc, boron, copper, molybdenum, and chlorine, are all required in small quantities, but most Southern soils contain adequate levels. Alkaline soil pH can cause these nutrients to be unavailable. A slightly acid soil will keep these nutrients in a form the plant can use.

Fertilizers

Fertilizers are identified by three numbers (for example: 13–13–13). This represents the percentages of nitrogen, phosphorus, and potash, in that order. A 100-pound bag of 13–13–13 has 39 pounds of nutrients. The rest is carrier, usually consisting of some kind of clay. Organic fertilizers are either derived from living organisms or mined from naturally occurring mineral deposits. Chemical fertilizers are man-made chemical salts or blends of chemical salts and mined minerals.

Plants have no way of determining which type of fertilizer you use, so selection will be determined by your gardening philosophy and what works for you.

Fertilizer recommendations usually center around the amount of actual nitrogen present in the fertilizer. The rate of .2 pounds of actual nitrogen per

VALUES FOR ORGANIC FERTILIZERS

Approximate Poundage/100 Pounds or Percentage

Fertilizer	Nitrogen (N)	Phosphorus (P2 O5)	Potash (K20)	Quantity Needed to Supply .2 Pounds N per 100 Sq. Ft.
Alfalfa Hay	.025	trace	.025	800 pounds
Bat Guano	10.0	4.0	2.0	2 pounds
Bone Meal	1.0	15.0	—	10 pounds
Cotton Seed Meal	6.0	3.0	1.5	3.0 pounds
Fish Meal	10.0	6.0	—	2.0 pounds
Kelp	1.0	0.5	9.0	20 pounds
Manures (Dried)				
Chicken	3.0	5.0	1.5	7 pounds
Cow	1.5	2.0	2.3	14 pounds
Horse	2.1	1.0	2.3	10 pounds
Pig	2.1	.4	.5	10 pounds
Sheep	4.2	2.5	6.0	5 pounds
Manures (Fresh)				
Chicken	1.5	1.0	.5	14 pounds
Cow	.5	.2	.5	40 pounds
Horse	.7	.3	.5	30 pounds
Pig	.7	.6	.7	30 pounds
Sheep	1.4	.7	1.5	15 pounds
Soybean Hay	.025	trace	trace	800 pounds
Used Mushroom Manure	1.0	1.0	1.0	20 pounds

100 square feet is a good rate for a single application. (The right-hand column of the charts gives the amount of each fertilizer needed to supply .2 pounds of actual nitrogen.)

VALUES FOR INORGANIC FERTILIZERS
Approximate Poundage/100 Pounds or Percentage

Material	Nitrogen (N)	Phosphorus (P2 O5)	Potash (K20)	Quantity Needed to Supply .2 Pounds N per 100 Sq. Ft.
Ammonium Nitrate	33.5	—	—	½ pound
Ammonium Sulfate	21.0	—	—	1 pound
Calcium Nitrate	15.5	—	—	1¼ pounds
Potassium Nitrate	13.0	—	44.0	1½ pounds
Urea	46.0	—	—	⅓ pound
Urea Formaldehyde	38.0	—	—	½ pound
Super Phosphate	—	18.0–20.0	—	N/A
Concentrated Super Phosphate	—	45.0 46.0	—	N/A
Potassium Chloride	—	—	60.0–62.0	N/A
Potassium Sulfate	—	—	50.0–53.0	N/A
13–13–13	13	13	13	1½ pounds
12–24–12	12	24	12	1½ pounds
15–5–10	15	5	10	1¼ pounds

Wood Ashes

Wood ash is a valuable source of potassium (potash) but is highly alkaline. Wood ash should never be used on alkaline soils and used only sparingly on acid soils. Five pounds or 1½ gallons of dry ash per 100 square feet is the maximum amount added per year. If you burn wood for heat, one winter can produce enough ashes to supply the average garden for a lifetime. Be careful not to overdo it.

Recipe for Your Own Organic Fertilizer

Mix together thoroughly 40 pounds blood meal, 30 pounds bone meal, and 10 pounds muriate of potash. This mixture makes a balanced organic fertilizer that should be used at a rate of 4 to 6 pounds per 100 square feet.

Foliar Feeding

Foliar feeding is a technique of delivering nutrients to the plant through the foliage. It is simple to do and generally overlooked by most gardeners.

The way to apply fertilizer for this purpose is with a hose-on sprayer, designed for water-soluble fertilizers. Water-soluble fertilizers like Peter's, Miracle Gro, Rapid Grow, or Greenlight 20–20–20 with micronutrients are available at most garden centers. Organic fertilizers like fish emulsion or seaweed extract also work well.

The idea is to spray the vegetables weekly with a diluted fertilizer solution, giving the plants a small but constant application. It should be used in combination with other fertilizer programs. Give it a try—you'll be amazed at the results!

TIME TO SIDE-DRESS WITH NITROGEN

Beans	At 3- to 4- leaf stage.
Beets, Carrots	Four to 6 weeks after planting.
Bell Peppers, Eggplants, Tomatoes	After first fruit set, and again every 4 to 6 weeks.
Broccoli, Cabbage, Cauliflower, Brussels Sprouts	Three weeks after planting and again 4 to 6 weeks later.
Corn	When 8 to 12 inches high and again when tassel is just beginning to show.
Cucumbers, Watermelons, Winter Squashes, Pumpkins	When plants begin to run.
English Peas	When plants are about 4 to 6 inches tall.
Irish Potatoes	When sprouts begin to break ground.
Leafy Greens (Mustard, Collards, Turnips, Chard)	Three weeks after planting and again following harvest, if plants are not pulled.
Lettuces, Chinese Cabbage	Two weeks after transplanting or 4 weeks after sowing.
Okra	After first harvest.
Onions	Once plants are established and again at the 7- to 10-leaf stage.
Southern Peas	No fertilizer needed.
Radishes	No fertilizer; grows too quickly to need it.
Summer Squashes	When plants are 8 to 10 inches tall.
Sweet Potatoes	No fertilizer needed.

Cover Crops

There are times when part or all of your garden will be fallow. One of the best uses of barren ground is to plant a cover crop. This is a crop that is planted for the purpose of plowing under before it matures to build up the soil and add needed nutrients.

Legumes (bean or pea family) are excellent because they add organic matter and nitrogen, which is fixed into the plant by *Rhizobia* bacteria from nitrogen found in the air. Legumes like clover or vetch are excellent for fall and winter planting. Southern peas work well in the summertime. For maximum nitrogen, always turn them under before they mature.

Winter cereal grains like wheat, elbon rye, or oats make excellent fall and winter cover crops. They add lots of organic material that help build up the soil. Like other grasses, they must be given generous amounts of nitrogen for good growth. One of elbon rye's extra benefits is that it helps reduce nematode populations that could damage vegetable plant roots.

Composting

Composting is the process of breaking down raw organic matter into a dark, rich, earthy material called humus. We generally think of composing as taking place in bins built for the purpose. Certainly, this is a common way, but it is not the only way. Good compost is produced by a variety of methods. All that is required is organic matter, nitrogen, oxygen, water, and microorganisms. The microorganisms feed on the organic matter, breaking it down into humus, which, as it oxides, releases needed nutrients to the plants.

C:N Ratios of Selected Organic Materials	
Grass clippings	12:1
Manure (fresh)	14:1
Straw	48 to 128:1
Sawdust (aged)	200:1
Sawdust (fresh)	500:1

All forms of organic matter can be described by their C:N ratio. This is the ratio of carbon to nitrogen. Microbes will work best on organic materials with a C:N ratio of 25 to 1. If it is greater than this, as it is with many materials, the process will go at a much slower rate.

By blending a variety of materials together, you can approach that magic 25:1 ratio needed to maximize the breakdown into humus. When using materials high in carbon, you can add additional nitrogen (ammonium nitrate, cotton seed meal, or blood meal) to help in the breakdown process.

When building a compost pile, build a large one to ensure good heating. A 4-ft. × 4-ft. × 4-ft pile is considered the minimum size. This will allow for enough bulk to easily regulate moisture, air, and nutrients. There's no question that a compost bin is the most common method of composting, but there are many others.

***S**HEET COMPOSTING*   Sheet composting involves laying down a thick layer of organic material (1 or 2 feet deep). This makes mixing or turning easy. Sheet composting can be done between garden rows, in walks, or even as a mulch over the garden. Sheet composting also helps reduce soil compaction. Water the compost regularly and add nitrogen to speed up the decomposition process.

***T**RENCH COMPOSTING*   Dig a shallow trench and fill it with leaves, grass clippings, or whatever is available. Lightly cover it with soil and sit back and wait. In a few months, you can dig or till the humus into the soil. This is an easy and efficient way of improving your garden soil.

Soil Building Tips

- The perfect garden soil is a loam or sandy loam with a pH of 6.0 to 6.5 (slightly acid).
- Organic matter, organic matter, organic matter—add lots and often.
- Good drainage is critical to healthy, vigorous plant growth. Use raised beds, organic matter, and sand to build up tight soils.
- Mulches add valuable organic matter, control weeds, conserve moisture, and moderate soil temperature.
- In the Southern garden, water is essential for seed germination and summer vegetables during short periods of drought. Water only when needed, and when you water, water deeply.
- Add fertilizer in small but regular doses to ensure quick, even growth.
- Composting is a great way to recycle organic yard waste while building healthy soils.

SLOW OR COLD COMPOSTING   This method is easy to do and fits into many gardeners' programs. Basically, you make a pile or mound of organic matter. Stack up as much material as possible, adding soil and nitrogen every so often to aid in the breakdown. Keep the pile watered and wait. If you want to turn it occasionally, that will speed up the process, but the whole point of cold composting is that it requires very little effort. The whole process may take as much as a year, but it will work. If the pile is not turned, the outer layer will not break down, but it can be added to next year's pile.

COMPOST BINS   Compost bins can be built out of a variety of materials like wood, concrete block, or wire mesh. (See photo on page 34.) A 4-ft. × 4-ft. × 4-ft. bin is generally considered to be the smallest size gardeners should use. Try to accumulate enough organic material to fill the bin all at once. Layer the organic matter with a little soil and nitrogen fertilizer every 6 inches or so until the bin is full. The pile should be turned every few weeks and kept moist. (It should feel wet, but you shouldn't be able to squeeze out water.)

After a few weeks, the volume of the pile will be reduced by more than one-half. Continue to turn the pile until it is ready to be used. This type of composting should take about 3 to 5 months. (When ready, the compost will be dark brown, the original ingredients will be relatively unrecognizable, and it will have an earthy odor.)

GARDENING AND THE WEATHER

Most gardening guides spend little or no time looking at the weather and its effect on the plants you are growing. One of the things that makes gardening in the South so different than gardening anywhere else is the weather. The Southern gardener is blessed with a long growing season, abundant rainfall, and mild winters, and cursed with long (really long) hot summers and high humidity.

Part of the challenge Southern gardeners face each year is the uncertainty of what's to come. Will it be rainy or the start of drought; will there be a late freeze or an early one? There's no way to predict what the future season will bring, so all we can do is rely on what's happened in the past.

Some gardeners, especially the old-timers, rely on the phases of the moon to time their plantings. It's fun to see what the almanac predicts and when the barren and fruitful dates will supposedly occur. However, if commercial farmers relied on this information, we might find ourselves standing in food lines. If planting by the moon interests you, give it a try, but we make our planting recommendations according to freeze dates. Planting dates are based on the average last freeze in the spring and the average first freeze in the fall. These dates are based on the probability of a freeze occurring.

Take a look at the following chart showing spring and fall freeze dates for selected Southern cities. (Also see maps on pages 35 and 36.) The 90-percent dates for the spring occur when there's a 90-percent chance of another freeze, the 50-percent dates occur when there's a 50–50 chance of another freeze, and the 10-percent dates are when there's only a 10-percent (1 out of 10 years) chance of another freeze occurring.

In the spring, we usually base our planting times on the 50-percent dates. This means we occasionally get wiped out by a late freeze. But with a little protection, we can usually get by. Those of you that lack the gambling spirit will want to use the 10-percent dates, or plan on covering tender plants.

In the fall, the 90-percent dates mean there's a 90-percent chance of a freeze hitting before this date. Again, the 50-percent freeze dates occur when there's a 50-percent chance of a freeze and the 10-percent dates are selected based on when there's a 10-percent chance of an earlier freeze.

To be conservative, and because vegetables don't generally develop as fast in the fall, base your fall plantings around the 10-percent dates.

Rainfall

Rainfall is another important factor that affects vegetables. Rainfall can be a blessing or a curse. Plants grow well in most of the South because of abundant rainfall, but the moisture and humidity contribute to a wide variety of fungal and bacterial diseases.

The rainfall in our region will range from less than 12 inches each year in West Texas and the Panhandle of Oklahoma to more than 80 inches each year in parts of Georgia and the Carolinas.

Tips for Weather Watchers

Weather plays an important role in vegetable growth and insect and disease problems. The nature of weather in the South creates unique problems and challenges for the Southern gardener. Remember:

- Plantings are always based around average freeze dates.
- Abundant rainfall in most of the South makes plants grow vigorously.
- Abundant rainfall and high humidity encourage disease problems and create soil drainage problems. So gardeners should build raised beds, except in very well-drained soils.

FREEZE DATES

STATE	SPRING (DATE)			FALL (DATE)		
City	Freeze Probability (Percentage)			Freeze Probability (Percentage)		
	90	50	10	10	50	90
ALABAMA						
Anniston	Mar. 15	Mar. 30	Apr. 13	Oct. 21	Nov. 1	Nov. 12
Birmingham	Mar. 13	Mar. 29	Apr. 14	Oct. 24	Nov. 6	Nov. 18
Dothan	Feb. 21	Mar. 13	Apr. 1	Oct. 31	Nov. 15	Nov. 30
Florence	Mar. 13	Mar. 27	Apr. 10	Oct. 22	Nov. 4	Nov. 17
Gadsden	Mar. 20	Apr. 4	Apr. 18	Oct. 18	Nov. 2	Nov. 17
Huntsville	Mar. 26	Apr. 9	Apr. 22	Oct. 9	Oct. 25	Nov. 10
Mobile	Feb. 6	Feb. 27	Mar. 19	Nov. 5	Nov. 26	Dec. 17
Montgomery	Feb. 22	Mar. 11	Mar. 28	Oct. 29	Nov. 12	Nov. 25
Tuscaloosa	Mar. 5	Mar. 22	Apr. 8	Oct. 20	Nov. 4	Nov. 20
ARKANSAS						
El Dorado	Mar. 14	Mar. 28	Apr. 11	Oct. 24	Nov. 5	Nov. 18
Fayetteville	Apr. 8	Apr. 21	May 3	Oct. 4	Oct. 17	Oct. 30
Fort Smith	Mar. 22	Apr. 3	Apr. 14	Oct. 18	Oct. 30	Nov. 12
Helena	Mar. 9	Mar. 25	Apr. 10	Oct. 20	Nov. 6	Nov. 23
Hot Springs	Mar. 7	Mar. 23	Apr. 8	Oct. 27	Nov. 9	Nov. 21
Jonesboro	Mar. 15	Mar. 29	Apr. 11	Oct. 23	Nov. 5	Nov. 19
Little Rock	Mar. 13	Mar. 28	Apr. 13	Oct. 15	Oct. 31	Nov. 15
Pine Bluff	Mar. 2	Mar. 19	Apr. 4	Oct. 26	Nov. 8	Nov. 22
Texarkana	Feb. 23	Mar. 12	Mar. 29	Oct. 29	Nov. 14	Nov. 30
FLORIDA						
Daytona Beach	Jan. 9	Feb. 8	Mar. 11	Dec. 1	Jan. 4	Feb. 9
Fort Myers	—	—	Feb. 10	Dec. 26	—	—
Gainesville	Feb. 5	Mar. 3	Mar. 29	Nov. 5	Nov. 27	Dec. 18
Jacksonville Beach	Jan. 17	Feb. 14	Mar. 14	Nov. 16	Dec. 14	Jan. 13
Lake City	Feb. 21	Mar. 10	Mar. 27	Nov. 5	Nov. 22	Dec. 8
Miami	—	—	—	—	—	—
Orlando	—	Jan. 28	Mar. 4	Dec. 3	Jan. 2	—
Pensacola	Jan. 26	Feb. 21	Mar. 20	Nov. 8	Nov. 29	Dec. 19
Tallahassee	Feb. 17	Mar. 12	Apr. 5	Oct. 28	Nov. 14	Dec. 2
Tampa	—	Jan. 28	Feb. 25	Dec. 3	Jan. 3	—
GEORGIA						
Albany	Feb. 21	Mar. 12	Mar. 31	Oct. 26	Nov. 13	Dec. 1
Atlanta	Mar. 16	Mar. 28	Apr. 10	Oct. 26	Nov. 8	Nov. 22
Augusta	Mar. 9	Mar. 28	Apr. 15	Oct. 23	Nov. 6	Nov. 20

continued

FREEZE DATES (CONT.)

STATE	SPRING (DATE)			FALL (DATE)		
City	Freeze Probability (Percentage)			Freeze Probability (Percentage)		
	90	50	10	10	50	90
Brunswick	Jan. 24	Feb. 20	Mar. 18	Nov. 15	Dec. 4	Dec. 24
Columbus	Mar. 3	Mar. 21	Apr. 8	Oct. 27	Nov. 9	Nov. 22
Macon	Feb. 27	Mar. 17	Apr. 4	Oct. 25	Nov. 8	Nov. 22
Savannah	Feb. 17	Mar. 10	Mar. 30	Oct. 31	Nov. 15	Dec. 1
Valdosta	Feb. 22	Mar. 12	Mar. 30	Oct. 27	Nov. 11	Nov. 26
LOUISIANA						
Alexandria	Feb. 12	Mar. 5	Mar. 26	Oct. 31	Nov. 16	Dec. 2
Baton Rouge	Feb. 26	Mar. 15	Apr. 1	Oct. 25	Nov. 10	Nov. 25
Lake Charles	Jan. 23	Feb. 19	Mar. 18	Nov. 6	Nov. 29	Dec. 21
Monroe	Feb. 18	Mar. 9	Mar. 27	Oct. 24	Nov. 7	Nov. 20
New Orleans	Jan. 21	Feb. 20	Mar. 21	Nov. 15	Dec. 5	Dec. 25
Shreveport	Mar. 9	Mar. 21	Apr. 2	Oct. 27	Nov. 10	Nov. 23
MISSISSIPPI						
Columbus	Mar. 11	Mar. 27	Apr. 11	Oct. 15	Oct. 29	Nov. 11
Greenville	Mar. 2	Mar. 18	Apr. 2	Oct. 27	Nov. 12	Nov. 28
Gulfport	Jan. 29	Feb. 22	Mar. 17	Nov. 7	Nov. 26	Dec. 16
Hattiesburg	Mar. 1	Mar. 17	Apr. 3	Oct. 24	Nov. 8	Nov. 23
Jackson	Mar. 12	Mar. 25	Apr. 7	Oct. 14	Oct. 29	Nov. 13
Meridian	Mar. 12	Mar. 27	Apr. 12	Oct. 19	Nov. 3	Nov. 17
Natchez	Feb. 10	Mar. 10	Apr. 7	Oct. 27	Nov. 14	Dec. 2
NORTH CAROLINA						
Asheville	Mar. 28	Apr. 10	Apr. 24	Oct. 11	Oct. 24	Nov. 6
Charlotte	Mar. 18	Apr. 6	Apr. 25	Oct. 14	Nov. 1	Nov. 19
Elizabeth City	Mar. 23	Apr. 6	Apr. 20	Oct. 21	Nov. 4	Nov. 17
Fayetteville	Mar. 18	Apr. 2	Apr. 17	Oct. 20	Oct. 31	Nov. 12
Greensboro	Mar. 31	Apr. 11	Apr. 22	Oct. 14	Oct. 27	Nov. 10
Raleigh-Durham	Mar. 24	Apr. 11	Apr. 29	Oct. 16	Oct. 27	Nov. 7
Wilmington	Feb. 28	Mar. 21	Apr. 12	Oct. 24	Nov. 11	Nov. 29
OKLAHOMA						
Boise City	Apr. 13	Apr. 28	May 12	Oct. 4	Oct. 16	Oct. 29
Enid	Mar. 24	Apr. 4	Apr. 15	Oct. 21	Nov. 3	Nov. 15
Lawton	Mar. 17	Apr. 1	Apr. 15	Oct. 21	Nov. 5	Nov. 19
McAlester	Mar. 19	Mar. 31	Apr. 12	Oct. 15	Oct. 31	Nov. 15
Muskogee	Mar. 21	Apr. 1	Apr. 11	Oct. 19	Nov. 2	Nov. 16
Oklahoma City	Mar. 22	Apr. 6	Apr. 20	Oct. 14	Oct. 27	Nov. 8
Ponca City	Mar. 29	Apr. 13	Apr. 27	Oct. 13	Oct. 26	Nov. 7

FREEZE DATES (CONT.)

STATE	SPRING (DATE)			FALL (DATE)		
City	Freeze Probability (Percentage)			Freeze Probability (Percentage)		
	90	50	10	10	50	90
Stillwater	Mar. 25	Apr. 7	Apr. 19	Oct. 14	Oct. 26	Nov. 17
Tulsa	Mar. 16	Mar. 30	Apr. 13	Oct. 21	Nov. 4	Nov. 17
SOUTH CAROLINA						
Anderson	Mar. 14	Mar. 29	Apr. 13	Oct. 24	Nov. 6	Nov. 20
Charleston	Feb. 27	Mar. 18	Apr. 6	Oct. 30	Nov. 12	Nov. 26
Chester	Mar. 18	Apr. 6	Apr. 25	Oct. 14	Oct. 30	Nov. 15
Columbia	Mar. 13	Mar. 30	Apr. 17	Oct. 16	Nov. 1	Nov. 17
Florence	Mar. 3	Mar. 20	Apr. 5	Oct. 26	Nov. 9	Nov. 23
Georgetown	Feb. 17	Mar. 11	Apr. 2	Nov. 4	Nov. 20	Dec. 6
Spartanburg	Apr. 2	Apr. 14	Apr. 25	Oct. 13	Oct. 29	Nov. 13
TENNESSEE						
Chattanooga	Mar. 23	Apr. 5	Apr. 18	Oct. 19	Nov. 1	Nov. 14
Clarksville	Mar. 29	Apr. 12	Apr. 27	Oct. 8	Oct. 22	Nov. 5
Greenville	Apr. 9	Apr. 23	May 8	Oct. 8	Oct. 20	Oct. 31
Kingsport	Apr. 3	Apr. 16	Apr. 29	Oct. 7	Oct. 20	Nov. 2
Knoxville	Mar. 18	Mar. 29	Apr. 9	Oct. 23	Nov. 6	Nov. 20
Memphis	Mar. 8	Mar. 23	Apr. 8	Oct. 27	Nov. 7	Nov. 19
Nashville	Mar. 24	Apr. 5	Apr. 16	Oct. 14	Oct. 29	Nov. 13
Union City	Mar. 23	Apr. 6	Apr. 20	Oct. 6	Oct. 20	Nov. 2
TEXAS						
Abilene	Mar. 10	Mar. 25	Apr. 8	Oct. 28	Nov. 13	Nov. 30
Amarillo	Mar. 29	Apr. 14	Apr. 30	Oct. 14	Oct. 29	Nov. 13
Austin	Feb. 14	Mar. 3	Mar. 21	Nov. 5	Nov. 28	Dec. 21
Beaumont	Jan. 24	Feb. 17	Mar. 16	Nov. 16	Dec. 9	Jan. 1
Brownsville	—	Dec. 31	Feb. 15	Dec. 17	Feb. 2	—
Conroe	Feb. 14	Mar. 5	Mar. 24	Nov. 6	Nov. 25	Dec. 14
Corpus Christi	—	Jan. 25	Feb. 23	Dec. 7	Jan. 11	—
Dallas	Feb. 18	Mar. 16	Apr. 4	Nov. 1	Nov. 20	Dec. 9
El Paso	Feb. 17	Mar. 9	Mar. 29	Oct. 27	Nov. 12	Nov. 29
Fort Worth	Mar. 10	Mar. 26	Apr. 11	Oct. 25	Nov. 11	Nov. 27
Houston	Jan. 20	Feb. 14	Mar. 11	Nov. 18	Dec. 11	Jan. 3
Longview	Feb. 28	Mar. 16	Apr. 2	Oct. 26	Nov. 15	Dec. 2
Lubbock	Mar. 25	Apr. 8	Apr. 22	Oct. 15	Nov. 1	Nov. 17
Midland-Odessa	Mar. 15	Mar. 28	Apr. 11	Oct. 21	Nov. 6	Nov. 23
San Antonio	Feb. 11	Mar. 3	Mar. 23	Nov. 6	Nov. 24	Dec. 11
Waco	Feb. 20	Mar. 12	Mar. 31	Nov. 4	Nov. 24	Dec. 13

The problem with rain is it doesn't always come when we need it, and quite often we find ourselves swimming in it. This feast-or-famine situation makes the job of soil building all the more important. Build your beds for the wettest of seasons and then be prepared to water if needed.

STARTING WITH SEED

Seed are where it all begins. If you're to become a good vegetable gardener, you must learn how to start plants from seed. Whether you are growing your own transplants or starting seed directly in the garden, there are a few things you'll need to do to be successful.

Direct Seeding

Most vegetables are seeded directly in the garden. Quite often you'll find it difficult to establish a full stand. By following a few simple principles of proper plant culture, you'll find establishing vegetable plants from seed to be easy and a great deal of fun.

The first step to success is selecting good seed. Remember that seed are living things. Fresh, high-quality seed are always the best choice. The cost of seed is insignificant when compared to the overall cost of gardening, so start off right with good seed.

There is nothing more frustrating than working up a bed and planting seed just to find out it was no good. If you save your seed from year to year, it's a good idea to check the germination percentage before each gardening season. This is easily done by laying 10 seed on a sheet of damp paper towel, rolling it up, and placing it in a plastic bag. In a few days, check the seed to see how many have sprouted. If less than seven seed sprout, plan on seeding heavily to account for the low germination percentage. If less than 4 seed sprout, throw them out and start off with a fresh batch.

Proper soil preparation is also very important. The bed should be well worked, loose, void of any large clods, and raked out until smooth.

Always plant the seed as shallow as possible. A good rule of thumb is to cover the seed 1 to 1½ times the diameter of the seed. This means that small seeds such as those of lettuces, mustard, or carrots should be scattered, only lightly raked in, and watered. Many seed, such as lettuce seed, require light for germination. Always plant more seed than you'll need to get a stand and thin to the final spacing before the plants begin to get crowded. Where heavy layers of mulch are used, be sure to rake it back away from the seed bed until the young plants are up and growing vigorously.

Water is very important to good seed germination. In the spring garden, you'll rarely need to water, except right after planting. In the summer and fall the seed bed will need daily applications of water for the seed to germinate.

Many Southern soils are prone to crusting. A hard crust will inhibit seedling development. By lightly sprinkling compost or vermiculite over the seed bed, you can reduce crusting and greatly enhance germination percentages.

Soil temperature is also a consideration when planting seed. Some seed germinate best in cool soils. These vegetables should not be planted too early in the fall when hot soils are still a problem. On the other hand, starting too early in the spring can be problematic for vegetables that require warm soil temperatures.

SOIL TEMPERATURE REQUIRED FOR GERMINATION

Vegetables	Soil Temperature Range (Degrees F)	Optimum (Degrees F)
Beans	60°–85°	80°
Beets	50°–85°	85°
Cabbage	45°–95°	85°
Carrots	45°–85°	80°
Chard, Swiss	50°–85°	85°
Corn	60°–95°	95°
Cucumbers	60°–95°	95°
Lettuces	40°–80°	75°
Muskmelons	75°–95°	90°
Okra	70°–95°	95°
Parsley	50°–85°	75°
Peas, English	40°–75°	75°
Peas, Southern	60°–95°	90°
Pumpkins	70°–90°	90°
Radishes	45°–90°	85°
Spinach	45°–75°	70°
Squashes	70°–95°	95°
Turnips	60°–105°	85°
Watermelons	70°–95°	95°

Seed Storage

Remember, seed are living things and the way they are treated can greatly affect their germination and storability. When you purchase seed, check the date on the package to make sure they are fresh. Place the seed in a cool, dry place as soon as possible, and keep them there until you are ready to plant them. Never leave packets of seed in the car, glove compartment, or store them in a hot garage. Some large seed, like bean or pea seed, can be damaged if the packet is dropped on a hard surface.

Seed will keep for a year or so in a dry place in an air-conditioned house. For longer storage, your seed should be refrigerated (at 40° to 50°) in a sealed bag or container. Make sure the seed are dry first and store them with a dessicant. Silica gel packets (they often come in electrical equipment) can be dried in the microwave for a minute or two, and placed in the container with the seed. A tablespoon of powered milk wrapped in tissue also acts as a dessicant. Many seed will keep for several years if some care is taken during storage.

Getting Difficult Seed Started

Some vegetable seed are extremely difficult to germinate. Gardeners have come up with all sorts of ways of handling this problem.

There are a number of ways to increase your chances for success. Spinach and beets don't like hot soils and okra doesn't like cool soil temperatures, so always plant at the recommended time of the year.

You can soak the seed overnight to help soften the seed coat and begin the germination process. Don't wait too long though, because once the seed germinate, they are very easily damaged. Covering the seed bed with row cover (a light-weight spun polyester fabric) will help hold in needed moisture, reduce crusting, and generally enhance seedling development. We've found row cover really helps get difficult seed off to a good start.

Growing Your Own Transplants

At some point, you may want to try your hand at growing your own transplants. There are numerous reasons for starting your own plants. You may want to grow some of the lesser-known or newer vegetable varieties or to at least try some of those varieties not found at your local nursery or garden center. Sometimes plants are not available at the best planting time, or you may just enjoy the challenge of starting plants yourself. (See photo on page 40.)

Whatever the reason, don't avoid giving this a try; it's really not that difficult. Plants can be grown in almost anything, including egg cartons, styrofoam cups, plastic pots, and clay pots. Any container will work, as long as it has drain holes.

The type of soil mix is very important. Generally, a peat-perlite mix is best. A number of these peat-lite or soilless mixes are available commercially. They are clean and free of weed seed and disease problems. If you prefer to mix your own, try a 50:50 mix of peat and perlite or a mix of one-third peat, one-third perlite, and one-third vermiculite. Garden soils, although great for growing plants in the ground, are not good for pot culture. They contain diseases, weeds, and insects, and tend to crust and pack badly. Never use garden soil when starting your own transplants.

One of the most difficult aspects of growing your own transplants is

EXPECTED LIFE OF VEGETABLE SEED STORED UNDER COOL, DRY CONDITIONS

Short-Lived Seed: Replace Each Season	Seed Can Be Stored 2 to 3 Years	Long-Lived Seed: Stores 4 to 5 Years
Celery	Beans	Beets
Leeks	Broccoli	Cabbage
Lettuces	Brussels Sprouts	Cauliflower
Onions	Carrots	Collards
Parsley	Chinese Cabbage	Cucumbers
Parsnips	Kohlrabi	Eggplant
Spinach	Okra	Endive
Sweet Corn	Peas	Kale
	Peppers	Muskmelons
	Southern Peas	Mustard
		Pumpkins
		Radishes
		Rutabagas
		Squashes
		Swiss Chard
		Tomatoes
		Turnips
		Watermelons

solving the problem of adequate light. Most homes don't have enough light to grow high-quality transplants without help. If plants are grown without a good light source, they will be tall, leggy, and poorly developed.

Plants grow best with light in the blue to red spectrums. It seems that red light stimulates stem and leaf development, while violet and blue light are required for most enzymatic functions and encourage short, stocky plants.

Fluorescent lights have made the job of growing plants indoors much easier. There are now a variety of types available that provide different qualities of light. Cool, white tubes give off a bluish-white light; warm, white tubes are pinkish in color; and grow lights are generally more bluish red. All fluorescent lights work well, but the plants produced under grow lights will look slightly better. A combination of warm and cool white tubes will give you excellent results without the added cost of grow lights.

It's very easy to set up a small lightbank under a shelf, in a pantry, or over the refrigerator by using a couple of double-tube fixtures suspended from the ceiling by chains or attached to the bottom of an upper shelf. By placing mirrors, aluminum foil, or white reflective paper on the bottom and sides of your indoor growing area, you can greatly increase the efficiency of the lights.

The lights can be plugged into a timer that automatically turns the lights on and off each day. A light schedule of 16 to 18 hours of light each day will produce excellent stocky plants.

The lights must be placed very close to the plants. Intensity of useable light decreases very rapidly as you move away from the source. As long as the plants don't touch the tubes they're not too close, but we'd suggest positioning the lights 4 to 6 inches above the foliage.

Many gardeners prefer to start their transplants in a cold frame or hot frame. (See illustration on page 27.) This is a small enclosure that is used specifically for starting transplants. In the case of hot frames, the mini-greenhouse is provided with bottom heat. Heating cables designed for this purpose are available from many gardening catalogs.

The frames are usually built out of wood and covered in polyethylene plastic. The lid is hinged so it can be ventilated on sunny winter days.

Vegetable seeds should be planted to a depth of about 1 to 1.5 times the diameter of the seed. The seed can be planted one or two to a pot and grown until ready to transplant in the garden or planted in a community pot to be transplanted into individual pots once the seedlings are large enough to handle easily. It takes 2 to 8 weeks to produce a nice transplant, depending on the type of vegetable.

Even though these plants are small and young, don't forget to give them a little fertilizer each week. There are a number of excellent water-soluble fertilizers on the market that will do a great job of producing healthy plants. Select a balanced fertilizer, like a 20–20–20 and mix it at half strength. Water the plants once a week with the solution. If you're growing your vegetables organically, use a weak fish emulsion or seaweed extract solution to provide the needed nutrition.

Plants grown indoors, or in a greenhouse, are very tender and must be acclimated or hardened off before being moved into the garden. This can be accomplished by taking the seedlings, once they are ready, to a protected spot outdoors, like a back porch. Over a couple of days, move the plants from the protected spot to an open, exposed location. This gives the plants a chance to become accustomed to the outdoor conditions and helps them make the transition from indoors to the garden.

Saving Your Own Seed

Each winter, when you're hit with a barrage of seed catalogs, it may seem strange to consider collecting your own seed. However, there are actually a number of good reasons to save seed.

There is a growing interest in antique or heirloom varieties. These are not widely available and are generally perpetuated and distributed by gardeners, to gardeners. The Seed Savers Exchange is a good example of gardeners keeping old varieties alive by saving their own seed. (Saving seed can give you the chance to become a backyard plant breeder, and, who knows, you may discover something really unique or worthwhile. Things to look for are:

earlyness, vigor, dwarfness, improved flavor, disease resistance, tolerance to local conditions, fruit size, and yield.) Seed are available through the Seed Savers Exchange (see the Appendices). Localized varieties are popular among seed savers. These varieties have been preserved over the years because of their tolerance to local conditions.

When starting out as a backyard plant breeder, it's important to use open-pollinated varieties instead of hybrids. Hybrids are created by making controlled crosses of two lines of plants to take advantage of the best characteristics of each. Unfortunately, this makes the seed saved from hybrids extremely variable. In other words, if you save seed of hybrid varieties you won't get what you started with.

When saving seed, always allow the fruit to ripen completely. Many vegetables are eaten before the fruit fully matures, so be sure to leave the fruit on until the seed have ripened. If the seed have not developed fully, they won't germinate and develop properly.

Plants used for seed must be isolated from other similar vegetables. Many members of the same family will cross with each other, making a mess of the seed you save. You can isolate varieties by distance, by changing planting dates, or covering the plants with something like row cover to prevent any mix-ups. If you cover plants that need insects for pollination, like the vine crops or peppers, you'll need to hand pollinate them. (For more information on hand pollinating, consult *Breed Your Own Vegetable Varieties,* by Carol Deppe, Little, Brown & Co.)

Once the fruit has matured, it should be picked and the seed removed. The seed should be washed thoroughly to remove any pieces of fruit. A strainer works well for cleaning the seed. By placing the cleaned seed into a glass of water, you can tell which ones are good. The seed that sink are solid and generally well developed. The ones that float on the top should be discarded.

The seed will need to be dried completely before they are stored. Spread them out in a well-ventilated, dry place for at least a week. Now, the seed are ready to bag and store for the coming gardening season.

Growing Your Own Sprouts

There has been a great deal of press lately on the health benefits of eating sprouts. It's true that sprouts can be very nutritious and many of them are quite good, as well.

Seed sprouting is really easy and makes a good weekend project for the younger gardeners in your house. Seed catalogs and health food stores have a variety of sprouting equipment available, but a homemade sprouter can be made out of things you already have around the house.

A 1-quart, wide-mouth jar makes an excellent sprouter. The mouth of the jar will need to be covered with something that breathes, like a piece of cheesecloth, an old piece of pantyhose, a piece of nylon window screen, or something similar that is secured in place with a rubber band.

Almost anything edible can be grown for sprouts. Alfalfa and mungbean are the most common seeds used for sprouts, but don't overlook chickpeas, fenugreek, sesame, oats, wheat, rye, soybeans, lentils, sunflowers, pumpkins, radishes (especially daikon), black mustard, red clover, corn, flax, garden peas, safflower, turnips, barley, Southern peas, buckwheat, Chinese cabbage, and others. Be creative, and don't be afraid to experiment.

Many garden seed are treated with a fungicide, like Captan or Thiram, to protect the developing seedlings from being attacked by damping off seedling disease. These fungicides help us in the garden, but have no place in sprout production, so be sure (very sure) to use untreated seed.

Wash the seed thoroughly and soak them for 6 to 8 hours, 10 to 12 hours for large seed. Discard the seed that float; the floaters are no good. They will only mold when placed in the sprouting chambers. A quart sprouter will take 2 to 3 tablespoons of small seed or one-fourth cup of large seed.

Place the seed, after soaking, into the clean seed chamber, place the mesh cover on, and then place the seed chamber in a warm, bright spot (but not sunny). Some seed, like mungbean and other bean seed, don't require light for successful sprouting.

Tips for Starting with Seed

- Always begin with good, high-quality seed.
- Provide the seed with adequate moisture, proper soil temperature, and a well-prepared soil.
- Never plant the seed too deep.
- Difficult seed can be presprouted to ensure success.
- Starting your own transplants will give you a chance to grow those hard-to-find vegetable varieties.
- Transplants should be grown in a sterile peat-lite mix, in containers with drain holes, under extremely good light, and with regular applications of a weak fertilizer solution.
- When saving your own seed, plants should be isolated to prevent crossing with other varieties, and the fruit should be allowed to ripen completely.
- Always dry the seed completely before storing.

The seed will need to be washed at least twice a day until they are ready to use. Spray water through the mesh lid, then drain off the water. It may take several rinsings to wash the seed thoroughly. This washing process is important because it reduces the development of mold on the sprouting seed.

It will take from 2 to 14 days for the sprouts to develop, depending on the seed used. Once the sprouts are ready, you can place a lid on the container and put it in the refrigerator. This will slow down their development. Once in the refrigerator, the sprouts will keep for a week or two.

By taking less than a square foot of counter space in the kitchen, you can produce several pounds of fresh sprouts each week. Not a bad way to garden!

GARDENING IN CONTAINERS

Container gardening is growing in popularity. With a growing number of apartment dwellers, and a highly mobile society, having a garden in containers is a wise choice for many. Container plants are also very easily moved to take advantage of seasonal changes in light and can be protected during short periods of freezing weather. A couple of tomato plants in 5–gallon buckets can produce fresh tomatoes until Christmas. When freezing weather approaches, you just move the containers inside until the weather improves.

Containers can be made out of almost anything. An old wheel barrow can be used to grow a fall tomato plant. When the weather turns cold, you can just wheel the plant to a protected spot.

Nursery pots work well, as do oak whiskey barrels, 55–gallon drums cut in half, or 5–gallon plastic buckets. Almost anything that will hold enough soil and that has drain holes can be used to grow vegetable plants. (See photos on page 41.)

The soil mix used for container gardening has a much greater effect on plant growth than the container docs. Soils for container culture must have different properties than those used in the garden. It is generally recommended that soils used for container gardening contain no soil. These soil-less mixes contain a variety of things including: peat, perlite, vermiculite, pine bark, calcined clay, and sharp sand.

There are a number of potting soils commercially available. Most of these are peat perlite or vermicu–lite mixes. They are light and airy with good moisture-holding ability. Commercial mixes are clean and free of diseases.

Many gardeners prefer to mix their own soil-less mix using any of the materials listed above. There are lots of reasons for making your own mixes. It gives you more control over the texture, weight, and moisture-holding capacity and can also help reduce the cost of the mix.

Growing Vegetables in Containers

Vegetable	Light Requirement	Minimum Pot Size	Minimum Plant Spacing (Inches)	Comments
Beans, Bush	Full sun	2 gallons	2–3	Plant a pot or two each week to spread out harvest.
Beans, Pole	Full sun	2 gallons	2–3	Place pots near trellis or provide some support.
Beets	Full to partial sun	1 gallon	2–3	Beets like fertile, organic soils high in nitrogen.
Carrots	Full to partial sun	1 gallon	2–3	Use deep pots to allow for better root development.
Cabbage and other Cole Crops	Full to partial sun	5 gallons	8–12	A very heavy feeder (includes broccoli, cauliflower, collards, and brussels sprouts).
Chard, Swiss	Full to partial sun	1 gallon	4–8	Just harvest a few leaves at a time to extend harvest period.
Cucumbers	Full sun	5 gallons	8–12	Provide a support or cage.
Eggplants	Full sun	5 gallons	1 plant per pot	Makes a nice ornamental when brightly colored fruit begin to develop.
Lettuces	Full to partial sun	1 gallon	6–10	Try these in a strawberry pot. Red-leaf varieties are very attractive.
Mustard and Turnips	Full to partial sun	2 gallons	4–6	Harvest the leaves to extend harvest period.
Onions	Full to partial sun	1 gallon	2–4	Avoid fertilizers high in sulfur for sweeter onions.
Peppers (all types)	Full sun	3 gallons	1 plant per pot	Requires an abundance of moisture during hot weather.
Radishes	Full to partial sun	1 gallon	1–2	Plant a pot or two each week to extend harvest season.
Squashes, Bush	Full sun	5 gallons	1 plant per pot	Don't forget bees are required for pollination, or keep a cotton swab handy.
Squashes, Vining	Full sun	5 gallons	1–2 plants per pot	Provide a trellis or other type of support.
Tomatoes (all types)	Full sun	5 gallons	1 plant per pot	Cage or stake for best results; large pots will produce better, more productive plants.
Watermelons (and other melons)	Full sun	5 gallons	1–3 plants per pot	Grow small-fruited varieties, and provide plants with support.

Container gardening is considerably different than gardening in the ground, especially when it comes to fertilizing and watering your vegetables. Soil-less mixes are almost inert. Whatever nutrition the plant receives must be supplied by you. This means that you will essentially be growing your vegetables hydroponically.

The term "hydroponics" was originally used to describe the culture of plants in a nutrient-rich water solution. It didn't take long for researchers to realize that problems associated with water culture could be lessened by growing plants in soil-less media while still providing the plants with a total nutrient package.

Before using the potting soil, mix 2 pounds (about 2 1/4 cups) of dolomite limestone for every 2 cubic feet of soil. Dolomitic lime provides the plants with needed calcium and magnesium. The rest of the required nutrients can be provided by using a water-soluble fertilizer high in nitrogen, phosphorus, and potash and adding soluble trace elements. These nutrients should be applied at the recommended rates, at least weekly. Many people prefer to use the fertilizer solution at half strength and apply it each time the plants are watered.

Watering is critical to plant survival and is much more critical for container-grown plants than those grown in the ground. The larger the container the less frequent the watering. If large plants are grown in small containers, you may find yourself watering several times a day just to keep up with water loss during our long, hot summers.

Many container vegetables can be grown quite nicely in a greenhouse. Greenhouses allow you to grow vegetables out of season, providing you with fresh vegetables when everyone else is bundling up or staying in out of the cold. A greenhouse can also be used to grow your own transplants.

Tips for Container Gardening

- The shape of container you select is not as important as whether it has drain holes and holds enough soil mix for the vegetable plants to thrive and grow.
- Never use garden soil in containers. Special mixes made for container gardening are available, or they can be mixed by using peat, perlite, vermiculite, calcined clay, pine bark, and sharp sand.
- Water-soluble fertilizers should be applied frequently to ensure vigorous, healthy growth. Slow-release fertilizers can also be used.
- Container gardens require more frequent watering, especially during our long, hot summers.

Vegetables Best Suited to Greenhouse Culture

Cucumbers	•	Mesclun
Green beans	•	Spinach
Lettuces	•	Tomatoes

When selecting a site for your greenhouse, look for a spot that receives at least 6 to 8 hours of direct sun during the winter months. Try to stay away from trees and other overhead obstructions.

Vegetables require a lot of light, so select a greenhouse covering that allows for good light transmission. Materials such as fiberglass, polyethylene, or Plexiglass all work well. Don't use green fiber glass; it screens out light that is needed by your vegetable plants. If shade is required, use shade cloth or a latex paint mixed with an equal amount of water.

When planning your backyard greenhouse, be sure to provide adequate ventilation. A few hours of sunshine can heat up an unventilated greenhouse to an unbearable temperature, even on a cold winter day.

You don't have to spend a fortune building a small hobby greenhouse. A nice greenhouse can be built out of inexpensive materials available at most lumber yards.

Warm-Season Vegetables

***A**SPARAGUS* This is one of the most elusive vegetables for most Southern gardeners, particularly for those living along the Gulf Coast. Though it is native to the seacoast regions of southern Europe, North Africa, and Asia, our domesticated asparagus needs a significant dormant period to force the production of large spears. In Northern gardens, winter does the job. And in some areas of the country, taking away the irrigation will suffice.

In the lower South, it just grows too much. Hot, often wet, summers are not conducive to the buildup of carbohydrates and the winters are not usually harsh enough to force dormancy. So, the asparagus just keeps growing; it limps through the summer and tries to grow off and on during warm spells in the winter. The few spears produced in the spring are usually spindly and not too numerous. Regardless, it's a delicious, gourmet vegetable and many Southern gardeners think it's worth the effort.

The challenge is to grow a healthy-size stand. Asparagus is a heavy feeder. It appreciates lots of organic matter mixed with the soil and plenty of

BASIC PLANTING INFORMATION FOR ASPARAGUS

Space Between Rows (Inches)	Seed Spacing (Inches)	Thin to (Inches)	Seed Depth (Inches)	Days to Reach Maturity	Comments/Planting Dates/Intensive Gardening (I.G.) Spacing
36–48	14–18 (crowns)		1–1½	Perennial, begin harvesting second or third year.	Asparagus can be started from seed but male plants tend to produce most heavily. Don't be afraid to fertilize. Asparagus is so salt tolerant that before the development of modern herbicides, salt (sodium chloride) was used to kill weeds in the vegetable's vicinity.

SPARAGUS VARIETIES

	Disease Resistance	Days to Reach Maturity	Comments
(WA)			Probably best in the upper South. Jersey King, Jersey Knight, and Jersey Centennial should also be tried.
UC 157 (WA)	Green	Rust, Fusarium Wilt	Strong, vigorous plant. One of the best varieties for the lower South.
VIKING KB3 (31)	Green	Rust, Fusarium Wilt	Primarily male variety with good heat tolerance.

fertilizer—at least 4 pounds per 100 square feet to start with. Use a complete fertilizer such as 13–13–13 or one of the high-nitrogen organics, like guano, at 1 to 3 pounds per 100 square feet.

Plant the crowns in a well-prepared bed at a depth of 3 to 4 inches, cover with lots of organic soil, and mulch heavily. A little afternoon shade may help, too.

Typically, asparagus is allowed to grow for two seasons before any harvesting is done. Then, the first year of harvesting, it is harvested continuously for 2 to 3 weeks, the second year for 3 to 4 weeks, and a mature bed for 6 to 8 weeks. This may sound a bit radical but, in the lower South, harvesting 2 to 3 times for 2 to 3 weeks at a time during the cool season (November through May) might result in a better yield, even though the spears may be small. During the typical spring harvest time, commercial asparagus is relatively inexpensive anyway. During the summer you would encourage good growth with plenty of water and fertilizer. After the first frost, cut the plants back to the ground even if the frost wasn't severe enough to kill the foliage.

Tips for Growing Asparagus

1. Incorporate 6 to 8 inches of organic matter and 2 to 4 pounds of a complete fertilizer like 13–13–13 before planting. Organic gardeners can use cotton seed meal, fish meal, blood meal or high-fertility manures like chicken manure. Remember, asparagus is salt tolerant and a heavy feeder.

2. Especially in the lower South, experiment with harvest intervals. Try harvesting periodically during the cool season.

3. Remember to harvest often or the spears will be tough and production will decrease.

Begin harvesting when new spears begin to appear, then let the plants grow for 4 to 6 weeks or until another hard freeze, continuing the process until spring. (See photo on page 108.)

Note: Asparagus plants grown from seed will include both males and females. The male plant produces more spears because it doesn't waste energy going to seed. However, it would be impractical to weed out the female plants from seedlings, because they're already producing by the time you know they're female.

GREEN BEANS

Beans have been a major food crop for centuries, and during all those years many different plants have been called beans. The Southern gardener, however, is primarily interested in green beans or snap beans. Dried beans, such as navy beans, require an arid climate to reach maturity without experiencing severe disease problems. Green beans and dried beans are in fact closely related and, along with limas, butter or Sieva beans, Scarlet runner beans, and the Tepary bean, are native to the New World. Some beans that will grow quite well in the South, such as the yard long bean (actually a Southern pea relative) and the edible soy bean, will be discussed in the Warm-Season Gourmet Selections section (page 142).

One advantage of all bean crops is their membership in the legume family. This means that they have the ability to fix atmospheric nitrogen in association with *Rhizobium* bacteria (nitrogen being one of the most essential plant elements). In order to do this they need close contact with the bacteria as the seeds germinate. Unless you have grown a particular type of bean on the same soil before, it is a good idea to ensure this contact by inoculating the

BASIC PLANTING INFORMATION
FOR BUSH BEANS

Space Between Rows (Inches)	Seed Spacing (Inches)	Thin to (Inches)	Seed Depth (Inches)	Days to Reach Maturity	Comments/Planting Dates/Intensive Gardening (I.G.) Spacing
18–36	2–4	4–6	½–1	45–60	Some gardeners plant on a double row, bedded up 2 feet across, 3 feet between rows. In this case, stagger plants 12 to 18 inches between rows on the bed and 4 to 6 inches apart in the rows. In spring: plant 8 to 10 weeks after last freeze. In fall: plant 10 to 12 weeks before first frost. I.G. spacing: 6 × 6 inches or 4 × 8 inches.

STANDARD BUSH BEAN VARIETIES

Name (Source)	Color	Disease Resistance	Days to Reach Maturity	Comments
Bush Kentucky Wonder (WA)	Dark Green		55	Bush form of one of the highest quality pole beans. Pods are held up off the ground and productivity is good.
Contender (WA)	Light Green		48	Very popular old-standby variety. It is very early, but the quality is substandard compared to newer varieties.
Derby (17, 19, 24)	Green	Tolerance to CBMV	57	This All-America selection is not only attractive with slim pods reaching up to 7 inches long, it is easy to pick because the pods slip easily from the stem. It's also a good producer with a concentrated fruit set.
E-Z Pick (19, 22, 35)	Dark Green	Tolerance to CBMV	55	Blue Lake-type beans are held high on the plant. Pods are also easy to separate from the plant.
Gator Green Improved (31, 35)	Green	Tolerance to CBMV	55	Concentrated set of 6- to 7-inch pods. Holds color and flavor when frozen.
Goldcrop (31)	Yellow	Tolerance to CBMV	50	5½-inch pods are held high on the plant. Stringless and good for canning and freezing. All-America selection.
Jade (12)	Dark Green	Tolerance to CBMV	53	Plants are upright with straight, slender 7-inch pods. Pods have good color, which holds well after picking.
Jumbo (9, 12, 17, 22, 24)	Green		55	Large, flat pods can be 8 to 10 inches long and still stringless. Rich Kentucky Wonder/Romano flavor. Very productive gourmet variety, tends to vine somewhat.
Provider (5, 9, 12)	Green	Tolerance to CBMV	50	Good home or market variety with a concentrated fruit set. The standard form has dark seeds—not great for canning—but varieties with dark seeds tend to be more vigorous. The 5-inch pods are round, stringless, and tender.
Roma II (WA)	Green	Tolerance to CBMV	56	Bush form of the Romano pole bean. Flat pods are 4 to 5 inches long with the same rich flavor that the Romano is known for.

Key to Disease and Pest Abbreviations
CBMV = common bean mosaic virus

STANDARD BUSH BEAN VARIETIES (CONT.)

Name (Source)	Color	Disease Resistance	Days to Reach Maturity	Comments
Royal Burgundy (WA)	Purple		51	Beans are stringless and purple. Fortunately, they turn green when cooked.
Topcrop (WA)	Green		48	This old favorite and All-America selection is still hard to beat. Pods are not as long and pretty as those produced by some of the newer varieties, but the quality and earliness is evident.

seed with a commercial preparation of the specific bacterium, also called a "garden blend," which typically includes *Rhizobium* species for green beans, English peas, and Southern peas. The bacterium causes the formation of root nodules on the plant that release soluble nitrogen the plant can use. At the same time, these nodules do little to impair the root function. Nematodes are microscopic round worms that attack the roots of many plants, including beans, and at first glance, the knots that form as a result of this pest might appear to be beneficial *Rhizobium* nodules. *Rhizobium* nodules, however, are more loosely attached whereas the nematodes cause large, disruptive knots to form that are more a part of the root. Also, don't plant too deep or cover the seed with compost if you have a clay soil. The bean seed lifts its cotyledons (seed leaves) out of the soil and can be stunted or even prevented from germinating in a heavy soil.

Bush beans are especially good in the fall since the pods mature with less fiber in cool weather. (See photo on page 109.) Beans need to be picked often to get the best quality of produce, particularly the French filet beans. (See photo on page 109.)

Tips for Growing Green Beans

1. Inoculate bean seed with nitrogen-fixing bacteria.
2. Don't plant too deep. Covering ½ to 1 inch is sufficient—bean seedlings have to push up through the soil as they germinate.
3. Try beans in the fall. The pods mature in cool weather and are even more tender and tasty.
4. Pick often, especially the filet beans. They are ready to harvest when only about ⅛ inch in diameter.

BASIC PLANTING INFORMATION FOR POLE BEANS

Space Between Rows (Inches)	Seed Spacing (Inches)	Thin to (Inches)	Seed Depth (Inches)	Days to Reach Maturity	Comments/Planting Dates/Intensive Gardening (I.G.) Spacing
36–48	2–4	6	½–1½	50–60	These varieties allow the use of vertical space. Put up a trellis of cedar lattice, woven wire, or even a teepee frame of bamboo poles. In spring: plant on average frost dates or 4 weeks after. In fall: plant 10 to 12 weeks before average frost dates. (Try using fiber row cover to get the seedlings started during the hot weather of August and September.)

POLE BEAN VARIETIES

Name (Source)	Color	Disease Resistance	Days to Reach Maturity	Comments
Emerite (28, 31)	Green	Tolerance to CBMV	53	Vertical gardening is a great way to make the most of limited garden space and this variety is not only a climber, it produces 7-inch, stringless filet beans.
Kentucky Blue (WA)	Green		51	This All-America selection combines the heat tolerance, vigor and quality of Kentucky Wonder with the quality of the Blue Lake variety. Pods are round and smooth.
Kentucky Wonder and Kentucky Wonder Wax (WA)	Green, Yellow		58	Pods are flat and brittle with a wonderful beany flavor. Good producer and heat tolerant.
Romano (WA)	Green		60	Short, flat beans with a distinctive nutty flavor. Pods are meaty yet tender and great for freezing.
Selma Star (19)	Mottled Green		60	There are a number of "old home" varieties with mottled pods, including Landfrauen (19), Alabama No. 1 (29), and Jeminez (12). There are even purple-podded pole beans like the Italian heirloom Trionfo Violetto (3, 12). Some may have strings but all have a following.

Key to Disease and Pest Abbreviations
CBMV = common bean mosaic virus

FILET BEAN VARIETIES

Name (Source)	Color	Disease Resistance	Days to Reach Maturity	Comments
Astrelle (Astrell) (5, 28)	Green		60	Reported to be an improvement over Label. Pods are short, 3 to 4½ inches in length and are produced on compact plants. Pick every other day to ensure stringless, gourmet beans.
Decibel (18, 31)	Green		50	Very early, very thin beans. They should be harvested often when 4 to 5 inches in length. This variety has a concentrated fruit set, so even though the beans are skinny, you can harvest a bunch at one time.
Dorabel (22, 31)	Yellow	Tolerance to CBMV	58	Considered a yellow filet (haricots verts) bean, this variety doesn't develop much yellow color until the pods are about the diameter of regular beans. Regardless, it is productive and the pods are stringless and of high quality.
Label (LaBelle) (17, 31)	Green		50	One of the first filet beans to be developed with a concentrated fruit set. New varieties like Astrelle have come along but this is still a good one. Pods are 4 to 5 inches in length and should be harvested when about ⅛ inch in diameter.
Tavera (12)	Green	Tolerance to A and CBMV	54	One of the newer varieties with both disease resistance and the same high quality beans. It grows 4 to 5 inches in length. Also has a concentrated fruit set. Good producer of very slender beans.
Triumph De Farcy (WA)	Green		48	This variety is a traditional standard for quality and earliness. It does, however, require frequent pickings. The tiny pods of this variety have a faint, purple mottling.

Key to Disease and Pest Abbreviations
A = anthracnose   CBMV = common bean mosaic virus

*L*IMA BEANS (BUSH AND POLE)   Most Southern gardeners find it difficult to harvest good crops of any type of lima, especially the bush varieties. They don't germinate well in cool soil (not colder than 65° F.) and don't set pods when temperatures are consistently in the 90° range. Probably the most successful is the speckled pole lima (either Florida or Christmas). Spring planting or midsummer planting for fall harvest will

BASIC PLANTING INFORMATION FOR BUSH LIMA BEANS

Space Between Rows (Inches)	Seed Spacing (Inches)	Thin to (Inches)	Seed Depth (Inches)	Days to Reach Maturity	Comments/Planting Dates/Intensive Gardening (I.G.) Spacing
30–36	1–2	4–6	1½	65–75	Can stagger plant on a double row as recommended for bush (green) beans. In spring: plant on or up to 4 weeks after day of last freeze. In fall: plant 10 to 12 weeks before first frost. I.G. spacing: 6 × 8 inches to 6 × 12 inches.

BASIC PLANTING INFORMATION FOR POLE LIMA BEANS

Space Between Rows (Inches)	Seed Spacing (Inches)	Thin to (Inches)	Seed Depth (Inches)	Days to Reach Maturity	Comments/Planting Dates/Intensive Gardening (I.G.) Spacing
36–48	4	8–12	1½	75–85	Speckled varieties are usually the most productive. In spring: plant on or up to 4 weeks after last freeze. In fall: plant 14 to 16 weeks before first frost. I.G. spacing: 6 × 12 inches.

result in enough production to make the effort worthwhile. Of the bush varieties, Dixie White Butterpea is one of the small-seeded limas that will produce better under heat stress and should be excellent when planted from mid-August through mid-September for a fall crop.

(See photo on page 109.)

Tips for Growing Limas (Bush and Pole)

1. The challenge is to have beans come into production during cool weather or produce before the heat of summer halts production. Hot caps or a black plastic mulch should get you off to a fast start in the spring. Use row cover to start seed as early as mid-summer for fall production. Don't forget limas are legumes. Inoculate them with a "garden blend" of *Rhizobium*.

2. A trellis in the form of a wooden lattice is an attractive way to grow pole limas but, of course, they can also be grown on poles. Set 3 bamboo poles every 3 to 4 feet in the row, teepee style. Plant 3 to 4 seeds at each pole and thin to 2 plants per pole.

BUSH LIMA BEAN VARIETIES

Name (Source)	Color	Disease Resistance	Days to Reach Maturity	Comments
Baby Fordhook (2)	Green		70	Pods are less than 3 inches long and slightly curved. Compact 12- to 14-inch plants.
Dixie White (13, 21, 24)	White to Light Green		65	Seeds round to broad oval shaped. Produces better than most in hot weather.
Eastland (19)	Light Green	Downy Mildew	68	Vigorous plants continue to yield after main harvest. Pods are 3 to 4 inches in length with large seeds.
Fordhook 242 (WA)	Light Green		75	An old standard and All-America selection. Better adapted to the upper South.
Henderson (WA)	Light Green		65	Large, green seeds. Good one to try in most areas of the South.
Jackson Wonder (Calico) (WA)	Speckled		65	Best known of the speckled bush types. Should be tried throughout the South. Fall crops will probably be the most productive.

POLE LIMA BEAN VARIETIES

Name (Source)	Color	Disease Resistance	Days to Reach Maturity	Comments
Christmas (Large Speckled) (WA)	Speckled		88	Produces large, flat, white beans with red blotches. Very good flavor; a favorite in the South.
Florida Butter (Calico or Florida Speckled) (1, 13, 24, 37)	Speckled		82	Beans are white with purplish markings. This is one of the most tolerant of hot, dry weather.
Fordhook (Burpee's Best) Pole (2)	Light Green		92	Large pods are 4 1/2 inches long and 1 1/4 inches across. Plants may grow to 12 feet or more.
King of the Garden (Large White) (WA)	White		88	Produces large pods up to 6 inches in length.
Prizetaker (Burpee) (2)	White to Light Green		90	Large 6-inch pods with 3 to 5 huge beans.

SWEET CORN

Corn is the only member of the grass family that is widely grown as a vegetable. It is also one of the few vegetables that originated in North America. Early expeditions brought a few ears back to New England as early as 1779. The early explorers found Native Americans from Canada to Florida growing corn and early settlers learned how to grow it from them.

Corn is not a difficult vegetable to grow, but like any other grass, it requires generous amounts of nitrogen. If you've done a good job of building up your soil, you'll find that nitrogen is the only thing that must be added.

Sweet corn prefers a well-drained sandy loam soil with an ideal pH of 6.0 to 6.8. Just remember that corn is very tolerant, and as long as the drainage is good, corn will do all right.

Prepare a good seed bed and rake it smooth. Dig a shallow trench the length of the row and place seeds every 3 to 4 inches. Lightly cover and pack the soil, keeping it watered until seedlings appear.

Once seedlings are up about 6 inches, thin plants to 8 to 12 inches apart. When the plants are 12 to 18 inches tall, bank up soil around the plants to help prevent them from blowing over as they mature.

When preparing the soil each spring, add a generous amount of nitrogen to the soil prior to planting. If a slow-release type is used, one application will probably suffice.

If an immediate-release fertilizer is used, you should side dress (sprinkle along the sides of the rows) with nitrogen when the plants are about 1 foot tall and again when the tassels begin to appear down in the whorl of the leaves. This will help ensure large ears at maturity.

Complete pollination is important if you want the ears to fill well. Each strand of silk goes to one kernel in the ear, and a pollen grain must land on each silk to fertilize its corresponding kernel. Corn is usually planted in blocks of 3 or 4 rows to allow for complete pollination. If anything happens to disrupt the process (strong winds, lots of rain, insect damage) your ears will be poorly formed. If you'll go out and shake the stalks on a very calm morning when the tassels are shedding pollen, it will help produce better filled ears.

Virtually every ear in a planting of one variety will ripen at the same time. Most gardeners will plant several short rows every week or so for several weeks to spread out the harvest. By making several plantings of 3 or 4 short rows grown side by side, you can get good pollination while spreading out the harvest.

A great deal has happened in the 200 years that corn has been in cultivation to improve the varieties available. Breeders continue to search for better, larger, sweeter, and more productive varieties.

BASIC PLANTING INFORMATION FOR CORN

Space Between Rows (Inches)	Seed Spacing (Inches)	Thin to (Inches)	Seed Depth (Inches)	Days to Reach Maturity	Comments/Planting Dates/Intensive Gardening (I.G.) Spacing
32–36	2–4	8–12	½–1	70–95	Newer varieties should be isolated. In spring: plant 1 to 2 weeks after last freeze. In fall: plant 3 to 4 months before first frost. I.G. spacing: rows 8 to 24 inches apart; plants placed 8 to 12 inches apart within rows.

Sweet corn varieties can be divided into three groups (sugary, sugary enhanced, or super sweet).

Sugary varieties (SU1) are traditional sweet corns. They produce sweet kernels that are tender with a creamy texture. The sugar is very rapidly converted to starch after harvest, so these varieties must be eaten very quickly. They should be harvested at just the right stage for peak quality.

Sugary enhanced varieties (Se) have much higher levels of sugar than standard varieties. The kernels are very tender and the texture is creamy. The combination of very sweet flavor, creamy texture, and tenderness makes these varieties much preferred over standard varieties. The conversion of sugar to starch is still very rapid, so the ears must be eaten quickly after

---

Tips for Growing Sweet Corn

- Sweet corn is a heavy feeder and requires generous amounts of nitrogen fertilizer.
- For best results, plant in a well-drained sandy loam soil with a pH between 6.0 and 6.8.
- Thin plants to 8 to 12 inches apart once they are about 6 inches tall.
- Pull soil up around the plants once they reach 12 inches in height.
- Always plant 3 to 4 rows side by side to ensure complete pollination.
- Stagger your planting every 2 weeks to spread out the harvest.
- Don't mix varieties; many sweet corn varieties must be isolated to retain high quality of product.

picking to enjoy their peak quality. It is suggested that these varieties be isolated from other varieties, but it is not absolutely required.

The newest group is the super-sweet varieties (sh2). These varieties produce two to four times more sugar than standard varieties, and the sugar is not converted into starch as it is with the other two types. Gardeners looking for corn with an extremely sweet taste will want to try these. The kernels have a unique crispness even after being frozen and stored for several months. These varieties are a little more challenging to grow because seedlings are weaker and more sensitive to cold soil. Plant seeds a little thick and shallow to ensure a good stand. These varieties *must* be isolated if quality is to be maintained.

Corn varieties also come in yellow, white, and yellow/white bicolors. Much of the decision on the color of varieties will depend on an individual gardener's preference.

Proper harvesting is critical if you want high-quality ears for the table. People use all kinds of tricks to tell when corn is ripe, but the only one that works all of the time is the thumbnail test. Pull back the shucks on an ear and puncture a few kernels with your thumbnail. If the liquid is milky, the ear of corn is ripe. If the liquid is clear, the ear is immature. If it is gummy, the ear is over-mature.

(See photo on page 110.)

SWEET CORN VARIETIES

Name (Source)	Color	Days to Reach Maturity	Comments
Bi-Queen Hybrid (35)	Bicolor	92	A bicolor Silver Queen with 8- to 9-inch ears on disease-resistant vigorous plants.
Bonanza Hybrid (37)	Yellow	82	Older variety with large 8- to 9-inch ears that fill well.
Calumet Hybrid (37)	Yellow	82	An old favorite that has good vigor, high yield, and shows some ear worm resistance.
Crisp 'N' Sweet Hybrid (22, 37)	Yellow	87	Large 9-inch ears with super-sweet quality on vigorous, high-yielding plants.
Florida Staysweet Hybrid	Yellow	87	This is an excellent variety with large ears and high yields. This variety must be isolated.
Funk's Sweet G-90	Bicolor	90	Excellent Southern sweet corn variety. Averages 2 ears per plant. Like a sugar-sweet field corn.
Golden Queen Hybrid (1, 35)	Yellow	92	A yellow version of Silver Queen. If you like Silver Queen, you'll like this one.

SWEET CORN VARIETIES (CONT.)

Name (Source)	Color	Days to Reach Maturity	Comments
Honey 'N' Pearl Hybrid (2, 12, 19, 35)	Bicolor	78	All-America winner, super-sweet type that keeps well. 9-inch ears. Isolate like other super-sweet types.
How Sweet It Is Hybrid (5, 8, 17, 19, 24, 35, 37)	White	88	All-America winner. A super-sweet type with excellent keeping quality. 8-inch ears. Normally produces 2 ears per plant. Plants require isolation.
Kandy Korn (2, 5, 28, 35)	Yellow	89	Very sweet 8-inch ear on purple-stalked plants. Good keeping quality.
Merit Hybrid (19, 37)	Yellow	75	A very dependable old variety that is still worth growing.
Miracle Hybrid (2, 8, 31)	Yellow	82	A sugar-enhanced, excellent variety with large 8½-inch ears. Very sweet and keeps well.
Platinum Lady Hybrid (2, 8, 17, 22, 31, 35)	White	78	Seven and one-half- to 8-inch ear with purple and green husks. Good growers.
Quicksilver	White	75	Similar to Silver Queen but two weeks earlier. Excellent for short-season areas.
Salsweet Hybrid (9)	Bicolor	83	Very vigorous, disease-resistant plants with good quality bicolor ears.
Seneca Star Hybrid (35)	Yellow	65	Very early variety with large 7½- to 8-inch ears. Good plant vigor.
Seneca Chief Hybrid	Yellow	82	An old standard that is still popular. 8½-inch ears with very thin cobs.
Silver Queen Hybrid (WA)	White	92	An old variety that sets the standard for other white-kernel varieties. Still an excellent Southern variety.
Summer Sweet Series (7620, 7710, 8601, 8701, 8502BC—see following descriptions) (35)			This series was developed to produce super-sweet kernels that hold their sweetness well during freezing or shipping. Isolate varieties to ensure best quality and highest sweetness.
Summer Sweet 7620	Yellow	82	Seven and three-quarter-inch ears with excellent quality and good disease resistance.
Summer Sweet 7710	Yellow	83	Seven and one-half-inch super-sweet ears with very small kernels. Vigorous plants with good disease resistance.
Summer Sweet 8601	White	86	Seven and one-half-inch ears with excellent sweetness and keeping quality. Some multiple ears.
Summer Sweet 8701	White	87	Very good well-adapted variety for the south. 7¼-inch ears.
Summer Sweet 8502BC	Bicolor	85	Very sweet widely adapted variety with good disease resistance. 7½-inch ears.

SWEET CORN VARIETIES (CONT.)

Name (Source)	Color	Days to Reach Maturity	Comments
Summer Flavor Series (79BC, 82Y—see following descriptions) (35)			This series was developed with full sugar-enhanced genes that yield a very high sugar content. These varieties don't need isolation, but it does improve quality.
Summer Flavor 79BC	Bicolor	79	A large 8-inch bicolor sweet corn with gourmet quality.
Summer Flavor 82Y	Yellow	82	A large high-quality yellow corn with large 8½-inch ears on large 8-foot plants.
Sundance Hybrid	Yellow	69	A very early 7½-inch ear with good quality on very disease-resistance plants.
Tender Treat E.H. Hybrid (5, 35)	Yellow	95	Late maturing, very large 9-inch ear with super-sweet quality on very large purple-stalked plants.

Other varieties that may merit attention include: Snow Belle, Sugar Loaf, Country Gentleman, Comet, and Spring Calico.

CUCURBITS: CUCUMBERS, SQUASHES, PUMPKINS, HONEYDEWS, CANTALOUPES, WATERMELONS, AND OTHER MELONS

The cucurbit, or vine crop, family is a group of tender annual plants grown for their fruit. They thrive in warm to hot conditions in full sun and respond poorly to cold weather. This group of plants shares similar cultural requirements and many of the same disease and insect problems. For this reason, it is important to rotate this family around the garden. Try not to plant any member of this family in the same plot year after year.

Most of the plants in the cucurbit family are monoecious, meaning they produce male and female flowers separately but on the same plant. Because pollination is important for fruit development, you must have bees or other pollinators present if you expect to harvest fruit.

The plant will usually develop a flurry of male flowers early in the season. As the plants mature they begin the formation of the female flowers, and then comes the fruit. If bees or other pollinators are absent, as is the case in many urban environments, you must pollinate the flowers by hand. This can be accomplished by placing the pollen from the male flowers on the stigma of the female flowers. The female flowers have miniature fruit behind the petals of the flowers.

Plant breeders have developed a number of all-female varieties (gynoecious). These female plants, when planted with a pollinator (a variety with male flowers), will set more fruit and do so earlier than other varieties.

Many gardeners worry about planting different members of the cucurbit family in the same bed for fear they might cross. It is true that some of the squashes and pumpkins do cross, but unless you plan to save the seed for next year, it will have no effect on this year's crop.

Fruit develops along the stem of the developing vine or bush. Because of this mulches are very beneficial. By mulching heavily before the fruit begins to develop, you can keep the fruit off the soil, thus reducing the problems with fruit rot. Trellises will also help keep the fruit off the ground.

Some members of the cucurbit family require a great deal of space, but are easy to care for and tolerate heat well enough to make them an ideal summer and early fall vegetable for the Southern gardener. Trellises can also be used as a space-saving method for smaller gardens. Those large-fruited varieties must have some sort of support for the developing fruit. Mesh bags, cheesecloth slings, or the legs of old washed pantyhose can all be used to hold up watermelons, muskmelons, winter squashes, and other large-fruited vine crops.

CUCUMBERS

Cucumbers originated in Asia and Africa, but have been in cultivation for more than 3,000 years. In fact, they were commonly grown in England as early as the fourteenth century.

The cucumber is a climbing or trailing vine with hairy, angular stems, and large leaves. Cucumbers will tolerate a wide range of soils, as long as the drainage is good. Sandy to sandy loam soils are best for early production, but don't hold enough moisture to encourage vigorous growth during the dry summer months. Heavier soils like clay loams will produce large yields for a longer period of time, but beds must be raised high enough to provide needed drainage during periods of wet weather. Although organic matter does not seem overly important in the production of cucumbers, you'll find that soils high in organic matter hold moisture better, as well as those needed nutrients.

Cucumbers are sun-loving plants that grow best in full or almost full sun under warm conditions. Don't start planting until well after the last freeze in the spring, once soils have warmed to about 60° F. Cucumber plants are extremely sensitive to temperature. If planted too early or left uncovered on cool nights, the plants will chill. After this occurs, they will resume growth very slowly.

BASIC PLANTING INFORMATION FOR CUCUMBERS

Space Between Rows (Inches)	Seed Spacing (Inches)	Thin to (Inches)	Seed Depth (Inches)	Days to Reach Maturity	Comments/Planting Dates/Intensive Gardening (I.G.) Spacing
48–72	6	12–18 (3 or 4 plants per hill)	1–1½	50–70	When planting in hills, place 4 to 6 seed per hill, with hills spaced 4 to 6 feet apart. In spring: plant 2 to 4 weeks after last freeze. In fall: plant 3 to 4 months before first freeze. (I.G.) spacing: place on trellis spaced 12 inches apart.

Cucumbers are ideal for trellises, cages, or some other form of support. They take up a great deal of space if allowed to vine, so trellises are best suited for the smaller garden.

The variety list notes two types of cucumbers: slicer and pickling types. Pickling types are just fine for fresh eating; long slicers are often used to make bread-and-butter pickles.

You'll also find some varieties listed as gynoecious (female). Most cucumbers are monoecious (they produce both male and female flowers on the same plant). Gynoecious varieties produce mostly female flowers. This makes them more productive, especially earlier in the season. Most of the gynoecious varieties are sold with a few monecious seeds mixed in to provide the needed pollen for fruit set. Always plant a few pollinators when planting a gynoecious variety in the garden.

You'll notice, too, that some varieties are listed as greenhouse cucumbers. These varieties were developed for greenhouse culture and should not be

---

Tips for Growing Cucumbers

- Plant in a well-drained, slightly acid soil. Ideal pH: 6.5 to 7.0.
- Wait until the soil has warmed to at least 60° F before planting. Plants will achieve best germination in 60° to 90° soil.
- Remember, cucumbers are moderate-to-heavy feeders.
- Place the cucumbers on a trellis or another support to reduce disease problems and to produce straight, unblemished fruit. Trellises are perfect for smaller gardens.
- Harvest fruit when they are slightly immature, and don't allow over-ripe fruit to remain on the plants.

CUCUMBER VARIETIES

Name (Source)	Type	Disease Resistance	Days to Reach Maturity	Comments
Burpee Hybrid II (2)	Slicer	CMV, DM	55	Straight green fruit 8½ inches long, with sweet, crisp flesh.
Burpless Hybrid (WA)	Slicer		62	Slender 2-foot-long fruit with tender skin. Ideal for trellis.
Bush Whopper (19)	Slicer		55	Six to 8-inch-long fruit on dwarf plants. Excellent for small gardens.
Calypso (22, 31, 35)	Pickling	S, DM, PM, CMV, A, LS	56	Medium green, slightly tapered fruit with white spines.
Comet II (31)	Slicer	S, DM, PM, CMV, A, LS	60	Improved burpless type with slim 7½- to 8-inch fruit; gynoecious (female) variety with pollinator.
Dasher II Hybrid (1, 24, 31, 35, 37)	Slicer	LS, A, DM, CMV, S	55	A gynoecious (female) 8- to 9-inch slicer with high yields; pollinator included in mix.
Fancipak Hybrid (19, 24)	Pickling	A, LS, DM, CMV, S	55	Very productive cukes, excellent shape for pickling.
Fanfare (WA)	Slicer	DM, PM, CMV, A, LS, S	63	1994 All-America winner. Excellent compact plants with good-quality, 8- to 9-inch cukes. Great for containers.
Jazzer (22, 31)	Slicer	CMV, PM, DM, S	48	An early burpless variety 7½ to 8 inches long.
Marketmore 76 (5, 8, 9, 12, 29, 31, 35, 37)	Slicer	CMV, DM, PM, S	68	An 8-inch, straight, glossy green cuke with white spines.
Maximore 103 (35)	Slicer	LS, PM, CMV, S	58	A blended gynoecious (female) hybrid with pollinator added to produce high yield.
Pickalot Hybrid (2)	Pickling	PM	54	Compact 4-foot plants that start bearing early.
Pickle-Dilly-Hybrid (19)	Pickling		50	Crisp, dark green, nearly spineless, 4½-inch fruit. Ideal for trellis.
Pioneer (31)	Pickling	S, CMV, DM, A, LS	51	A black-spined gynoecious (female) variety that bears heavy crop of medium-size fruit.

Key to Disease and Pest Abbreviations
A = anthracnose   BW = bacterial wilt   CMV = cucumber mosaic virus   DM = downy mildew
LS = leaf spot   PM powdery mildew   S = scab   TLS = target leaf spot   WMV1, 2 = watermelon mosaic virus 1, 2

CUCUMBER VARIETIES (CONT.)

Name (Source)	Type	Disease Resistance	Days to Reach Maturity	Comments
Poinsett (WA)	Slicer	PM, DM, A, LS	65	A gynoecious (female) vigorous plant that fruits over a long season. Plant with a pollinator.
Salad Bush Hybrid (WA)	Slicer	PM, DM, LS, S, CMV	57	All-America winner. Compact plants with uniform, 8-inch fruit.
Saladin (28)	Pickling	CMV, PM, BW	55	All-America winner. High yields of crisp, good-tasting, knobby fruit.
Salty (31)	Pickling	S, CMV, PM, DM	53	A gynoecious (female) variety; excellent for pickling.
Slice Master Select (8, 22, 24, 35, 37)	Slicer	DM, PM, CMV, S, LS, TLS	61	An improved Slice Master with better fruit shape, color, and yield.
Straight Eight (2, 5, 8, 24, 37)	Slicer	CMV	58	All-America winner. High-quality, even deeper green color, 8 inches long.
Streamliner Hybrid (2)	Slicer	CMV, DM, PM	60	Slender, slicing-type up to $10\frac{1}{2}$ inches long, thick flesh, and small seed cavity.
Supersett (1, 12, 31, 35)	Slicer	S, CMV, PM, DM, A, LS	60	Cylindrical, slightly tapered, 8- to $8\frac{1}{2}$-inch long, dark green fruit. Early gynoecious plants; pollinator required.
Soo Yoh Long (pronounced "suyo") (12, 17, 29, 31)	Slicer	PM	61	Sweet-flavored, ridged Chinese variety is burpless and high quality.
Sweet Success Hybrid (WA)	Slicer	CMV, WMV1 & 2, S, LS	58	All-America winner. Dark green, 14-inch fruit with crisp flesh.
Sweet Slice (WA)	Slicer	S, LS, A, CMV, PM, DM	62	Long 10- to 12-inch burpless fruit that's very sweet.
Vert De Massy (3, 12, 17, 29)	(Fancy) Slicer	S	53	Gourmet French variety used for slicing or pickling (comichons).

grown outside. They are called parthenocapic (developing fruit without pollination). There are no insects in a greenhouse to pollinate the flowers, so these varieties were developed with this in mind. If pollination does occur, it actually reduces the fruit quality.

Cucumbers are moderate-to-heavy feeders, benefiting from a regular application of a fertilizer high in nitrogen with a moderate level of phos-

EUROPEAN GREENHOUSE CUCUMBER VARIETIES

Name (Source)	Type	Disease Resistance	Days to Reach Maturity	Comments
Aricia (31)	Slicer			Excellent for fall/winter greenhouse production.
Beauty (17)	Slicer	LS, S	60	Tasty, crisp, sweet greenhouse cucumber.
Carmen (31, 33)	Slicer	DM, PM, S		Long, slender, nicely shaped fruit, gynoecious (female).
Dynasty (35)	Slicer	LS, A, CMV, PM, DM, S	55	Very productive gynoecious variety with uniform, smooth fruit.

Key to Disease and Pest Abbreviations
A = anthracnose   CMV = cucumber mosaic virus   DM = downy mildew   LS = leaf spot
PM = powdery mildew   S = scab

phorus and potash. Fertilizer (see the Soil Building chapter) should be mixed into the garden before planting, again once the plants begin to vine, and once again when the plants begin producing. When slow-release fertilizers are used, a single application will usually suffice with an occasional foliar feeding applied.

Many of the newer varieties are resistant to the common cucumber diseases like downy and powdery mildew, anthracnose, angular leaf spot, and a variety of viruses. Selecting resistant varieties is the best way to reduce the use of pesticides in the garden.

Cucumbers are generally harvested when immature, before the seeds become hard. The fruit should be harvested when it is dark green, firm, and crisp. Pickling types are harvested from when they're very small until they're 4 to 6 inches in length, depending on the use. Slicers are usually harvested when they are about 1½ inches in diameter and 8 to 10 inches long. You'll need to pick them at least once every other day to get the fruit at its prime. (The quality is at its peak in the morning.) Don't allow over-ripe fruit to stay on the vine. It will cause the vines to stop producing.

(See photos on page 111.)

*S*QUASHES AND PUMPKINS
Squashes and pumpkins are both native to tropical and subtropical America. Their care and culture are very similar. Winter squashes are actually more closely related to pumpkins than they are to crookneck, straight-neck, or zucchini-type squashes.

The squash and pumpkin family is made up of four species: *Cucurbita pepo, Cucurbita moschata, Cucurbita maxima,* and *Cucurbita mixta.* These groups can generally be divided into two types: Summer squashes range from bush to vining plants and their fruit is used when it is immature. Winter squashes (including pumpkins) are usually harvested when the fruit are fully mature, the rinds are tough and durable, and the fruit will keep for months. Some winter squashes are also used as summer squashes or harvested when immature. A good example of a winter/summer squash is Peter Pan, a scalloped squash that is eaten either when immature or mature.

Squashes and pumpkins are heavy feeders and prefer a well-drained loamy soil. Organic matter is beneficial in breaking up tight, poorly drained soils and should be added well in advance of planting. The addition of a fertilizer high in nitrogen, phosphorus, and potassium prior to planting will ensure a bountiful harvest. A slow-release fertilizer will provide needed nutrition throughout the growing season. More immediately available fertilizers must be reapplied every 4 to 6 weeks. Squash and pumpkin seeds germinate quickly in warm soils, so transplanting should only be necessary in the higher altitudes where the growing season is very short.

Bush and semibush types are best adapted to smaller gardens, but vining types will easily climb a trellis or other support if space is limited. If you decide to trellis the large-fruited varieties, be prepared to provide some type of support for the fruit.

Summer squashes should be harvested almost every other day to enjoy their maximum quality. The fruit are at their peak 3 to 5 days after flowering. Some gourmet chefs actually prepare baby squash, which are harvested before the female blossom even opens. The fruit are useable as long as the skin is still tender and can easily be pierced by a thumbnail. Don't allow over-ripe summer squashes to remain on the vine. These developing fruit will cause the vine to stop producing.

BASIC PLANTING INFORMATION FOR SQUASHES AND PUMPKINS

Space Between Rows (Inches)	Seed Spacing (Inches)	Thin to (Inches)	Seed Depth (Inches)	Days to Reach Maturity	Comments/Planting Dates/Intensive Gardening (I.G.) Spacing
24–36 for bush types, 48–72 for trailing types	6–12	24–36 (2–3 plants per hill)	1–2	45–120	Plant 4 to 6 seeds per hill. In spring: plant 4 to 6 weeks after last frost. In fall: plant (summer squash) 60 to 90 days before first frost. Plant winter squash/pumpkins 4 to 5 months before first frost. I.G. spacing: 12 to 24 inches, if trellised or caged.

ZUCCHINI VARIETIES

Name (Source)	Days to Reach Maturity	Comments
Aristocrat Zucchini (17)	48	An early, heavy producer of dark green, cylindrical fruit on an upright plant.
Burpee Hybrid Zucchini (2)	50	High yields of medium green, tender-skinned fruit on a compact bush.
Cocozelle (12, 17, 30)	55	Long, slender, dark green zucchini with light green stripes.
Condor (12)	48	Medium green, early, high-quality fruit on vigorous, open, nearly spineless stem that is easy to pick.
French White Bush Zucchini (17)	50	A vigorous, white zucchini with a mild flavor.
Gold Rush (WA)	52	A deep-golden, zucchini-type plant. Uniform, cylindrical, straight fruit on easy-to-pick plant.
Gourmet Globe Hybrid (19, 35)	50	Unique round fruit; light green and slightly tapered fruit.
Greyzini (22, 31)	50	Excellent quality; light green and slightly tapered fruit.
President Hybrid (1, 24, 37)	50–55	Easy-to-harvest fruit on open plants. Very uniform, dark green fruit with light green flecks.
Senator Hybrid (24, 37)	48	Early, green zucchini on vigorous bushes.
Seneca Zucchini (1, 17, 31, 35, 37)	47	An early medium green fruit with light green flecks. Compact, open plants with long-stemmed fruit for easy harvest.

Winter squashes and pumpkins, on the other hand, should be harvested once the fruit have matured. Many gardening books suggest harvesting just before the first snow of the season, but the Southern gardener may find this difficult. Our long growing season allows for several pickings.

Select fully developed fruit with a tough rind. The mature fruit should be cured at 85° to 90° F for several days to encourage hardening of the rind if you plan to store them for a while. Store your harvest under cool (50° to 60° F), humid conditions.

If you want pumpkins for Halloween, don't plant too early. Hybrids planted in mid-June will ripen before October 31. They will develop a burnt orange color when ripened under as cool a temperature as possible.

Squash blossoms are edible, too! Try them fried with scrambled eggs or deep-fried in an egg batter.

(See photos on page 113.)

YELLOW SQUASH VARIETIES

Name (Source)	Type	Days to Reach Maturity	Comments
Butter Swan Hybrid (19)	Crookneck	48	Small plant produces abundant, smooth, crookneck fruit; very uniform and high quality.
Butterbar Hybrid (24)	Straight Neck	50	Long, slender, buttery yellow fruit; excellent quality on a vigorous, open bush.
Butterstick Hybrid (2)	Straight Neck	50	Bright yellow, firm texture, sweet fruit.
Dixie Hybrid (19, 24, 37)	Crookneck	45	Compact plant; bears heavy crop of uniform high-quality fruit.
Early Prolific Straight Neck (WA)	Straight Neck	50	All-America winner. Yellow fruit, 6 inches long, and a heavy producer.
Early Summer Crookneck (WA)	Crookneck	50	Bright yellow, tender, small-seeded fruit on an open plant for easy harvest.
Goldbar Hybrid (1, 22, 24, 37)	Straight Neck	53	Golden-yellow; cylindrical fruit; very uniform; vigorous and productive.
Goldie Hybrid (1, 37)	Crookneck	55	A medium-early, high-yielding, semi-crookneck with creamy flesh.
Multipick Hybrid (1, 9, 24, 37)	Straight Neck	50	Strong bush type, very productive, and resistant to Mosaic virus.
Pic-N-Pic Hybrid (19)	Crookneck	50	Tender yellow fruit with a smooth skin. Open plant habit allows for easy harvest; very productive.
Seneca Butterbar Hybrid (19)	Straight Neck	49	High quality. Tender flesh and long cylindrical fruit on a vigorous bush.
Smoothie Hybrid (35)	Straight Neck	47	A very early, long, smooth fruit on compact plants. Plants are productive and open habit makes harvesting easy.
Sun Drop Hybrid (17, 19, 24, 35)	Novelty	48	All-America winner. Compact bush with small yellow oval fruit with excellent quality.
Sunbar (1, 31)	Straight Neck	54	Very productive. Glossy yellow, slightly tapered fruit.
Sundance Hybrid (1, 3, 17, 31, 35, 37)	Crookneck	50	Early, attractive, very uniform, high-quality, smooth fruit on compact, high-yielding plants.
Supersett Hybrid (9, 28, 37)	Crookneck	50	Yellow, fine-textured fruit with smooth skin; very productive.

Tips for Growing Squash and Pumpkins

- Squash and pumpkins should be planted during warm weather. (Soil temperature for best germination: 60° to 90° F.)
- Ideal pH: 6.0 to 7.0.
- These vegetables are heavy feeders, so apply fertilizer generously.
- Summer squash quality is best when picked 3 to 5 days after flowering.
- Bush-type or trellised plants are best suited to small gardens.
- Floating row cover can be used to cover young plants to prevent aphid-transmitted viruses.
- Bees are important for pollination, so be cautious about using pesticides when they are active.

WINTER SQUASH VARIETIES

Name (Source)	Type	Days to Reach Maturity	Comments
Autumn Queen (31)	Acorn	71	A very early acorn type; semi-bush with dark green fruit, about the size of Table Queen.
Buttercup (WA)	Buttercup	90	Dark green fruit with orange flesh on vigorous vines.
Butternut Supreme Hybrid (31)	Butternut	87	Uniform, blocky, 12-inch fruit with tan rind.
Cream of the Crop (9, 12, 19, 24, 33, 35)	Acorn	85	A novelty All-America winner. Creamy yellow fruit with creamy white flesh. Good keeper with very high quality.
Delicata (3, 8, 12, 22, 31)	Cushaw	100	Small, cream-colored fruit with dark green stripes. Excellent keeper.
Early Butternut Hybrid (1, 5, 19, 22, 31, 35, 37)	Butternut	85	All-America winner. High yields on semibush type plant. Excellent fruit quality that stores 2 months.
Golden Hubbard (22, 31)	Hubbard	90	Orange-red, warted fruit with deep orange flesh; 10 to 12 pounds.
Hubbard Improved Green (31)	Hubbard	120	Ten- to 12-pound fruit; slightly warted; dark green with orange, thick flesh.
Pasta Hybrid (17)	Spaghetti	90	Large 12-inch, creamy white cylindrical fruit.

WINTER SQUASH VARIETIES (CONT.)

Name (Source)	Type	Days to Reach Maturity	Comments
Peter Pan Hybrid (2, 9, 17, 19, 28, 35, 37)	Scallop or Patty Pan	48	A very uniform, light green, scallop-type that is eaten when immature (1 to 2 inches) or mature.
Pink Jumbo Banana (1, 5, 8, 24, 30, 37)	Banana	100	Large, banana-type squash, weighing up to 75 pounds. Flesh is light orange, fine grain, sweet-flavored, and excellent for pumpkin pies.
Scallopini Hybrid (3, 24, 31)	Scallop or Patty Pan	70	Flavorful scalloped fruit; excellent for eating when immature or fully ripe.
Sugar Loaf (12, 17)	Cushaw	100	Very high-quality, blocky fruit; average 1 to 2 pounds. Rusty brown with green stripes.
Sunburst Hybrid (WA)	Scallop or Patty Pan	75	All-America winner. Bright yellow scalloped fruit with green coloring at both ends. Excellent when immature or mature.
Sweet Mama (17, 19, 24, 31)	Buttercup	85	All-America winner. Compact vines with high yields of 2 to 3 pounds of mild-flavored fruit. Vines tolerate vine bores and Fusarium wilt.
Table Ace (WA)	Acorn	78	A semibush-type acorn with black-green fruit. Thick, orange flesh.
Table Queen (WA)	Acorn	90	An old standard that is still hard to beat. Dark green fruit with nutty flavor.
Table King (31)	Acorn	80	Good-size acorn squash on a compact bush.
Table Gold (5, 8, 35)	Acorn	90	A novelty acorn with bright orange fruit when fully ripe; yellow when immature. Bush type.
Tivoli Hybrid (5, 8, 22, 33, 35)	Spaghetti	100	All-America winner. A bush type with 3 to 4 pound fruit.
Turk's Turban (24, 35, 37)	Turban	100	Colorful ornamental that is fine for stuffing or baking. Bright orange-red fruit; average weight is 8 to 10 pounds.
Watham Butternut (WA)	Butternut	82	Uniform 8-inch, tan fruit with deep orange flesh. A good keeper.
White Bush Scallop (1, 29, 30, 37)	Scallop or Patty Pan	60	Flattened scallop-type; creamy white when mature.

PUMPKIN VARIETIES

Name (Source)	Size in Pounds	Days to Reach Maturity	Comments
Autumn Gold Hybrid (WA)	10	90	All-America winner. Ripens gold to deep orange; globe shaped.
Big Max (WA)	50–100	120	Very large fruit with pinkish orange rind and bright orange flesh that is excellent for cooking.
Connecticut Field (WA)	15–25	115	A large pumpkin for pies; hard, ribbed, deep orange fruit.
Frosty Hybrid (WA)	15–20	95	High-quality, bright orange fruit on semibush plant for smaller gardens.
Funny Face Hybrid (24, 35, 37)	10–15	100	Very attractive, uniform, bright orange fruit on semibush plants. Thick flesh for carving or cooking.
Jack O' Lantern (WA)	10–15	110	Excellent shape; very popular for Halloween.
Lumina (WA)	8–10	110	Novelty white fruit with bright orange flesh. Harvest slightly immature.
Prizewinner Hybrid (2)	100+	120	Even larger than Big Max. Great for shows or to amaze your friends.
Small Sugar (WA)	7	115	Excellent for pies. Deep orange flesh; sweet flavor.
Spirit Hybrid (WA)	15	99	High yields of bright orange, oval fruit on semibush plants.
Spookie Hybrid (9)	10–15	90	Perfect for carving or cooking. Bright orange, globe-shaped fruit on vigorous vines.

MINIATURE PUMPKIN VARIETIES

Name (Source)	Days to Reach Maturity	Comments
Baby Boo (19, 28)	95	Creamy white, 3-inch-diameter fruit; excellent for holiday decorating; white flesh is edible.
Jack Be Little (WA)	90	Rich orange color on deeply ribbed 2 × 3-inch fruit.
Little Lantern (31)	100	Miniature Jack-O-Lantern-shaped fruit; 5 inches in diameter.
Sweetie Pie (31)	110	A little flattened, deep-ribbed pumpkin; 3 × 2 inch. An improved Jack Be Little.

HONEYDEWS, MUSKMELONS, AND OTHER MELONS

This group of plants is believed to have originated in Asia, but their existence in the Americas dates back to before the 1500s. The fruit we know in America as a cantaloupe is more correctly named muskmelon. The muskmelon is a nettled melon with small ribs and a stem that slips freely from the fruit when it is fully ripe. A European or French melon is the true cantaloupe or charantais melon. Charantais melons have a rough, scaly rind that doesn't slip from the stem. Honeydew and crenshaw melons lack the powerful aroma characteristic of cantaloupes, but their sweet, smooth flesh is hard to beat.

Honeydews, muskmelons, and cantaloupes are the most demanding of the vegetables in the cucurbit family. They prefer a very well-drained sandy to sandy loam soil with a pH of 6.0 to 6.5. They do not like high-acid soils. Lime may be used to raise the pH of very acid soils.

The high humidity and abundant moisture encourage disease problems and dilute the sweetness and flavor of the fruit. One of the things we can do to help encourage better quality and reduce disease problems is to delay planting so the fruit ripens during our usually drier weather in July and August.

You'll find that warm soils are required to germinate the seed. Seed will germinate best with soil temperatures of 80° F. The soil should be well prepared by deeply tilling along with the addition of generous amounts of organic matter. Fertilizer high in nitrogen with moderate amounts of phosphorus and potassium should be tilled into the soil just prior to planting. Additional fertilizer should be added once the plants begin to vine and again as soon as the fruit have set. Generally, each plant will set 3 to 8 fruit all at once. Any other fruit that appears will usually shrivel and drop off. Stag-

BASIC PLANTING INFORMATION FOR HONEYDEWS, MUSKMELONS, AND OTHER MELONS

Space Between Rows (Inches)	Seed Spacing (Inches)	Thin to (Inches)	Seed Depth (Inches)	Days to Reach Maturity	Comments/Planting Dates/Intensive Gardening (I.G.) Spacing
48–72	6–12 in row, 3–4 in hill	18–24 in row (2–3 seed per hill)	½–1	60–90	This group of melons does best when grown under dry, hot conditions. Plant 3 to 6 weeks after last spring freeze or up until 4 to 5 months before the first fall freeze. (I.G.) spacing: 12 inches apart on trellis.

CANTALOUPE, HONEYDEW, AND OTHER MELON VARIETIES

Name (Source)	Type	Days to Reach Maturity	Comments
Ambrosia Hybrid (2, 19, 22, 24, 35)	Muskmelon	86	Thick, salmon orange-fleshed fruit on vigorous, powdery mildew-resistant plants. An excellent quality variety.
Burpee Hybrid (2, 31, 35)	Muskmelon	82	Heavily netted, 4½-pound, high-quality melons on vigorous vines.
Classic Hybrid (24, 35, 37)	Muskmelon	85	Four- to 4½-pound fruit with fine-grained, salmon flesh; high-quality, and vigorous.
Earli-Dew (WA)	Honeydew	80	Lime green flesh with smooth, creamy green rind when fully ripe. Productive.
Earlisweet (3, 17, 31, 35)	Muskmelon	68	A very early variety with very sweet salmon-colored flesh.
Early Hybrid Crenshaw (2, 35)	Crenshaw	90	Delicious, flavorful, salmon pink flesh with yellowish green skin when ripe. Large 14-pound fruit.
French Charantais and Hybrids (3, 12, 17, 22, 28, 31, 33, 37)	Cantaloupe	68–80	French Charantais are high-quality, gormet varieties. Unavailable at markets because they don't keep well. Other varieties like it are: Chamel (78), Pancho (80), Alienor (75), Early Chaca (68), Savor Hybrid (78), and Flyer (68).
Gold Star Hybrid (9)	Muskmelon	87	Tolerant of fusarium wilt (race 1). This is a vigorous, heavy-yielding variety. Fruit quality is very good.
Harper Hybrid (9)	Muskmelon	86	Considered by some to be the best-quality melon around. Sweet, rich flavor on a high-yielding, vigorous vine. A honeydew-muskmelon hybrid.
Honey Brew Hybrid (1, 35)	Honeydew	90	High-yielding, good-quality honeydew on vigorous, powdery mildew- and fusarium wilt-resistant plants.
Honeyshaw (17)	Crenshaw	90	Large 16-pound crenshaw with salmon pink, very juicy sweet flesh. Skin is mottled yellow at maturity.
Imperial #4–50 (37)	Muskmelon	90	Large, oval fruit with good netting. Pick at full slip stage for best quality.
Israeli (24, 37)	Israeli	90–95	Very sweet, creamy colored flesh with thin yellow-orange rind that has very little netting.
Jumbo Hale's Best (37)	Muskmelon	82	Good-flavored cantaloupe for roadside market. Firm flesh; holds up well.
Magnum 45 Hybrid (1, 24, 35, 37)	Muskmelon	80	An early large cantaloupe that produces well over a long period. Tolerant of powdery mildew.

continued

CANTALOUPE, HONEYDEW, AND OTHER MELON VARIETIES (CONT.)

Name (Source)	Type	Days to Reach Maturity	Comments
Mainstream (37)	Muskmelon	90	Well adapted to humid climates. Three- to 4-pound fruit on downy and powdery mildew-tolerant vines.
Mission Hybrid (24, 37)	Muskmelon	80	A vigorous, powdery and downy mildew-resistant vine with 4-pound, well-netted, deep salmon-colored fruit.
Perlita (1, 24, 37)	Muskmelon	80	An early ripening cantaloupe with tolerance to downy and powdery mildew. Fruit is firm with medium thickness and good flavor.
Planters Jumbo (37)	Muskmelon	85	Four-pound fruit with good flavor. Downy and powdery mildew-tolerant vines. Very small seed cavity.
Primo Hybrid (24, 31, 35)	Muskmelon	79	Very large 5- to 7-pound fruit. Excellent high sugar, dark orange flesh.
Saticoy Hybrid (9, 35, 37)	Muskmelon	85–90	Tolerant of powdery mildew and fusarium wilt. Dark orange, high-quality fruit that is harvested over a long period of time.
Star Headliner Hybrid (35)	Muskmelon	84	Good-quality 4- to 4½-pound fruit on high-yielding, vigorous vines.
Summet (31)	Muskmelon	75	Vigorous vines that tolerate fusarium wilt, downy mildew, and powdery mildew. Fruit is best picked at full slip.
Sweet Dream Hybrid (2)	Muskmelon	79	Excellent-quality, large 5-pound fruit on vigorous, mildew-resistant vines. Sweet Dream is a lime green cantaloupe.
Tam-Dew (1, 24, 37)	Honeydew	100	Medium, oval, smooth-rinded fruit that turns ivory when ripe.
Tam-Uvalde (1, 24, 37)	Muskmelon	85	Concentrates its harvest over short period. Fruit are medium size, oval-round with strong flavor. Harvest at full slip.

gered planting, starting a few vines at a time, will help spread the harvest over a longer period of time.

These melons are usually grown in hills spaced 4 to 6 feet apart with 3 to 4 plants per hill. The vines spread and will cover considerable territory before harvest. Don't cross these delicious melons off your list just because you have a small garden. Trellises are a great way to grow cantaloupes, muskmelons, and the like. They take up less space, and by getting them up off the ground you'll greatly reduce the problems with disease. Plant the seed 6 inches apart and thin them to about 12 inches along the trellis. Plan to support the fruit as it grows.

Don't forget to mulch the plants heavily before they start to vine. Mulches control weeds, help regulate moisture, and keep the fruit up off the ground. For gardens in areas with a short growing season, try starting plants indoors about two weeks before planting time. The use of black plastic mulches and row cover will also allow for an earlier start.

Harvesting muskmelons is easy because the fruit tells you when it is ripe. The stem, where it attaches to fruit, has a layer of cells that slip from or release the fruit at maturity. Muskmelons are fully ripe when the fruit releases or slips free of the vine with little effort. If you have to pull the fruit free, it is not ripe.

True cantaloupes (charantais), honeydews, and crenshaws are not as easy to harvest because the changes that occur as the fruit ripen are subtle and unclear. These melons do not develop a slip. You should notice a slight color change from green to yellow or green to white, and the blossom end of the fruit will begin to soften.

Harvesting is a large part of fruit quality, but quality is greatly affected by the environment. Heavy rains just prior to harvest will dilute the flavor and sugars, reducing the fruit to nearly inedible. These fruit will not improve in quality after harvest, so remember: What you pick is what you get. (See photos on page 114.)

Tips for Growing Honeydews, Muskmelons, and Other Melons

- Melon seed germinate best once the soil temperature reaches 80° F.

- Ideal pH: 6.0 to 6.5.

- Dry, hot weather will produce sweeter, higher-quality melons with less disease problems.

- Good drainage is critical to production of quality melons.

- Bees are important to the pollination of all melons.

- Trellising helps conserve space and reduce disease.

- Wet weather near harvest will reduce fruit quality.

- Harvest when fully ripe; quality does not improve after harvest.

BASIC PLANTING INFORMATION
FOR WATERMELONS

Space Between Rows of Hills (Feet)	Seed Spacing (Inches)	Thin to (Inches)	Seed Depth (Inches)	Days to Reach Maturity	Comments/Planting Dates/Intensive Gardening (I.G.) Spacing
8–12	6–12 hills (6–8 seed per hill) 36–48 inches	row 18–24 per hill (3–4 plants per hill)	½–1	65–90	Plant from 2 to 4 weeks after the last spring freeze until 4 to 5 months before the first fall freeze. I.G. spacing: 12 to 15 inches × 24 to 36 inches, grown on a trellis.

WATERMELONS   Watermelons are considered by most to be native to Africa but were found growing wild in the Americas in the mid-1600s. Watermelons, like the other members of the cucurbit family, prefer a long, warm growing season. They are more tolerant of the moist, humid climate of the Southeast than their more finicky relatives, the honeydew and muskmelon. They also tolerate a much wider range of pH and soil. Because of their deep root system, watermelons will rarely need irrigation in the Southeastern climate. Watermelon care and culture is identical to that of the other melons already discussed.

Seedless varieties do require a little more attention. Seedless watermelon seed are expensive (25¢ to 50¢ per seed). They are weak and it is often difficult to get a good stand when planting directly in the garden. Seed should be planted indoors 2 to 3 weeks before you plan to set them out. Plant the seed in fairly large containers because they don't respond well to being transplanted. The pollen produced by seedless varieties are sterile, so pollinator plants must be planted with seedless ones. Pollinators are usually provided when you order the seed. With a little extra care you'll have no difficulty

Tips for Growing Watermelons

- For best germination, wait until the soil temperature reaches at least 70° F, but doesn't exeed 95° F.
- Moderate feeders that require a balanced fertilizer.
- Ideal pH: 5.0 to 7.0.
- Try small-fruited varieties on a trellis, especially in small gardens.
- Warm weather is the key to good production.
- Plant a few hills with the kids—they'll love it!

WATERMELON VARIETIES

Name (Source)	Size in Pounds	Days to Reach Maturity	Comments
Allsweet (1, 24, 35, 37)	25–30	90	Crimson, sweet type. Oblong, striped fruit. Bright red, very sweet flesh. Tolerant to anthracnose and fusarium.
Bush Jubilee	11–13	95	Ideal for small gardens. Vines only spread 4 to 6 feet. A striped melon with dark red, very sweet flesh.
Calhoun Gray (35, 37)	25–35	85	Improved Charleston Gray type with smoother rind; better shape and flesh color.
Charleston Gray (WA)	25–35	85	A good old variety that is still very popular. Light green rind; long melon with sweet red flesh.
Congo (35, 37)	90	90	Some tolerance to anthracnose. Oblong, dark green fruit with darker stripes. Medium texture; bright red, sweet flesh.
Crimson Sweet (WA)	15–25	96	Oval, light green fruit with dark stripes. Tolerates fusarium and anthracnose. High-sugar, bright red flesh.
Desert King (8, 37)	85	85	Very drought-tolerant, vigorous vines. Light green, almost round fruit with very sweet, deep yellow flesh.
Dixielee (35, 37)	25–30	92	Oblong-round, light green melon; very sweet flesh. Tolerance to anthracnose and fusarium wilt.
Golden Crown Hybrid (2, 35)	7–9	75	All-America winner. Unique golden rind when ripe. Oval icebox type with very sweet red flesh.
Jack of Hearts (17, 24, 31)	11–13	85	A fair-quality seedless watermelon. Oval, light green with dark stripes. Start seed in pots, seedlings have low vigor.
Jubilee (WA)	30–35	90	Vigorous vines resistant to anthracnose and fusarium wilt. Large, oblong, light green, striped fruit with excellent-textured, sweet red flesh and large black seed.
Louisiana Sweet (37)	25–30	90	Round-oblong, medium green fruit with dark stripes. Some tolerance to anthracnose and fusarium wilt. Flesh is bright red, crisp, and very sweet.
Mickylee (22, 31, 37)	6–7	75	Small, round icebox type; light green skin with darker flecks; bright red flesh with good quality.
Minilee (24, 37)	4–12	75	Light gray-green icebox-type melon with bright red, excellent-flavored flesh. Vines show some tolerance to anthracnose and fusarium wilt.

continued

WATERMELON VARIETIES (CONT.)

Name (Source)	Size in Pounds	Days to Reach Maturity	Comments
Mirage Hybrid (37)	25–30	85	A crimson-sweet type; oblong, light green melon with dark green stripes. Flesh is dark red, very high quality.
Nova (12)	10–13	84	Round-oval seedless, light green, striped fruit with very good quality, deep red flesh. Start indoors. Seedlings are not very vigorous, like most seedless varieties.
Royal Charleston Hybrid (37)	20–25	84	Tolerant of fusarium wilt, mildew, and anthracnose. Oblong, striped melons with very sweet red flesh.
Royal Sweet Hybrid (1, 35, 37)	20–25	85	Large oblong, medium green striped melon with sweet red flesh. Vigorous vines with some resistance to fusarium wilt.
Royal Jubilee Hybrid (1, 24, 35, 37)	25–30	95	Elongated, medium green with dark stripes. Bright red flesh; high yields; good resistance to fusarium wilt.
Sugar Baby (WA)	7–10	75	Small, round icebox type with almost black rind. Flesh is crisp, sweet, and bright red.
Sweet Favorite Hybrid (5, 12, 31, 35)	18–20	82	All-America winner. Oblong, light green, striped fruit. Red flesh, very sweet, with small seed. Good resistance to fusarium and anthracnose.
Tendersweet (WA)	25–30	85	Very tasty, orange-yellow flesh with white seed. Oblong, medium green striped melon.
Top Yield Hybrid (35)	25–35	80	Large, gray-green, oblong melons. Very productive. Red flesh; very sweet; fine texture with small black seed. Resistant to anthracnose and fusarium wilt.
Yellow Baby Hybrid (9, 19, 28, 31)	6–8	70	Very sweet, yellow-fleshed icebox type. Light green with dark flesh. All-America winner.
Yellow Doll Hybrid (5, 17, 24, 35, 37)	5–8	65	Very early, productive, compact vines with lemon yellow, crisp, sweet flesh.
You Sweet Thing Hybrid (17)	8–13	70	Small, round, striped fruit, resistant to fusarium wilt and anthracnose. Very sweet, bright red flesh.

growing these seedless varieties, but be aware they are not as productive as other types.

One of the biggest problems you'll encounter when growing watermelons is determining when they are ripe. You can thump them, roll them over to look for a color change in the spot that rests on the ground, and still harvest them when they're over-ripe or under-ripe. Many of the new varieties have red flesh even when they are very immature. The only way we've consistently been able to harvest ripe melons is to look at the tendril closest to where the fruit stem attaches to the vine. The tendril is the curly-Q that grabs the trellis, other vines, or anything nearby. The fruit has a stem that attaches to the vine. At the base of this stem is a tendril. In most cases, the fruit is ripe when this tendril turns completely brown.

*E*GGPLANT   This member of the solanaceae family, which also includes tomatoes, peppers, and potatoes, probably originated in India or southern China. (The other members are from the Americas.) Much like the tomato, the eggplant was grown as an ornamental in Europe and the United States for a long time. Even today there are red- and orange-fruited varieties that are probably best used for ornamental purposes (they are likely to be bitter).

Most gardeners are less than fond of eggplant. Probably because their first experience with the vegetable was a mushy casserole. But eggplant are actually quite elegant table fare. They have a subtle flavor that is more like that of an oyster than the oyster plant (salsify) can claim.

For best quality, pick the fruit anytime while the skin is still glossy. Even the best varieties can be bitter if picked when the plants are suffering from heat stress or after the skin starts to turn dull.

Eggplant casseroles are all right, but they are best when combined with Italian sausage, marinara sauce, bubbly mozzarella and provolone cheeses blended with Italian bread crumbs, and topped off with freshly grated romano and Parmesan cheeses. Another variation that even the kids will scarf

BASIC PLANTING INFORMATION FOR EGGPLANT

Space Between Rows (Inches)	Seed Spacing (Inches)	Thin to (Inches)	Seed Depth (Inches)	Days to Reach Maturity	Comments/Planting Dates/Intensive Gardening (I.G.) Spacing
24–36	Transplants	18–24	1/4–1/2	90	Keep eggplants growing vigorously with weekly to biweekly applications of fertilizer and they will be less likely to produce bitter fruit. Don't plant as early as tomatoes; cold weather can stunt the plants. However, if taken care of (i.e., keep the spider mites under control) they will often come back for a glorious fall crop. In spring: plant 4 to 6 weeks after last freeze. In fall: plant 16 weeks before first frost. I.G. spacing: 18 × 24 inches.

EGGPLANT VARIETIES

Name (Source)	Color	Disease Resistance	Days to Reach Maturity	Comments
Black Beauty (WA)	Purple-Black		73	The standard Black Beauty variety is notorious for developing bitter fruit when growing under stress in the summer. Look for hybrid or improved selections of Black Beauty.
Classic (9)	Purple-Black		76	One of the large-fruited varieties but with an elongated, teardrop shape. Plants are vigorous with good stress resistance.
Ichiban (8, 19)	Purple-Black		61	Typical of many Asian varieties that are long and skinny. Usually they are less likely to become bitter in the summer (although lots of water and fertilizer are recommended for all eggplants to keep them growing vigorously). Similar varieties include: Little Fingers (9), Kurume (4, 14), and Millionaire (2).
Florida Market (1, 13)	Purple-Black	Some to Fruit Rots	85	This is an old standard commercial variety of which there are several strains. Produces large, typical fruit.
Listada de Gandia (29)	Purple Marbled with White Stripes		75	One of the most beautiful of all eggplants—almost too pretty to eat. Fortunately it is very good to eat (with thin skin), and it's a good producer. Plants are medium size, vigorous with good heat tolerance. Rosa Bianca (18, 27) and Italian Pink Bicolor (18, 31) are similar varieties with white fruits lightly striped with pink. Rosa Bianca is more variable and some plants may produce pale pink fruit.
Pingtung Long (4, 15, 19)	Violet-Purple	Fruit Rot	65	This variety is similar to Ichiban, but it is much longer (foot-long hotdog size) and the skin is perhaps even more tender. Plants are very productive and, like most Asian varieties, they seem to have fewer seeds.
Thai Long Green (4, 29)	Light Green		80	This is an 8- to 10-inch green eggplant. This may not sound too appetizing, but the skin is tender (unlike most white-skinned varieties) and it cooks to a bright green. A similar variety is Louisiana Long Green (29). Harabegan (37) is also a long green hybrid variety.

Key to Disease and Pest Abbreviations
TMV = tobacco mosaic virus

EGGPLANT VARIETIES (CONT.)

Name (Source)	Color	Disease Resistance	Days to Reach Maturity	Comments
Vittoria (2, 31)	Dark Purple	TMV	61	This variety is typical of European varieties. They are long like the Asian varieties but usually a bit thicker. Others include: Prelane (17, 28), De Barbentane (15), and Rosita (18, 31). They often have good disease resistance and are of excellent quality.

down involves dipping eggplant slices in an egg batter, coating them with Italian-seasoned bread crumbs, and frying the breaded "vegetarian medallions" in a 50/50 mixture of olive and canola oils. Before serving, sprinkle on a bit of seasoned salt and forget to tell them what they're eating until they've had a second or third helping.

(See photo on page 115.)

Tips for Growing Eggplant

- Don't plant too early. Wait 4 to 6 weeks after the average spring frost date before setting out transplants. Eggplants really perform better in the fall, so they can also be used to replace spring crops like beans from May through July.
- Watch out for spider mites. The leaves will show tiny stippled areas where the leaf cells have died due to the sucking action of this pest. Eventually, the leaves will yellow and you may see a fine webbing. High-pressure water sprays will control this pest or try one of the insecticidal soaps or wettable sulfurs for low-toxicity pest control.
- Harvest often. You don't want the fruit to lose its glossy look.

There are many other varieties of eggplant. Some, like Turkish Orange (29) and Sweet Red (27), are of doubtful culinary value. Others like the Ping-Pong ball-sized "crispy eggplant" (seed is sometimes available in Asian grocery stores) and Lao Green Grape (29) will require considerable research of Southeast Asian cuisine before most gardeners will know how to prepare them. As previously suggested, the white-skinned varieties look pretty but they are usually second rate for eating. The skins are tough and the fruit is often seedy.

OKRA

Okra is one of several vegetables, along with Southern peas and sweet potatoes, that are best grown in the South. Okra thrives on high humidity and heat. (What would you expect of a vegetable native to Africa and related to cotton?) And no wonder we think of it as a Southern vegetable; it's probably been cultivated in the region since the late eighteenth century.

Okra varieties were pretty boring for many years—Clemson spineless, Emerald, and an occasional white or red form showed up in some neglected corner of the average seed catalog. Then the University of Arkansas released Lee, a very productive, branching variety. Now we even have a hybrid variety, Annie Oakley, which has already been improved to Annie Oakley II.

Tips for Growing Okra

- Wait until the soil warms up in April or May before planting. Seedlings or transplants placed in cold soil are often stunted.
- Nematodes are a problem, especially in sandy soils. Work lots of organic matter into the soil to encourage a healthy microorganism population.
- Virtually all okra varieties have some spines that cause itching, so it is a good idea to wear long sleeves when picking.

Okra doesn't just grow best in a hot climate, it demands it. If seed are planted too early, when the soil temperature is below 68° F, the okra may come up but is likely to be stunted even after temperatures warm up. An even better idea is to wait until the soil temperature is about 75° F, soak the seed overnight in warm water, and then plant. Seedling emergence will be faster and more uniform, plus chances are harvest time will come earlier than it does for plants that were seeded beforehand. Also, okra seed don't have good longevity, so even when stored cool (see the Starting with Seed chapter), they shouldn't be kept for more than two seasons or you can expect them to produce uneven stands when planted.

Good drainage is important, so be certain to plant on ridges, especially when the soil is heavy and the rains are frequent. Lots of organic matter in the soil is also important. If you have a sandy soil, enriching it with organic matter may be one of your main defenses against nematodes—microscopic roundworms that attack the plants' root system. A rich, organic soil encourages soil fungi, which attack nematodes.

(See photo on page 115.)

BASIC PLANTING INFORMATION FOR OKRA

Space Between Rows (Inches)	Seed Spacing (Inches)	Thin to (Inches)	Seed Depth (Inches)	Days to Reach Maturity	Comments/Planting Dates/Intensive Gardening (I.G.) Spacing
36–42	4–6	15–24	½–1	48–60	Transplants are a waste of time. Use seed, but wait until the soil temperature is 75° F or warmer. Don't try to save seed of the hybrid variety Annie Oakley II (it won't come true) or of standard varieties unless you have only one variety that is isolated from others because cross-pollination is likely. In spring: plant 4 to 12 weeks after last freeze. In fall: plant at least 16 weeks before first frost. I.G. spacing: 15 × 24 inches.

OKRA VARIETIES

Name (Source)	Color	Days to Reach Maturity	Comments
Annie Oakley II (WA)	Medium Green	48	Early and very productive with Clemson Spineless-like, ribbed pods. Pods get woody and hollow faster than Emerald types but quality is excellent if the pods are picked at 4 inches or shorter.
Blondy (5, 8, 13, 24)	Light Green	55	Compact plants with good production of meaty pods.
Burgundy (WA)	Red	60	Pods are red, ribbed, and remain tender when actively growing up to 6 inches. Plants even have red stems and some red on the leaves. Pods turn green when cooked.
Candelabra (19)	Medium Green	60	Ribbed variety with good base and branching habit provided it is spaced at least 20 inches. Developed by home gardener Mr. L.S. Jennings. Park Seed Company exclusive.
Clemson Spineless (WA)	Medium Green	56	Old standard with ribbed pods free of spines. The rest of the plant has spines, so it is still a good idea to wear long sleeves when picking.
Cowhorn (21, 24)	Medium Green	60–65	There are a number of local varieties, such as Cowhorn. Some are thick and stubby. Others, like Cowhorn, are reported to develop long, skinny pods that remain tender when plants are growing actively.
Emerald (21, 24)	Dark Green	60	This is the gourmet variety of okra. Pods are long, smooth, and meaty. Plants can get fairly tall. Kind of an improved Green Velvet variety.

continued

OKRA VARIETIES (CONT.)

Name (Source)	Color	Days to Reach Maturity	Comments
Lee (5, 19, 21, 24)	Medium Green	50	This is one of the first improved varieties developed by the University of Arkansas. Plants are compact and branching with high-quality, ribbed, spineless pods.
Perkins Long Pod (21, 24)	Medium Green	60	One of the old varieties with long, slender, ribbed pods.

Gold Coast (21, 29), Jade (29), Star of David (29), Rani #6 Hybrid (37), and Mita #7 Hybrid (37) are also worth trying.

*S*OUTHERN PEAS   This vegetable is actually closer to a bean than a pea, though both are legumes. As a group, the category of Southern peas includes a variety of forms: blackeyes, purple hulls, creams, and crowders. (The Yard-long bean is a close relative but it is discussed under warm-season gourmet selections.)

Not only are Southern peas good to eat, they are good for the soil. With the aid of *Rhizobium* bacteria, this legume fixes atmospheric nitrogen in the soil. Seed should be inoculated at planting time with a garden blend of the bacteria. This product comes in the form of a black powder (for seed coating)

BASIC PLANTING INFORMATION FOR SOUTHERN PEAS

Space Between Rows (Inches)	Seed Spacing (Inches)	Thin to (Inches)	Seed Depth (Inches)	Days to Reach Maturity	Comments/Planting Dates/Intensive Gardening (I.G.) Spacing
24–36	2	4–6	1–2	60–70	Use of a general-purpose nitrogen-fixing, bacterial inoculant is recommended. As with all legumes, this symbiotic relationship with the *Rhizobium* bacteria reduces or eliminates the need for supplemental nitrogen with these crops. In spring: plant 4 to 12 weeks after last freeze. In fall: plant 10 to 14 weeks before first frost. I.G. spacing: 6 × 6 inches to 8 × 8 inches.

Tips for Growing Southern Peas

- Inoculate seed with *Rhizobium* before planting. If using the powder form, dampen the seed slightly, sprinkle the powder on, and shake the bag for good coverage just before planting. The granular inoculant is also sprinkled down the row before covering the seed.
- The major home garden pest of this vegetable is the stinkbug—both the regular green stinkbug and the leaf-footed bug. They feed on the developing pods and cause a significant reduction in quality. The key for control is to start early. Hand removal (you may want to wear gloves, they do stink), organic or chemical pesticide sprays, and planting trap crops like sunflowers may be necessary.
- Remember, this is a hot-weather vegetable. Don't plant until soil temperatures are in the 70° to 85° F range.

---

or a granular material to sprinkle over the row. The same material can be used on other garden crops like green beans and English peas. (See photo on page 108.)

SOUTHERN PEA VARIETIES

Name (Source)	Color	Disease Resistance	Days to Reach Maturity	Comments
Big Boy (13, 21, 24)	Light Green		75	Large peas in pods longer than 10 inches will make this one popular with market gardeners and those growing for the pick-your-own market.
Blackeye (CA #5, WR, WA)	Cream, Dark Eye	CW	75–95	This is an extremely popular Southern vegetable. Try some of the new disease-resistant varieties.
Dixie Lee (21)	Brown	N	65	Pods are mature when light green and about 8 inches in length. Yields over a long time—second harvest often possible.
Elite (21, 37)	Cream		75	Extremely productive cream-type variety with pods held above the foliage.

continued

Key to Disease and Pest Abbreviations
CW = common wilt   N = nematodes   SB = stinkbugs

SOUTHERN PEA VARIETIES (CONT.)

Name (Source)	Color	Disease Resistance	Days to Reach Maturity	Comments
Mississippi Silver (WA)	Brown	N	65	Upright plants are very productive. Pods are held above the foliage and the crowder-type peas are easy to shell.
Purple Hull Pinkeye (WA)	White, Pink Eye		80	One of the reasons this variety is so popular in the South is that it is easy to shell. It also tastes great!
Texas Cream 40 (21, 37)	White, Orange Eye		65–75	Semibush variety with medium-size pods.
Whippoorwill (37)	Light Green		75	A smooth-skinned variety with long seed pods. Prolific and long bearing.
Zipper Cream (21, 24, 37)	White	SB	75	Another easy one to shell. This time in a cream type.

_B_ELL PEPPERS   The bell pepper is one of many vegetables that originated in the Americas. And, although it is extremely popular in many cuisines, it is not easy to grow. It won't prosper as early in the spring as will its relative, the tomato, and it suffers even more in the heat of summer. To get the most from this vegetable, plant vigorous, early hybrids and push them almost to the point of burning the roots with fertilizer. Don't be afraid to use a fertilizer with plenty of nitrogen. In fact, using soluble fertilizers in a hose-

BASIC PLANTING INFORMATION FOR BELL PEPPERS

Space Between Rows (Inches)	Seed Spacing (Inches)	Thin to (Inches)	Seed Depth (Inches)	Days to Reach Maturity	Comments/Planting Dates/Intensive Gardening (I.G.) Spacing
20–35	N/A	Set Transplants— 12–24	1/4	70–100	This is a crop that demands high fertility. Mulching and providing plenty of water (with good drainage) are also important. In spring: plant 2 to 4 weeks after last freeze. In fall: plant 16 to 20 weeks before first frost. I.G. spacing: 12 × 18 inches.

on fertilizer sprayer to supplement good soil fertility is often the key to success.

Most gardeners strive to produce the big, blocky bell peppers usually sold at ridiculously high prices in the produce market. Some varieties that don't have this good-for-stuffing shape, such as Big Bertha, are better producers. (You'll just have to lay them on their sides for stuffing.) Also, as temperatures warm up in the summer, the size of all varieties decreases. The plants are struggling enough to stay alive that small "bells" are all they're capable of.

Different-colored bells have also become increasingly popular. Most bell peppers will eventually turn red if left on the plant long enough, but some varieties have been developed especially for a tendency to color early (including white, yellow, and purple varieties) and uniformly. It's actually a more nutritious vegetable when it develops color, but overall production is reduced when it stays on the plant longer. Don't fret early in the season though; they all start out in some shade of green.

(See photos on page 116.)

Tips for Growing Bell Peppers

- Plant early hybrid varieties.
- Wait to plant until the soil warms up (at least to 55° F), 2 to 4 weeks after setting tomato plants.
- Fertilize heavily to promote early and heavy fruit set that will mature before hot weather.
- Virus infections are a serious problem with all members of the solanaceae family. Look for plants that appear abnormally mottled in color or that have abnormal growth-wrinkled leaves, shoestring leaf tips, or stunting and pull them out as early as possible. The potential for production from a few seemingly diseased plants isn't worth the risk of infecting other plants.
- Use fiber row cover around the planting cages when you first set out plants. This will not only reduce damage from drying winds, it will also exclude insects like aphids that can spread virus diseases early in the season. To keep the bugs out, tie the row cover off at the top of the cage until plants begin flowering.
- Sunscald damage on the fruit is a common problem in the summer. Try building a frame over the row with 2 × 2s, bamboo poles, etc., and drape fiber row cover over the top to reduce the sun's intensity during midday.

BELL PEPPER VARIETIES

Name (Source)	Color	Disease Resistance	Days to Reach Maturity	Comments
Bell Tower (12)	Green	TMV, PVY	70	Early enough to produce large peppers before the heat of summer; plants also produce heavy foliage to protect fruit from sunscalding. Bell Boy (5) and Bell Captain (1, 34) are also good.
Big Bertha (WA)	Green	TMV	70	This is a large, elongated bell that is extremely productive. While this shape may not be the preferred form, the quality and production is outstanding. Fruits will eventually turn red if left on the plant long enough.
Canape (9, 17, 33, 36)	Green		65	This variety produces a small, tapered fruit but production is outstanding and early.
Capistrano (1, 31)	Green		65	One of the new commercial hybrids. It will perform equally well in the home garden.
Dove (31)	Pale Yellow		71	Pale yellow fruits will eventually turn orange-red but this one is prettiest at the immature stage. Good leaf cover reduces sunscald damage.
Golden Summer (3, 5, 8, 19, 24)	Light Green to Yellow	TMV	70	Good foliage is important for pepper varieties grown in the South and this is one of the best. Flavor and production are also excellent.
Gypsy (WA)	Yellow to Orange-Red	TMV	65	This is another elongated bell. Even though this isn't the preferred form, it was so productive and attractive that it was awarded All-America Selection status. Flesh is thick and tasty.
Jupiter (J. Elite) (1, 24, 31, 35)	Green	TMV	75	This is a large, 4-lobed commercial-type pepper. It is a little later to fruit, but because it is also productive and its fruit are of high quality, it is often included in variety lists from most Southern states.
Keystone Resistant Giant #3 (WA)	Green	TMV	75	Another typical bell variety, it is not as commonly listed in catalogs as it once was. It seems almost every catalog has a number of proprietary varieties and some of them may be similar if not synonymous.
Lady Bell (9)	Green to Red	TMV	70	Another early bell, but this one is more blocky and closer to medium than small in size. Good, sweet flavor.

Key to Disease and Pest Abbreviations
TMV = tobacco mosaic virus

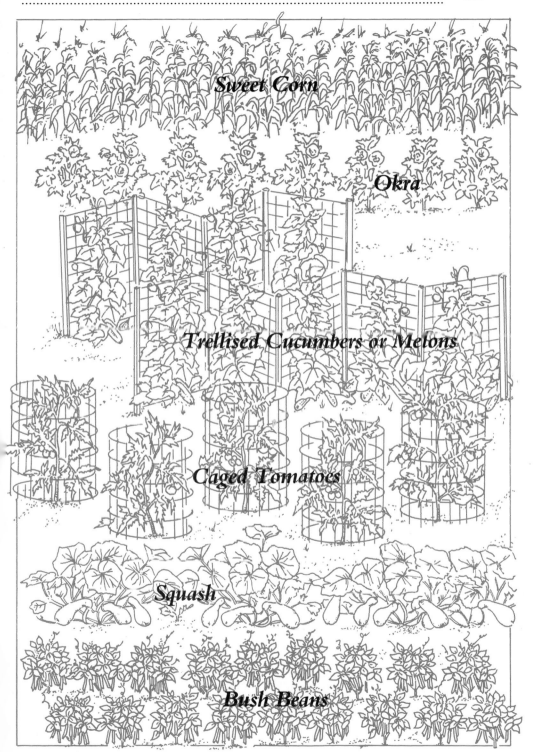

Sweet Corn

Okra

Trellised Cucumbers or Melons

Caged Tomatoes

Squash

Bush Beans

Warm-Season Garden Plan.

Whippoorwill Southern

Asparagus.

Florida Speckled lima beans. Photo by Mary Stewart.

Tavera French filet beans.

Derby bush beans.

Florida Staysweet sweet corn.

Specialty baby corn ear.

Soo Yoh Long cucumbers.

Salad Bush cucumbers.

Bitterstick squash blossoms (female, left; male, right).

Left: Small zucchini with male flower (left) and female flower. Right: Dixie squash.

Cream of the Crop winter (acorn) squash.

Sunburst winter squash.

Newly harvested pumpkins.

Magnum 45 cantaloupe.

Minilee watermelon.

Assorted eggplants (clockwise from the upper left: Louisiana Green Oval, Violette Lunga, Thai Long Green, Ping Tunig Long, De Barbentane, C. histada de gardia)

Lee dwarf okra.

Above: Dove sweet (bell) peppers. Right: Golden Summer sweet (bell) peppers.

Laparie sweet peppers.

Habanero hot peppers.

Ancho hot peppers.

Super pimento sweet peppers.

Super Cayenne hot peppers.

Red Lasoda potatoes.

Vardaman sweet potatoes.

Tomato cages wrapped with
fiber row cover.

Sweet Chelsea cherry tomatoes.

Dona tomatoes supported
by wire cage.

Planting tomato transplants
by laying stem in trench.

Trombocino squash.

Royal Burgundy green beans.

Cucuzzi gourd.

Above: Fuzzy melon gourd.
Right: Climbing okra gourd.

Bitter melon.

Winged beans.

Water spinach.

Climbing, or Malabar, spinach.

Tomatillos.

Sunroots.

BELL PEPPER VARIETIES (CONT.)

Name (Source)	Color	Disease Resistance	Days to Reach Maturity	Comments
Oriole (31)	Green to Orange	TMV	75	Ripe color is a brilliant orange. Fruits are 4-lobed and medium large.
Orobelle (12, 18, 34)	Green to Yellow	TMV	70	Fruits are 3- to 4-lobed and small to medium size. Plants have strong foliage for good fruit coverage.
Summer Sweet 860 (35)	Green to Yellow	TMV, PVY	75	Blocky, 4-lobed fruits that are typically bigger than 4 inches in diameter and length. Good foliage.
Yellow Belle (31)	Green to Yellow		65	Very early and productive with heavy foliage. This and other early yellows, such as Gold Crest (12), which matures in 62 days, should be tried in Southern gardens to beat the heat.

Gator Belle (34), Rampage (34), Shamrock (24), and Marengo have also been recommended for Southern gardens.

OTHER SWEET PEPPERS Not all sweet peppers are bells. For example, there are the Italian Ramshorn types, which are popular in the Northeast but easily grown in Southern gardens. Sweet cherries, pimentos, and sweet yellows are just some of the other classifications used. Peppers are very likely the most diverse group of vegetables we grow. Some are used for frying, others for pizza toppings; some are canned (pimentos), and others (cherries) are often pickled.

(See photos on pages 116 and 117.)

HOT PEPPERS Recently, numerous books have been written on this subject. Hot peppers seem to be addictive and every culture and cuisine has taken to them in one form or another. And guess what? All peppers probably originated in the Americas! China, however, claims some of the credit and maybe that would help to explain the popularity of this vegetable in Asian and Indian cuisine. Regardless, ships have been sailing to faraway ports for a long time and it certainly wouldn't take people long to recognize the value of the pepper, especially back in the days prior to refrigeration when meat tended to get a bit gamey before consumption.

Scientists even suspect that the fire of the hot pepper, capsaicin to be exact, is soothing to the digestive system. Taken in moderation, it seems to be

OTHER SWEET PEPPER VARIETIES

Name (Source)	Color	Disease Resistance	Days to Reach Maturity	Comments
Sweet Banana (WA)	Pale Yellow		60	This is the pepper that often surprises gardeners. Instead of being sweet, it turns out to be fiery hot. The Hungarian Wax looks identical. There is also a Sweet Hungarian variety. The plants also look identical, so beware of pranksters who may switch plants in the trays at the nursery.
Sweet Cherry (WA)	Green to Red	TMV	75	Super Sweet Cherry is an improved variety with resistance to tobacco mosaic virus and also to cracking. This variety is most often pickled.
Cheese Peppers (27, 31)	Yellow or Red	TMV	68–73	Essentially, a pimento pepper grown for fresh use. Super Greygo Hybrid is a red type and Yellow Cheese is a green to yellow-orange type. Both have thick flesh and are great for stuffing.
Cubanelle (WA)	Yellow-Green		68	This is one of the sweet yellow peppers popular for frying. The hybrid Italian Ramshorns are more productive.
Laparie (31)	Green to Dark Red		72	One of the most outstanding hybrid Ramshorn types. The tapered fruit are up to 8 inches long and as sweet as candy. This is one of the few peppers that most people will enjoy eating fresh in the field.
Pimento (WA)	Red	TMV	70	Why not grow your own? Mary Stewart (one of Houston's gardening legends) does. Especially consider trying the Super Red Pimento variety. It tends to be more blocky, like the cheese variety. Regular pimentos have an elongated top. Roast them in a 350° oven, remove when blackened, and place in a paper bag to cool. When cool, remove the skins, then cut up and process your own pimentos.
Szegedi (31)	Yellow-Orange		70	A popular thick-fleshed Hungarian sweet pepper. The fruit is shaped like a top and has a distinctive flavor.

Key to Disease and Pest Abbreviations
PVY = potato virus Y   TMV = tobacco mosaic virus

BASIC PLANTING INFORMATION FOR HOT PEPPERS

Space Between Rows (Inches)	Seed Spacing (Inches)	Thin to (Inches)	Seed Depth (Inches)	Days to Reach Maturity	Comments/Planting Dates/Intensive Gardening (I.G.) Spacing
20–36	Set Transplants Only 12–24	12–24	¼	60–75	Don't plant too early. Wait several weeks past the planting time for early tomatoes. Fertilize almost to the point of burning the plants to encourage rapid growth and early production. In spring: plant 3 to 8 weeks after last freeze. In fall: plant 16 to 18 weeks before first frost. I.G. spacing: 12 × 18 inches.

calming and may do more to settle the stomach than to stir it up, as some twinky-tummied individuals would caution.

(See photos on page 117.)

HOT PEPPER VARIETIES

Name (Source)	Color	Disease Resistance	Days to Reach Maturity	Comments
Anaheim (and similar New Mexico chiles) (WA)	Green-Red		70–80	Many varieties fit in this category. Typically, they are picked green, roasted on the grill to remove the skins, and then frozen for later use. They are also allowed to mature to a red color and then dried for ristras (a string of dried peppers). The degree of pungency produced varies considerably. Big Jim and R. Naky are 6 to 8 inches long and comparatively mild, while the shorter Sandia variety is much hotter. In New Mexico, these peppers are put on everything. In fact, if you order a hamburger you will have to declare "Hold the peppers!" as they are often a standard garnish on such dishes. Be bold instead; you'll be addicted before you know it.
Ancho (Poblano when fresh, green) (WA)	Red or Green		65 (fresh)	This medium to large, top-shaped pepper is one of the staples of Mexican cuisine. Though Anaheims or other chiles may be substituted for Poblanos, they are the genuine article in authentic chile rellenos. The dried ancho is used in stews or, especially, in chile con carne.

Key to Disease and Pest Abbreviations
TMV = tobacco mosaic virus

continued

HOT PEPPER VARIETIES (CONT.)

Name (Source)	Color	Disease Resistance	Days to Reach Maturity	Comments
Cayenne (WA)	Red		60–75	Hot pepper lovers know there are distinct differences in the flavor of the various "hots." Cayenne is the one associated with the pungency of dried chile powder. It is widely available as a dried product even in the far reaches of civilization, like New York City. Connoisseurs know that there are many subtle differences and that fresh cayenne is very different from the dried product. New varieties like Super Cayenne Hybrid are extremely productive.
Cherry, Hot (WA)	Green to Red		75	Another identity crisis! First you had to worry about Yellow Bananas actually being Hungarian Hots. Now you can lose sleep wondering if your Sweet Cherry peppers are actually Hot Cherry peppers. If it's any consolation, nurseries rarely offer Hot Cherry pepper plants.
Chiltepine (Bird's Eye, Chile Pequin) (10, 11, 16, 23, 25, 27, 34)	Green to Red		75	Various forms of this pepper are found growing wild in the Southwest and in Mexico. The tiny peppers vary in shape from almost round to elongated and, without fail, they are brutally hot, rivaling the Habanero. Six of these peppers in a small bottle of vinegar should suffice for hot sauce to sprinkle on your collard greens.
Chimayo (10, 11, 23, 25, 27, 34)	Green to Red		95	There are many regional pepper varieties around the world, but they are especially abundant in Mexico. The Chimayo is one such variety. The thin-fleshed fruits are mild when green but become hot when they turn red. Others include: Mulato (10, 27)—a medium-hot pepper, shaped like a top, that can be used fresh or dried; and Mirasol (10, 25)—another Mexican variety with small peppers borne erect that can be used green or dried to add heat and yellow coloring to stews.
Habanero (12, 17, 18, 19, 23, 31, 34)	Green to Orange		85–95	This variety is often claimed to be the hottest of the "hots," but there are a few other contenders for the crown. Chiltepin, Scotch Bonnet, and Thai Hot are other super hot varieties. The Habanero is a small (1 1/2-inch long, 3/4-inch wide), bull-nosed variety that should be treated with due respect.
Hungarian Hot (Wax) (WA)	Light Green to Yellow		60	This is the one that folks often get by mistake when they really want Sweet Hungarian. It's really not that hot but it benefits from its surprise value. The fruits can be 6 inches long and an inch or so at the shoulder. If left on the plant long enough they will eventually turn red.

HOT PEPPER VARIETIES (CONT.)

Name (Source)	Color	Disease Resistance	Days to Reach Maturity	Comments
Jalapeno (WA)	Green to Red		70	The popularity of Tex-Mex food and nachos has made this type of pepper the best known of all. It actually has flavor in addition to heat and there are even mild varieties like the TAM Jalapeno 1 Mild (1, 24) and Jalapa (1, 19, 24) available. If you really like jalapenos, you will probably find them too mild. Mitla Hybrid (1, 24, 31) is a larger fruited jalapeno that is still hot.
Mexibell (35)	Green to Red	TMV	70–75	These small bell peppers are actually quite hot. If you are careful to remove the core and veins, the heat can be tempered somewhat. They are too hot for playing jokes on unsuspecting friends.
Paprika (17, 27, 28, 34)	Red		70	It's hard to know where to place this type of pepper. It really should be spicy and flavorful as opposed to tongue-bitingly hot. Several companies claim to have the jealously guarded Hungarian strain. Freshly ground paprika is a joy to the senses.
Pasilla (10, 23, 28)	Dark Green to Chocolate-Red		75	Long, 1/2- to 3/4-inch diameter pods have a distinctive flavor. It is typically used, second to drying, for sauces
Pepperoncini (10, 17)	Light Green		65	This pepper is really quite mild. It is generally used pickled and develops a mild bite.
Serrano (WA)	Green to Red		70	These are small (2 inches × 3/8 inch), very hot peppers that are a must in salsas like pico de gallo. They are used in a wide variety of ways and are the most popular hot pepper in Mexico. TAM Hidalgo is a mildly pungent serrano type.
Super Chili Hybrid (5, 8, 19)	Green to Red		75	This 1988 All-America Selection is one of several new hybrid or improved hot pepper types. This one makes a good substitute for serranos or cayennes. Other varieties for similar uses include: Diablo Grande (31)—a 7 × 2-inch very hot wax type; and Hot Stuff Hybrid (31)—a medium-hot variety for pickling or sauces.
Tabasco (28)	Red		80	This is the legendary pepper of Avery Island, LA, where they make Tabasco pepper sauce. Their proprietary brand is claimed to be superior and unique.
Thai Hot (4, 14, 18, 19, 32, 34)	Green to Red		40	This tiny, elongated Asian pepper is super hot. One plant should suffice for all but the most daring. Yatsafusa (17), a Japanese variety, is 3 inches long and also quite hot.

Tips for Growing Peppers

- Don't plant too many. One or two plants will suffice for most families.
- Don't plant too early. Wait until temperatures warm up in late March or April.
- Fertilize. Hot peppers need to be fertilized almost to the point of burning them, just as with bell peppers. Try a foliar hose-on feeder once a week, plus start with 2 to 4 pounds of a complete fertilizer, like 15-5-10, per 100 square feet (incorporated into the soil).
- Wear rubber gloves when handling peppers and especially when processing them. Not only will the capsaicin burn your hands, it will burn any other part of the body that you touch with your hands.

*P*OTATOES   This South American native has become a staple around the world, and for good reason. It consists of 20% carbohydrates, 2% to 7% protein, and vitamin C, iron, thiamine, niacin, phosphorus, and trace minerals. It can also be grown almost anywhere from sea level to high elevations. Even though it likes cool growing conditions, it is adaptable. In the South we can grow potatoes successfully by planting them in late winter or in late summer so the tubers can mature in a cool soil.

As popular as the potato is, most people think it exists only in the form of red ones harvested for new potatoes or as white ones for bakers. Actually, there are many forms that differ considerably from the traditional spud. In Peruvian markets you would see purple ones, red ones, yellow ones—in all shapes and sizes. As the potato has been spread around the world for the last 400 years, many of these forms have been developed into locally popular varieties. The common red and white potatoes are still predominant, but fingerling or crescent-shaped potatoes are now popular, especially in Europe.

Getting seed potatoes to cut up and plant is not always easy for the Southern gardener, especially for fall planting. They are more likely to be available in the spring. Seed potatoes must be grown and carefully monitored to ensure that they are free of disease. Unlike store potatoes, they have not been treated with a growth inhibitor to retard sprouting. Seed pieces should be cut to contain 1 to 2 eyes and should weigh 1 to 2 ounces. Allow the cut pieces to dry and callous (develop a layer of protective tissue) for 24 to 48 hours before planting. Dust with sulfur or wood ashes to reduce pest problems. Small seed potatoes, weighing less than 2 ounces, should be planted whole.

Allowing the potatoes to green up and sprout before planting is a good idea for the home gardener. Spread the pieces out in flats so they are not touching, and keep them in a location where the temperature is 70° and there's good light. Some gardeners even bed them in a damp, loose potting soil or peat moss with the eyes exposed to speed up sprouting. Using this technique, the potatoes can be planted later in the season, protecting them from a late frost, and they will still get off to a fast start.

Fall-planted potatoes are also very successful, but it is hard to find seed potatoes that have had enough dormancy to take off and grow rapidly when you need them. The best solution is to save small potatoes from the spring crop, store them in the refrigerator until mid–August, and plant them whole. Cut pieces planted in warm soil are much more likely to decay. Don't bother to clean up these small potatoes before storing because washing will expose them to a greater chance of storage-rot organisms.

Potatoes do best in a slightly acid soil (pH 6.0), which decreases the chance of scab fungus infection. The seed potato is usually planted about 3 inches deep, and after 4 to 6 inches of growth has emerged, soil is pulled up leaving 1 inch of growth exposed. Several weeks later, the process, sometimes referred to as "dirting" is repeated.

A small plot in the home garden can be grown very successfully in mulch. Seed pieces are planted on a loose soil prepared with lots of organic matter (compost is best), and then they are covered with a foot or more of hay or other suitable mulch. Add to the mulch as needed so the tubers won't green up (they develop alkaloids that are bad for you), and in early May pull

BASIC PLANTING INFORMATION FOR POTATOES

Space Between Rows (Inches)	Seed Spacing (Inches)	Thin to (Inches)	Seed Depth (Inches)	Days to Reach Maturity	Comments/Planting Dates/Intensive Gardening (I.G.) Spacing
36–42	8–12	N/A	3–4	85–110	Potatoes need good drainage. Plant in raised beds or mound up the soil and plant on the ridges. Be sure to let seed pieces callous for 24 to 48 hours before planting to decrease the chance of decay. In spring: plant 2 weeks before to 2 weeks after last freeze. In fall: plant 12 to 14 weeks before first frost. I.G. spacing: 12 × 12 inches to 18 × 18 inches.

back the mulch to find "new potatoes" that can be pulled, leaving the bigger ones down deep for harvest later in the month.

(See photo on page 118.)

This is a limited list of potato varieties. There are hundreds more available from catalogs like Ronniger's (see resource section for address). The big problem is getting the seed potatoes at the proper time for planting. It's too cold to ship in mid-February, and production will be limited if you plant in March or April. If you want to try some of the gourmet varieties, like the purple ones or fingerlings, you may have to plant a bit late in the spring and save your own seeds for fall and the following spring.

POTATO VARIETIES

Name (Source)	Color	Disease Resistance	Days to Reach Maturity	Comments
Bison (26)	Red		70	Many varieties of potatoes have been developed in recent years and this is one of the best. It's early, has great flavor, and shallow eyes.
Kennebec (WA)	White		85	This is the standard white variety for Southern gardeners. You might not grow potatoes the size of Idaho or Maine spuds, but Kennebecs will develop into adequate baking size before the soil warms up.
Red Lasoda (WA)	Red		85	Probably the most commonly planted potato variety in the South. It has smooth skin and tastes great. In fact, fresh potatoes from the garden are almost like another vegetable—sweeter, fresher, too good to describe. You'll just have to grow your own.
Norgold M (26)	White/ Russet		70	Good Southern variety because it continues to grow even as the weather gets hot. Produces good bakers with tough skin.
Russet Norkotah (26)	White/ Russet	S	70	Relatively new variety, excellent for baking, boiling, frying, making chips, etc. Good production and good for storage.
Viking, Red or Purple (8, 26)	Red/ Purple		85	New varieties with good yields and good keeping qualities. The Purple Viking has purple skin with pinkish splashes. Perfect for gourmands.
Yukon Gold (5, 8, 26)	Yellow		60	This variety is already available in produce markets and its earliness, thin skin, and good yields should make it a real hit with Southern gardeners.

Key to Disease and Pest Abbreviations
S = scab

Tips for Growing Potatoes

- Potatoes need to mature in cool soil. Don't fool with planting by the moon if it causes you to miss the early planting season (2 weeks before to 2 weeks after the average spring frost date).
- After cutting seed potatoes for spring planting, allow them to callous for at least 24 hours. Then dust with sulfur or wood ashes to reduce the chance of decay.
- Don't be afraid to harvest a few new potatoes early in May. This is especially easy if you are growing them in mulch. Just pull the mulch back and steal a few. You can still get the big ones later in the month.

S*WEET POTATOES*   This is not a vegetable for the small garden (even when planting compact-growing varieties like Vardaman) because it roots wherever it touches the soil and foliage rapidly covers everything in sight. Sweet potato weevils are another problem. But even with two strikes against it, this is a great vegetable. Nematodes may be strike three for some gardeners, but not many Southerners are this pessimistic—it's still a widely

---

BASIC PLANTING INFORMATION
FOR SWEET POTATOES

Space Between Rows (Inches)	Seed Spacing (Inches)	Thin to (Inches)	Seed Depth (Inches)	Days to Reach Maturity	Comments/Planting Dates/Intensive Gardening (I.G.) Spacing
48–54	N/A	12–14	N/A	120–140	This crop obviously needs a lot of room. To try a few slips in a small garden, build a sturdy wire fence (i.e., with hardware cloth) around a small bed to support the vines and keep them out of the other beds. To lessen the chance of infestation with sweet potato weevils, start with certified pest-free slips. In spring: plant 8 to 12 weeks after last freeze. In fall: don't plant. I.G. spacing: use compact varieties and grow with wire enclosure. Set plants 12 × 12 inches to 24 × 24 inches apart.

grown Southern vegetable. The sweet potato probably originated in tropical America although it is grown throughout the tropics today.

The favorite varieties today have yellow to reddish orange flesh, though there are also white-fleshed varieties. They grow best in a loose, organic, sandy soil. Sweet potatoes are planted from slips (adventitious shoots sprouted from last year's crop) which shouldn't be set out until the soil is thoroughly warm—in late April or early May.

Work up beds 30 inches wide and 8 to 12 inches high. Slips get off to a better start if the tender roots are healed in (set in a shallow trench) first in a

---

Tips for Growing Sweet Potatoes

- This is a vegetable for large gardens, but compact varieties like Bush Porto Rico and Vardaman can be grown in smaller gardens or even in whiskey barrels.

- Sweet potato weevils are a limiting factor in the production of this vegetable. Be sure to get certified pest-free slips. Chemical control isn't practical for the home gardener.

- Set the slips deep with at least 3 leaf joints below the surface. Be sure to follow with a good watering immediately. Using a soaker hose to mist the foliage for a few days wouldn't even be a bad idea.

- Mulch the plants heavily to save water, control weeds, and reduce the tendency to continually root where the vines touch the soil. In sandy soils, many varieties produce their smoothest roots at these points.

- Four months after planting, carefully (i.e., with a hand trowel) check the roots for development. Once they are large enough, and before soil temperature drops below 50° F, it's time to carefully dig the crop. Any roots that are damaged should be set aside for immediate consumption because they won't cure and store well.

- It's usually warm enough at harvest time to cure the potatoes in the garage. Don't wash or even brush off the soil. Cover the roots with damp burlap, row cover, etc., and store for two weeks at about 80° F. After curing, the potatoes can be kept at storage temperatures above 50° F for 3 to 4 months.

SWEET POTATO VARIETIES

Name (Source)	Color	Disease Resistance	Days to Reach Maturity	Comments
Beauregard (19)	Light Purple Skin, Dark Orange Flesh		120	High-yielding Louisiana State University release. Not a compact grower, however, so this one is for large gardens. As with most sweet potatoes, the quality improves in storage.
Centennial (5, 8, 19)	Orange Skin, Orange Flesh		140	Strong grower. Good for short-season areas of the upper South.
Jewell (5, 8)	Copper Skin, Orange Flesh	N	120	Good high-yielding variety with some resistance to nematodes. Vining growth habit. Jewell is probably the most commonly planted commercial variety.
Vardaman (5, 8, 19)	Yellow Skin, Red-Orange Flesh		120–140	Not only compact, this one has purplish leaves. You might even try it in the flower bed. Vines will grow up some so it could be used on a small trellis.

Key to Disease and Pest Abbreviations
N = nematodes

muddy section of the garden. This coats the roots and protects them from drying. If the soil is dry, make a muddy spot by running the hose for a few minutes. A modern variation of this technique would be to use a water-absorbing polymer to coat the roots. This is often done with seedling trees, and it should work equally well with sweet potatoes. Open small holes in the row 3 to 4 inches deep and space the plants 12 to 18 inches apart. The 18-inch spacing will produce larger potatoes. Be sure to water in the slips as you plant.

The sweet potato plant is a heavy feeder so don't be afraid to side dress every 2 to 4 weeks during the season. Foliar fertilizer sprayers will work well if the planting isn't too large.

It is usually October before the roots have formed. To tell if roots are mature, break a few roots and set them out on the counter. If the broken areas turn black, say within a 24-hour period, they're not mature. Be careful in digging them—bruises or punches from a spading fork will invite storage rot. Sweet potatoes need to be cured 12 to 15 days at 80° F. This toughens the skin and reduces rot. After this treatment they can be stored for 5 to 6 months, provided they are kept at a temperature between 55° and 60° F.

(See photo on page 118.)

*T*OMATOES   The tomato is America's favorite garden vegetable—and for good reason. Perhaps no vegetable differs more from its commercial counterpart than the homegrown tomato. Tomatoes from the produce counter are often bland and mushy because most have been ripened artificially in storage—picked green at what is called the "chow-chow" stage. Eating a BLT sandwich made with one of these technological wonders is a sacrilege. BLTs and, for that matter, any other food that calls for fresh tomatoes should be made with tomatoes like the ones Grandma used to grow.

Americans haven't always been so enamored with tomatoes. Along with the potato and pepper, tomatoes originated in the Americas but they came back to the United States via Europe. Thomas Jefferson suggested the use of tomatoes for food in 1781, but tomatoes were primarily grown as ornamentals until 1835.

Today's tomato is not only America's favorite vegetable, it is also one of the country's most genetically advanced. Plant breeders have established varieties with multiple disease resistance that, in most cases, are still good quality. A gene that will allow tomatoes to be picked closer to fully ripe and not rapidly decay at the marketplace is on the horizon, even for home gardeners. Genetic advancements have also given us determinate varieties (those that stop growing once they reach between 24 and 30 inches in height), as well as new indeterminate ones (which continue to grow, sometimes getting as tall as 8 to 10 feet high).

In spite of all the genetic technology there is increased availability of heirloom varieties. Many are ugly by popular standards—odd-shaped fruits with pleated shoulders, yellow streaks, or even purple coloring—but the flavor is often excellent and future plant breeders may need some of these di-

BASIC PLANTING INFORMATION FOR TOMATOES

Space Between Rows (Inches)	Seed Spacing (Inches)	Thin to (Inches)	Seed Depth (Inches)	Days to Reach Maturity	Comments/Planting Dates/Intensive Gardening (I.G.) Spacing
36–48	N/A	24–36	1/4	65–90	Seed are typically planted in the greenhouse in January for early spring transplants. If started indoors under fluorescent lights, be sure to keep the seedlings close to the lights (2 to 6 inches), otherwise they will get leggy. In spring: plant any time from average last frost date to 8 weeks later. In fall: plant 16 to 20 weeks before first frost. I.G. spacing: 24 × 24 inches.

verse genetic traits in years to come. All this variety makes tomato growing fun, but it also makes it frustrating because some of us would like to grow them all.

Most home gardeners buy their tomato plants at the local nursery. This works fine until you want to grow new or unusual varieties. Then you need to find a place in the landscape for a greenhouse, or at the least a cold frame, and start your own seedlings.

The time to begin planting out in the garden usually begins 2 to 4 weeks after the average last spring frost date—between March 1 and April 1 for most Southern gardeners. However, if you are only planting a dozen plants or less, take a chance and plant on or before the average frost date. If you have a hard freeze, and all the mulch, old blankets, etc., that you can find won't save them, just go out and buy some more. The cost will be minimal. If you do save the plants, you'll have earlier tomatoes and more of them. Unlike peppers and eggplant (close relatives), tomatoes are tolerant of cool soils and marginal growing temperatures. When it does warm up they will have a good root system established and will outproduce the same varieties planted later.

Tomatoes do best in a rich, organic soil with plenty of water but good drainage. For some gardeners, this means installing raised beds or at least planting on top of ridges in the garden. Transplants that have become lanky do best if their stems are laid down in a trench with the leafy portion staked up. (See photo on page 119.) This allows the stem to root along its length, whereas planting the stem in a deep hole may cause the existing roots, which are used to more oxygen, to die off in the bottom of the hole. It's also a good idea to put a slow-release fertilizer in the planting hole to ensure that the young, developing roots will have an adequate supply of nutrients. This can be a compressed, commercial fertilizer tablet; a tablespoon of fertilizer like Osmacote; or, for the strictly organic, a similar amount of blood meal or fish meal. Finish the planting with a starter solution, such as one-third-strength soluble fertilizer, or use a similar dilution of fish emulsion.

Most home gardeners have discovered the reinforced wire tomato cage. By supporting the plant it solves a lot of problems. Disease problems are reduced with good air circulation, and by keeping the fruit off the soil, plants are easier to spray and the fruit is easier to find and harvest. Wrap the cage with fiber row cover in the spring and you eliminate wind damage, get a few degrees of frost protection, and keep disease-spreading insects like aphids out the first month or two. (See photos on page 119.)

Hanging red Christmas tree balls on the tomato plants just before they begin to ripen discourages mockingbirds from coming back for more. Or, you can still get a very flavorful tomato if it is picked at the pink blush stage and allowed to ripen on the kitchen counter.

LARGE-FRUITED TOMATO VARIETIES

Name (Source)	Color	Disease Resistance	Days to Reach Maturity	Comments
Better Boy (WA)	Red	V, F, N, FW	70	One of the first of the disease-resistant hybrids. It's still a good one even though as an indeterminate-size variety it will grow for the sky. Best of all, it not only looks good it tastes good, and the fruits are fairly large—weighing up to a pound—early in the season.
Better Bush (19)	Red	V, FW, N	75	This is becoming a popular home variety because the plants will not grow higher than 42 inches. Quality is also good from medium-large (3 to 4 inch) fruits. Not a heavy producer.
Big Beef Hybrid (WA)	Red	V, FW, N, TMV, ASC, GLS	73	Beefsteak varieties are typically a waste of time for the Southern gardener. The demand for this type of tomato variety is considerable, however, and the plant breeders have been hard at work to produce good ones. This one received the All-America Selections banner, so it's worth a try if you must have tomato slices that will overlap on your BLT sandwiches. In our trials, the small- to medium-size varieties produced 40 to 50 pounds of tomatoes per plant while the "beefsteaks" produced a few big, distorted fruits.
Bingo (37)	Red	V, FW, TMV, A, GLS	75	This is one of the determinate-size, small- to medium-size varieties with large, meaty, globe-shaped fruits.
Carmello (18, 28)	Red	V, FW, N, TMV	70	One of several French varieties that have good disease resistance, excellent productivity, and outstanding flavor. This is an indeterminate-size variety capable of producing 50 pounds of tomatoes per plant that are truly of gourmet quality—meaty, juicy, and acid enough to awaken the palate, and flavorful enough to make you stand guard at the garden gate. Not a beefsteak type, but the fruits are large and crack resistant.
Carnival (WA)	Red	V, FW2, N, TMV	75	This semideterminate-size variety has great disease resistance and produces larger and more uniform tomatoes than its rival, Celebrity. Its flavor is not quite as good but it's worth growing.

Key to Disease and Pest Abbreviations
A = anthracnose   ASC = alternaria stem canker   FCR = fusarium crown rot   FW1, 2 = fusarium wilt 1, 2   GLS = gray leaf spot   LS = leaf spot   N = nematodes   R = russeting   TMV = tobacco mosaic virus   V = verticillium

LARGE-FRUITED TOMATO VARIETIES (CONT.)

Name (Source)	Color	Disease Resistance	Days to Reach Maturity	Comments
Celebrity (WA)	Red	V, FW2, N, TMV	72	Celebrity won an All-America award for its heavy production of large, good-quality tomatoes on a determinate-size plant. It's still a popular variety with homeowners. However in some areas of the South, tomato spotted wilt virus has limited its commercial production.
Champion (34)	Red	V, FW, N, TMV	75	This was one of the early semideterminate-size hybrids. It almost fell through the cracks with the popularity of Celebrity and others, probably because it is hard to find in consumer seed catalogs. Fortunately, it is readily available to bedding plant growers and is often available as a transplant at the nursery. It is consistently one of the heaviest producers in our trials and is highly rated in taste tests. This variety should be included in any tomato planting.
Dona (3, 18, 28, 34)	Red	V, FW2, N, TMV	65	Dona was one of the first French varieties that we tested, and it really got our attention. It is an indeterminate-size variety developed for the fresh market. Thus, these medium-size, slightly flattened, juicy, scrumptious tomatoes will probably never show up at the local grocery market. Most surprisingly, the plant has good disease resistance and tolerates heat about as well as any large-fruited variety.
Heat Wave (1, 2, 34)	Red	V, FW2, A	70	This is a determinate, heat-tolerant variety. Frankly, in the midst of a lower South summer nothing but the cherry types will set much fruit and the fruit on the large-fruited types is smaller when it matures.
Fantastic (WA)	Red		70	This older hybrid is still popular with many home gardeners because of its good quality and productivity. It's an indeterminate-size variety and it doesn't have the disease resistance of newer hybrids. Regardless, it often produces lots of tomatoes and they make for good eating. Terrific (V, F, N) and Super Fantastic (V, F, N) have a similar following and some disease resistance.
Merced	Red	V, FW2, GLS, TMV	70	Large 9- to 10-ounce fruit are produced well into the summer on determinate-size plants. Fruits are globe shaped and ripen to an even red.

continued

LARGE-FRUITED TOMATO VARIETIES (CONT.)

Name (Source)	Color	Disease Resistance	Days to Reach Maturity	Comments
President (34)	Red	V, FW2, N, TMV	70	A determinate-size variety producing large, high-quality fruit. Also has good foliage to reduce sunscald. Productivity is less than can be expected from indeterminates like Champion but the plant is also smaller. Should be a good one for large containers.
Spitfire (37)	Red	V, FW2, A, LS	75	Another of the hot weather-tolerant varieties, this one is produced on a semideterminate-size bush. This is an obvious commercial variety. It produces a lot of No. 1 grade, attractive fruit with good quality and crack resistance.
Summer Flavor 5000 (34, 35)	Red	V, FW2, N	75	This is a large-fruited determinate variety. Even though a proprietary variety from a Pennsylvania seed co., it has produced high-quality fruit in Southern trials.
Valencia (12, 34)	Orange		70–80	This is an indeterminate-size, heirloom variety that did surprisingly well compared with modern hybrids. It also has attractive yellow-orange fruit. Plants are large with lots of foliage cover to protect the fruit. There are a number of yellow, striped, and even white varieties that will be discussed more under warm-season gourmet vegetables.
Whirlaway	Red	V, FW2, A, GLS	70–80	This is a determinate-size variety with strong foliage and, as would be expected, less tendency for the fruit to sunscald. Fruits are medium to large and crack resistant.

Many new tomato varieties come out each year, and it's always exciting to grow them to see if they're any better than your old favorites. Recently, varieties that look promising are Acclaim (13)—a new hybrid bred for the South with outstanding disease resistance; Hayslip (13, 34)—a determinate-size, fresh-market variety from Florida; and Sunny (34)—another new one from Florida.

Greenhouse tomato varieties are often tasteless and mushy. Perhaps growing conditions are a major factor—low light, short days, and marginal temperatures—but not entirely. Homeowners wanting just a few tomatoes to get them through the winter will probably do best with the varieties they liked from last summer's garden. Mosaic virus, whiteflies, spider mites, pinworms, leaf miners, and gray leaf mold are major concerns. All too often

GREENHOUSE TOMATO

Name (Source)	Color	Disease Resistance	Days to Reach Maturity	Comments
Caruso (31)	Red	TMV, V, FW2	75	This greenhouse tomato is a small- to medium-size variety, unlike most indeterminate types.
Cobra (31, 35)	Red	TMV, V, FW2	75	Supposedly the best tasting of the greenhouse varieties. Based on this factor alone, it goes to the top of the recommended list. It also has great disease resistance, as do most greenhouse varieties. This one should be tried outside the greenhouse, too.
Jumbo (31)	Red	V, FW2	80	Big beefsteak-type fruits. May not be very pretty but they will appeal to some who miss this type of fruit in the winter.
Match (31)	Red	TMV, V, FW2, FCR, R	80	Large-fruited variety on a vigorous, indeterminate-size plant. Fruits are globe shaped, uniform, and tolerant to fusarium crown rot and russeting.
Tropic (WA)	Red	V, FW, TMV	85	This tomato is attractive, but tasteless and mushy. It's nasty tasting even when grown outdoors. So, don't waste valuable greenhouse space on this dog. It may be pretty and it does have tremendous disease resistance, but will customers or friends ask for more?

Key to Disease and Pest Abbreviations
FCR = fusarium crown rot   FW, FW2 = fusarium wilt, fusarium wilt 2   R = rust   TMV = tobacco mosaic virus   V = verticillium

PASTE TOMATO

Name (Source)	Color	Disease Resistance	Days to Reach Maturity	Comments
Bellstar (12, 31, 34)	Red		70	Large size for a processing tomato. Good for sauce or juice, but also good fresh.
Enchantment (22, 28, 34)	Red	V, FW2, N	70	Typical egg-shaped processing tomato, but this one has flavor and juiciness. Even the acidity is good and the plant has outstanding disease resistance.
Hybrid 882 (35)	Red	V, FW2, N, ASC	75	Heavy production on a strong, determinate-size plant. Fruits are attractive, but are processing quality only.
Royal Chico (1, 34)	Red		75	Very compact, determinate-size vines and larger fruit than most paste types.
Viva Italia (WA)	Red	V, FW, N, A, GLS	70	Good yields on a determinate-size plant with excellent disease resistance.

Key to Disease and Pest Abbreviations
A = anthracnose   ASC = alternaria stem canker   FW, FW2 = fusarium wilt, fusarium wilt 2
GLS = gray leaf spot   N = nematodes   V = verticillium

CHERRY TOMATO

Name (Source)	Color	Disease Resistance	Days to Reach Maturity	Comments
Baxter's Early Bush (1, 34)	Red		70	Early and heavily productive, semideterminate-size variety. Average to large-size, cherry-type fruit. Excellent quality.
Currant and Droplet Varieties (3, 11, 12, 17, 18, 27, 28, 29, 34)	Red, Yellow, or Pink		65–70	Some of these fruits are so small, it hardly seems worth the effort to pick them. However, they are often some of the most delicious, and one plant in the garden shouldn't be too much of a burden. Some of our Master Gardener volunteers still remember the tedium of picking Pink Droplet but they also remember how great it tasted. These varieties tend to be indeterminate and rather large.
Gardeners Delight (2, 12, 27, 33)	Red	Cracking	70	Determinate plant with 1- to 1½-inch, sugar-sweet fruits.
Pear Tomatoes (WA)	Red or Yellow		75	These mild-flavored fruits are usually not much larger than the large cherries. Plants are typically healthy and vigorous.
Porter (34)	Pink		75	This tough, productive variety has been around for a long time. It is not a highly flavored tomato but it is juicy and good. Best of all, it will continue to produce in the heat of summer.
Red Cherry (WA)	Red		75	This variety is typical of indeterminate cherry varieties. If you only plant one tomato, this one would be a good choice. It will produce lots of salad tomatoes all season long. (Of course, they tend to fall out of a sandwich when sliced.)
SuperSweet 100 (WA)	Red	V, FW	65	One of the newer indeterminate varieties. This one has very sweet fruits 1 inch in diameter and lots of them. Sweet Million is similar but has increased disease resistance to FNTL.
Sweet Chelsea (33, 34)	Red	V, FW, N, TMV	70	Indeterminate variety with large fruit for a cherry variety. In addition to good disease resistance, the fruit resists cracking.
Toy Boy (34)	Red	V, FW	60	Several of these varieties only grow 12 inches or so high. Tiny Tim (34) and Red Robin (34) are similar. All are primarily novelties since the amount of fruit harvested from container-grown plants of this sort is negligible.

Key to Disease and Pest Abbreviations
FW = fusarium wilt   N = nematodes   TMV = tobacco mosaic virus   V = verticillium

enthusiastic home gardeners harbor the misconception that growing in a greenhouse eliminates pest problems. It does not!

In spite of small fruit size, cherry tomato plants (see photo on page 119) often produce more pounds of fruit than the large tomatoes—as much or more than 60 pounds per plant in some trials.

Tips for Growing Tomatoes

- Plant good-tasting, disease-resistant varieties. Check with your local extension agent for recommendations, label your plants, and keep notes.

- If you are only planting a few plants, take a chance and plant a few weeks before the average last frost date. Then, protect them if necessary.

- When you set transplants, use a slow-release fertilizer in the bottom of the hole (about an inch under the roots), water the plants in with a starter solution (one-third-strength soluble fertilizer), and start foliar feeding a week or two after planting.

- Use fiber row cover or clear plastic to wrap the tomato cages. The small plants will think they never left the greenhouse.

- Spray early in the season with preventative fungicides. Early blight often turns tomato plants yellow, then brown from the bottom up almost before you know it is happening. Later on as fruits begin to ripen you will probably need fewer sprays. Be sure to direct sprays to the underside of the leaf as well as to the top.

- Hand pick early populations of stinkbugs (especially leaf-footed bugs). Yes, you can use rubber gloves and the sole of your shoe. These large overwintering adults will quickly start a population boom. Try a trap crop like sunflowers—this may be the only plant they love more than tomatoes.

- Tomato-growing diehards may want to construct a frame over the row to hold a layer of fiber row cover for sunscald protection at midday in midsummer.

- Fall tomatoes are tough to grow—viruses are everywhere and so are the bugs and mites. Masochists and tomato lovers that must try should start early. Set plants out as early as June or July and shade them, if necessary. Use early varieties and keep the green tomato chow-chow recipes handy.

WARM-SEASON GOURMET SELECTIONS

This section covers a wide range of vegetables, most of which are grown only on a limited basis and often are little known. Some of them may become common staples one of these days because they're quite good. Also included in this section are some of the more unusual color variations of the more common vegetables.

Variations on a Color Theme

CUCUMBERS. Fortunately, most are green, but white cucumbers do exist. White Wonder (27, 29) is the only variety offered, and it is reportedly good fresh or could make some "ghostly" pickles for Halloween. Oh yes, there's also a Lemon cucumber (17, 27), a round apple-shaped curiosity that's supposed to be easy to digest.

EGGPLANT. This gets complicated. Most of the variations on the standard eggplant theme (large, purple, and semiteardrop shaped) are color variations but shape also plays a role. Long, skinny eggplants are becoming more common. We think of these as Asian varieties, but the French seem to appreciate the elongated shape as well. Then there are the little ones—round ones ranging from marble to Ping-Pong ball size and lance-shaped ones 2 to 3 inches long. Oh, and there's the half-long size, some of which are white. Ignoring shapes, the colors of the most edible ones are purple or purple-striped with white tinges or suffused with pink, white, or green. Red and orange eggplants are also available, but their culinary value is suspect. Remember that eggplants belong to the solanaceae family, which includes poisonous plants like the Deadly Nightshade. These red and orange varieties aren't poisonous, but some are reportedly bitter.

GREEN BEANS. Not all bush and pole beans are green, of course. Yellow is probably the most popular variation of this vegetable, also known as the wax bean. Productivity usually isn't on par with the green varieties but we have seen good production from Goldcrop (31), Goldkist (WA), and Dorabel (22, 31). Best of all, they taste great and add a new color dimension. Purple-podded beans are another variation. Unless used fresh or pickled, the purple pigment breaks down to dark green with cooking, however. Good varieties include: Royal Burgundy (WA) (see photo on page 120) and Purple Teepee (19). Some beans also have purple mottling on the pods; this color also breaks down to green with cooking. Landfrauen (19) and Selma Star (19) are examples of pole beans with this coloration. The filet or haricot vert variety Triumph de Farcy (WA) is a skinny French bush bean with mottled pods.

OKRA.   The major color variation in this vegetable is red. There are several of them, including an All-America Selection Burgundy (WA). A variety Blondy (WA) is, at best, pale green rather than white.

PEPPERS.   This group of vegetables is one of the most genetically diverse in the garden. If you consider the green bell pepper to be the only standard variety then the chart of unusuals would fill up numerous pages of this book. You'd have reds, yellows, purples, hot ones, long ones, and little ones plus every variation inbetween. We've covered most variations in separate charts earlier in this chapter.

POTATOES.   The most striking color variation in this vegetable is purple, except for All Blue (26), which has blue skin and flesh. Some varieties have purple skin with white flesh and when prepared for the table won't startle anyone.

In recent years yellow-fleshed potatoes like Yukon Gold (WA) have begun to appear on grocers' shelves. This color variation has some potential. Golden yellow mashed potatoes might pass the test with less butter. Green, however, is not a good color variation and all potato tubers will start to turn green if they aren't stored in the dark. You wouldn't eat potato foliage (remember: solanaceae family), and green potatoes aren't good either. Often the green parts can be trimmed off and are in no way as toxic as the leaves, but why chance even a slight allergic reaction?

SQUASHES (WINTER, SUMMER, AND PUMPKINS).   This is another extremely variable group of vegetables that comes in many colors. Color variations of the standard types also occur. For example, we usually think of zucchini as a green vegetable. Now, however, we have golden yellow zucchinis like Burpee's Golden (2) and Golden Dawn II (19) that are not only productive but appetizing as well. Acorn squashes now come in white, such as the All-America Selection Cream of the Crop (WA), and in yellow, such as Golden Acorn (WA). Patty pan squashes don't just come in pale green anymore, as evidenced by Sunburst Hybrid (WA), which is golden yellow with a green center. And not all pumpkins are golden orange; Lumina (WA) is a 10 to 12 pound white-skinned variety and Baby Boo (19, 31) is a miniature white.

SWEET CORN.   Most corn is, of course, yellow, but white super-sweet varieties like How Sweet It Is (WA) have sure garnered some attention. Bicolors like Honey 'n' Pearl (19) are also available. Brightly colored "Indian" corns and colored popcorns are listed in most catalogs, but they are mostly for use as mature dried corn and often just for show. Some, like the blue

UNUSUAL TOMATO VARIETIES

Name (Source)	Color	Days to Reach Maturity	Comments
Calabash (27)	Purple	85	This variety has deeply ribbed shoulders and a color that many people find unappetizing. The flesh almost looks like raw meat. As repulsive as this may sound, the tomato is excellent. The flavor is sweet, complex, and tart enough to taste like a homegrown tomato. Fruits are medium to large in size and the indeterminate plant is relatively vigorous and productive.
Costoluto Genovese, Italian (27, 28, 29, 34)	Red	78	Strong-growing, indeterminate variety with deeply ribbed, flavorful tomatoes. An Italian heirloom adapted to hot weather.
Eva Purple Ball (29)	Purple	78	An heirloom German variety that is reportedly adapted to hot, humid conditions. Hot and humid in Germany may not be comparable to Gulf Coast weather, but this should be a fun one to try. Fruits are medium-size and are produced on an indeterminate plant. Cherokee Purple (12, 29, 34) is another purple heirloom—this time from Tennessee. These fruits are in the large category and so is the plant.
Garden Peach (27, 34)	Yellow/ Pink	75–85	Another curiosity. This one has fuzz. Not exactly what most folks want on a BLT, but there's a good chance you'll have the only ones on the block. Flavor is mild and the plant is indeterminate.
Georgia Streak (29)	Yellow/ Red	90	Georgia heirloom, beefsteak type similar to Striped German. The colors here won't appeal to most people but the quality is excellent. Both varieties are indeterminate and moderately productive.
German Johnson (29)	Pink	75	Heirloom variety with large pink fruits produced on an indeterminate variety.
Green Grape (18, 29, 34)	Green	70	Plants are compact with quarter-size, yellow-green fruits. Sweet and juicy but they look like the kind you get on your hamburger at some fast food restaurants. Evergreen (27) is another one that is green when ripe.
Green Zebra (18, 29)	Green, Striped	85	Another green one but this one is striped—with yellow and green. Reportedly of gourmet quality and sure to get attention at the table. Plants are indeterminate and fruits are small to medium size.
Mini Orange (29)	Orange	65	Indeterminate variety with golf ball-size, bright orange fruits. Supposed to set fruit when night temperatures rise above 70° F.
Persimmon (3, 7, 27, 29)	Rose/ Orange	90	Vigorous, indeterminate vines produce large fruits that rate high in taste tests.

Unusual Tomato Varieties (cont.)

Name (Source)	Color	Days to Reach Maturity	Comments
Riesenstraube (29)	Red	75	Cherry-size tomatoes are produced in bunches of 20 to 40 fruits. Indeterminate variety with good foliage. Might be a good one to try in the fall garden.
White Wonder (5, 27, 29, 34)	White	85	Medium-size white fruits are produced on an indeterminate plant.

corns (16, 23), which make great nacho chips, and colored popcorns (WA) that actually pop, have culinary uses but are easiest to grow in the dry climate of the Southwest. The strange "baby" corns (4) are a form of popcorn (see photo on page 110). Pick the ears about 5 days after silks appear.

TOMATOES. Yellow and pink tomatoes aren't big news but white and permanently green ones would get some attention. White Wonder and Evergreen are good examples of how diverse tomato genetics can be. Red tomatoes that remain striped with yellow, even when ripe, may not appeal to the senses, but the flavor can be excellent. Striped German is just such an heirloom variety. Tomatoes are almost every gardener's favorite because growing a weird-looking, good-tasting tomato is almost as appealing as growing the pretty red ones.

WATERMELONS. Yellow-fleshed watermelons like Yellow Baby (WA) probably don't come as much of a surprise to most gardeners. These even show up at roadside markets with regularity. But how about yellow skin and red flesh? One good melon with this combination is All-America Selection Golden Crown (2, 19). The orange-fleshed melons Orangeglo (37) and Tastigold (37) are also worth a try.

More Specialty Warm-Season Selections

The United States's melting pot is constantly being stirred. Most recently, we have welcomed a large population of Southeast Asians to our shores—Vietnamese, Cambodians, Laotians, and others—who've brought many exciting new vegetables and herbs with them. In addition, we already had quite a few other vegetables—gourds, chayotes, yard-long beans, Malabar spinach, and the like—that most gardeners weren't familiar with. Here, then, are the unusual varieties that shouldn't be overlooked.

CHAYOTE *(Mirlitons, vegetable pears)* (30 or from produce market). Chayotes are actually in the squash family, but they are considerably different in a few cultural aspects. To begin with, their seeds sprout while still in the fruit. Buy one at the produce market and leave it on the kitchen counter for 6 to 8 weeks. A sprout will begin to emerge from the large end. Time your purchase so the sprouted fruit will be ready to plant in mid- to late March when the soil is good and warm. This plant, like many tropical vegetables, is day-length sensitive. Unfortunately, except in the extreme South where the 12-hour or so days needed to initiate blooming come earlier, chayotes won't begin to bloom until fall. As a result, only gardeners living in the lower South will be able to grow them.

This is a very mild-tasting vegetable that's widely grown in Mexico and is common in the produce markets of larger cities, which is probably the best place to get them. The fruits are typically light green but there is a rare ivory-colored variety.

EDIBLE CHRYSANTHEMUM *(Shungiku)* (WA).   This is certainly an acquired taste, though this form is much milder smelling than commercial potted mums. Masochistic gardeners may want to try stir-frying Shungiku with bitter melon.

EDIBLE SOYBEANS (WA).   The adjective "edible" is used in this case to distinguish them from varieties grown for oil or meal. Whether they are truly edible is a matter of opinion. They are darn hard to get out of the shell and, once extracted, they taste like little pieces of green cardboard. A fellow gardener once remarked that they should be cooked with sausage, butter, sour cream, peppers, etc. Well, cook an old shoe long enough with that stuff and it would be edible. But, if you're an adventurous gardener you will probably want to try edible soybeans. At least they are good for you, and you could always use them for sprouts.

EXOTIC SQUASHES.   This is another large family of vegetables.

Calabaza (*C. moschata*) (30) is the Cuban winter squash and it may be the best adapted of the storage or winter varieties. (At least it was developed in the tropics.) The fruits are somewhat pumpkinlike—round, flattened, and with a hard buff-cream skin. The flesh is light yellow, firm, and meaty. This squash is gaining in popularity and is already grown to some extent in southern Florida's Dade County. Seeds are not readily available, so you may have to buy one of the squashes at a specialty market and save the seed.

Tahitian Squash (19) is similar to the Banana squash in texture and flavor (maybe sweeter) but is crooked and has a bulbous end measuring 4 to 5 inches in diameter. Great for baking or pumpkin pies.

Tromboncino (3) is used as a summer squash. (See photo on page 120.) It is one of the most vigorous of squashes and does best when trained on a trellis. The fruits are long and skinny—1½ to 2 inches in diameter at the prime picking stage—and have a bulbous end 3 to 4 inches in diameter. Cut up and prepared like zucchini, they have a rich, smooth, buttery texture and flavor that is unattainable with any other summer squash. Best of all, they grow like weeds in Southern gardens. They even seem to outgrow squash vine borers.

Tatume (1, 30) is another vining summer squash. This one is popular with hispanic gardeners. It looks like a short cylindrical to round-shaped zucchini and in fact fills a similar place at the table.

Vegetable Spaghetti (WA). This one is in a culinary category of its own. The cylindrical, tan-colored fruits are boiled or baked, then cut open, the seeds removed, and what remains can be forked out in the form of a vegetable spaghetti, hence the name. It's quite easy to grow and is becoming increasingly popular with gardeners everywhere.

GARDEN HUCKLEBERRY (8, 27).

A tomato relative, the garden huckleberry produces small, black fruits that range from tasteless to slightly bitter when fresh and used to make preserves or pies. Grow and space them as you would determinate tomato varieties.

GINGER.

Commercial gingerroot (*Zingiber officinale*) can be grown with some success from sprouted roots purchased at the grocery store. It's a long-season perennial native to the tropics though. So, except in the lower South, it may not grow long enough to produce much root. If you have a greenhouse, try some in a large container like a whiskey barrel. Other gingers like turmeric can be grown with some success in the lower South, but most ornamental gingers are probably best not used in the kitchen even though they may have edible relatives.

GOURDS.

Most people immediately think of bright, shellacked, round, warty ornamental gourds when you mention this vegetable, but there are a number of edible gourds we can grow very successfully in our Southern gardens. Of course we can grow the ornamental ones, too, but sometimes drying them in our typically humid climate isn't easy. If you decide to grow a crop of ornamental gourds, let them develop to full maturity and cut them with a good portion of vine attached, because this helps with drying. If you have an empty room in the house to store them, the lower humidity will also speed up the job.

First, wash the fruit with a disinfectant like household bleach (1 part bleach to 10 parts water) or Lysol to reduce the chance of surface decay. When fully dry, paint with several coats of marine varnish.

Lagenaria Gourds include Calabash (4, 14), Cucuzzi (WA) (see photo on page 120), and New Guinea Butter Vine (17), which are some of the alternate names you may see listed for this vegetable. Dipper (WA) and some Bird House gourds (WA) fit in this genus, too. Usually, the edible forms are long (36 inches is not unusual), and they vary in diameter from 2 to 6 inches. They are best when picked at 18 to 24 inches and even then, most first-time tasters will think them a bit bland. They can be used as a zucchini substitute though they will benefit from spicier treatment. The vines grow rampantly, sometimes covering small trees and houses in a single season, so give them plenty of room—36 to 48 inches apart in the row along the fence is about right. You shouldn't have to worry about insect and disease pests. The foliage has a musty odor and nothing seems to bother it. Organic gardeners might want to try grinding it up in the blender, combining with water, straining the solution through cheese cloth, and spraying it on other crops to repel insects.

Luffa Gourds (Cee Gwa, Climbing Okra, Vegetable Sponge) (WA) come in two basic types: the smooth ones and the ones with angular ridges. (See photo on page 121.) Both can be eaten when young (8 to 10 inches long and 1 inch or so in diameter), or can be processed into sponges when mature. To produce your own "upscale" sponges, remove the skin (you may want to soak them in water for a couple of days), rinse in a 10% household bleach–90% water mixture, and hang up to dry.

Wax Gourds and Winter Melons (becoming WA, Asian seed catalogs are good sources). Shape is the main distinguishing characteristic between these two vegetables known by the scientific name *Benincasa hispida*.

Wax Gourds (Fuzzy melon, Mao Gwa) are usually harvested when 6 to 8 inches long and 2 inches in diameter. (See photo on page 121.) If allowed to stay on the vine (grow this one on a trellis), they may grow to 36 inches in length and 10 to 12 inches in diameter. At this stage they will weigh 50 pounds or so, and your trellis will be history. When picked at the recommended size, the fruit is medium green and covered with fuzz. The fuzz is easily wiped off. Then, prepare the fruit like a zucchini. The flavor is more bland and the texture is crispier than zucchini, but this vegetable has potential to become much more popular. Just remember to be diligent about harvesting. It only takes a few days for these fruits to grow like Jack's bean stalk. Another benefit is that insects and diseases don't seem to like either vegetable.

Winter Melons (Doan Gwa) are usually grown on the ground like watermelons. They are very similar to Fuzzy gourds except for shape. These melons mature to become stocky cylinders, 18 to 24 inches long and 12 to 18 inches in diameter. They look a lot like watermelons with a waxy bloom on the skin. In fact, kids have been known to mistakenly steal these melons only to be disappointed when cutting open their booty to find it's more zucchini-like than red and juicy like a watermelon.

Traditionally, winter melon is used to make a specialty Chinese soup, which is often served in an elaborately carved winter melon rind.

Bitter Melon (Balsam Pear, Foo Gwa) (WA, Asian seed catalogs 4, 14, 32, 37) (See photo on page 121.) is a vegetable that demands an acquired taste. (It isn't called Bitter melon for nothing.) This one's been grown in the United States for a long time but mainly as an ornamental. The fruits are light green, shiny, and warty. When mature, they open to reveal a bright red pulp. To cook this interesting vegetable, harvest when only 6 to 8 inches long, cut and remove the seed cavity, boil briefly in two changes of water to remove some of the bitterness, then stir-fry. (Hopefully, our Asian and Indian friends will overlook such culinary abuse in deference to the fast food palate of most Americans.)

*J*ACKBEAN.   This isn't much of a vegetable. Apparently, small quantities of the immature seeds can be cooked with a change of water if you're desperate for something to eat, but consumption of these large, pink lima-looking beans is generally discouraged. The only reason for even mentioning jackbean is that this is one of those plants that is so fascinating people save the seeds and pass them around to their friends. The vines grow 20 to 30 feet in one season. But trust us, there are better vegetables. Grow these 8- to 12-inch pods as a curiosity only.

*J*ICAMA (10, 30).   This tropical vine does produce a delicious, underground tuber that looks like an overgrown, leather-covered turnip. When the skin is removed, however, a white, crisp flesh is revealed, the taste of which has a hint of English peas and apples. It is great in salads or cut into sticks for dips. Outside of Southern Florida this vegetable doesn't have time to produce large tubers. You'll need to continually remove flowers to prevent seed set, which reduces tuber production. It's a wonderful vegetable but you might save your energy for more productive crops.

*O*THER MELONS.   We're not including all the various colored watermelons, because we could fill a book. Some of the most interesting, however, include:

Asian Crispy Melons (4, 14, 32, 37), which are small, 4 to 6 inches long, 3 to 4 inches in diameter and typically white fleshed. The skin usually matures to a bright yellow. The flavor is sweet, mild (bland compared with a muskmelon), and aromatic.

Israeli Melons (Ogen) (WA) grow very well in the South. At maturity it varies in color from orange to orange with green striping and is cantaloupe shaped. The flesh is white and very tasty. It's a true gourmet melon.

Crenshaw Melons (1, 2, 27, 31, 37) are yellow-gold when mature and somewhat wrinkled looking. The shape is almost nutlike, but this is a comparatively large melon and the orange flesh is to die for.

Charantais Melons (pronounced SHARE-n-tay) (2, 3, 12, 27, 28, 37) have the strong, perfumy, muskmelon flavor of a crenshaw. However, they're not the easiest to grow—decay and cracking tend to be a problem. But they are wonderful tasting, and new hybrids like Primo (24), Pancha (28), and Savor (37) make this gray-green-on-the-outside, bright orange-on-the-inside melon worth trying.

Casabas, Persians, and other Melons are sometimes offered in the produce markets. Seed could be saved from these melons but the quality is usually inferior compared with that of the wonderful muskmelons and honeydews also available.

*R*OSELLE *(Hibiscus sabdariffa)* (30). This okra relative is sometimes called the Florida Cranberry because the flowers (calyx and sepals) are used to flavor sauces, jellies, and teas. Plants are large, like okra, with red-tinged foliage. In fact, this one should be good to grow just for its ornamental value.

*S*ORREL (WA) is a cultivated form of the noxious weed dock. It has a tart flavor that has traditionally been used in cream soups. It grows well in Southern gardens, but you probably won't want to plant too much.

*S*UMMER GREENS (WA). Cool-season greens like collard, mustard, and spinach are just plain better than their summer substitutes. If, however, you get a hankering for greens around the Fourth of July, you can make do with some of the following.

Climbing Spinach (Malabar spinach, Basella alba or rubra) (WA) has developed quite a following in the last few years. (See photo on page 122.) It is easy to grow, ornamental (with shiny green, heart-shaped leaves), and the flavor is good—a lot like spinach's. It does, however, have an unpleasant texture. It's slick, so it goes down quickly.

Reportedly, climbing spinach also has medicinal value for those unfortunate gardeners with intestinal problems. Try it as part of a salad with mostly lettuce. It can even be cooked, but then it's warm and even more slick. A little vinegar and pepper sauce improves it, though, as should steaming.

New Zealand Spinach (WA) is sometimes called Summer spinach (must be describing a summer in England). This one grows best in cool weather and won't survive a hard frost like real spinach will. Its fuzzy leaves do taste good, like spinach leaves, but it won't grow much except in mild weather.

Purslane (3, 18, 28) is a weed. Chances are you already have a good supply, but there are cultivated varieties available. A little bit is good in salads but you may have to sneak it in and tell your guests what they're eating after dinner.

Water Spinach (Ipomea aquatica) (4, 14, 32) is perhaps the best of the bunch and it is only being discovered by most American gardeners. (See photo on page 122.) It doesn't have to be grown in water-filled beds—that's mostly for weed control—but it can be, and, of course does need plenty of moisture. Seeds are available from Asian specialty catalogs or often from Asian grocery stores. The plants, if fresh, could be rooted and grown from cuttings. Only the tender young shoots and leaves are eaten.

*S*UNROOTS (SUNCHOKES, JERUSALEM ARTICHOKES) (2, 5, 8, 12, 17, 19, 26, 29).

(See photo on page 122.) Be careful with this vegetable; it can become a weed. In fact, it's a native sunflower that produces edible tubers in late summer and early fall. Leave a few tubers unharvested, however, and next year they will be back. The tubers can be scrubbed clean and cut up for salads or cooked with a roast. This has become a popular health food item because the tubers contain inulin (*not* insulin), which is easy for people with diabetes to digest. Lots of gardeners must like them because there are now several varieties available, including Stampede (12) and Fuseau (26, 29). It used to be you had to plant the ones from the grocery store and that will still work, but it's wise to plant several varieties to see which one produces best in your area. They begin to form tubers in response to the shorter days of fall and so latitude may influence your success with a particular variety. There are also differences in flavor.

*T*OMATILLOS (WA).

(See photo on page 122.) There would be no Mexican green sauce without this vegetable. It's another member of the tomato family and is quite happy in the Southern garden. The small green fruits have a papery shell and they lend a uniquely tart taste to many south-of-the-border sauces. Start like you would with tomatoes and set the plants 18 to 24 inches apart in the row.

*W*INGED BEANS (Psophocarpus tetragonolobus) (4, 11, 30).

(See photo on page 121.) This tropical vine is day-length sensitive so it doesn't begin to produce the delicious, winged pods it is named for until fall. Reportedly, there are day-neutral varieties, but it is hard to find seed for any variety. This is the kind of vegetable that gets written up in the *Wall Street Journal* with a headline like: Winged Bean: The Vegetable That Could End World Hunger. Why? Well not only are the pods edible, the tender growing shoots taste like

English peas (the pods do, too) and in the tropics the plant produces an edible, underground tuber.

YAMS *(Dioscorea spp.)*.   Most Southern gardeners are not likely to ever grow true yams in their garden. The yam of commerce is actually a sweet potato. Yams on the other hand are tropical vines that produce underground or aerial tubers that are best described as bland compared to sweet potatoes. The Air Potato *(D. bulbifera)* is a fairly common ornamental yam often grown in the South. It has beautiful glossy, heart-shaped leaves, and leathery tubers are produced in the leaf axils. Some true yams have medicinal value and others are downright toxic, including the Air Potato.

YARD-LONG BEANS *(Dow Gauk)* (WA).   Closely related to Southern peas, this is an extremely productive vegetable for the Southern garden. Hint: Don't let them get a yard long or you'll need bionic jaws. They're best at 12 to 18 inches. Basically, two types exist. The black-seeded ones are slimmer and are picked longer than are the red-seeded types. This vegetable obviously needs a trellis and regular picking. Thin the plants 12 to 18 inches apart in the row and inoculate with a garden *Rhizobium* at planting. The finished product is identical to young green "snaps" from other Southern peas, like Purple Hulls. This makes a great vertical space vegetable!

Cool-Season Vegetables

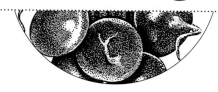

BEETS   Beets are far from being one of America's favorite vegetables. Perhaps their popularity would improve if more people grew and cooked them fresh from the garden. Most people grow beets for the roots, but the tops are equally delicious. In fact, Swiss chard is nothing more than a beet that doesn't form an attractive, edible root. Both of these vegetables like a neutral to slightly alkaline soil pH (7 to 7.5). If a soil test shows your soil to be acid (most common in sandy, Southeastern soils), then adding agricultural lime (CaCo3), at 5 pounds per 100 square feet, is a good way to start amend-

BASIC PLANTING INFORMATION FOR BEETS

Space Between Rows (Inches)	Seed Spacing (Inches)	Thin to (Inches)	Seed Depth (Inches)	Days to Reach Maturity	Comments/Planting Dates/Intensive Gardening (I.G.) Spacing
14–24	1	3–5	$1/4–1/2$	50–65	Plenty of moisture is important for good seed emergence. Try using fiber row cover floated over the row and wettened daily until seeds have germinated. The row cover can be left in place for several weeks and it is often a good idea to leave it attached to one side of the row and pull it back on bright, sunny days, but to have it handy in case of a late freeze. In spring: plant 4 to 6 weeks before last freeze. In fall: plant 8 to 10 weeks before first frost. I.G. spacing: 3 × 3 inches to 5 × 5 inches.

BEET VARIETIES

Name (Source)	Color	Disease Resistance	Days to Reach Maturity	Comments
Big Red (31)	Red	CLS	55	This hybrid variety was developed for factory canners so you can bet it's great for home processing, too. Roots are shaped like tops with blood red interiors.
Cylindra (Formovana) (WA)	Red		60	Stocky, carrotlike variety that is great for slicing.
Detroit Dark Red (WA)	Red		60	This variety has been the standard by which other varieties have been measured for many years. It's still a good variety and there are improved forms like Detroit Supreme (Stokes) that are more uniform.
Early Wonder (Green Top Bunching) (WA)	Red		50	An old variety but still on most recommended lists.
Monopoly (28)	Red		55	Beets typically produce several plants per seed. This one was developed to have only one sprout per seed. It will save you the arduous task of thinning (as much) and the quality is excellent.
Pacemaker III (WA)	Red	LS	50	This variety produces sweet, uniform, very early beets. It is rapidly becoming a favorite of home gardeners.
Red Ace (1, 19, 22, 31, 35)	Red	LS	55	This hybrid is an improved Detroit type. Tops are relatively short and resistant to bolting.
Ruby Queen (WA)	Red		55	An old variety, but it is still one of the sweetest and the texture is finely grained. All-America Selections winner.
Sangria (5, 28)	Red		55	One of the newer hybrids. Good as baby beets and at full maturity. Very finely textured and sweet.
Warrior (1, 9)	Red		55	Another new hybrid. This one is especially dark red with some sugar beet background.

Key to Disease and Pest Abbreviations
CLS = cercospera leaf spot   LS = leaf spot

ing the soil. Calcium hydroxide (CaOH), called hydrated lime, is often the only lime product available in small packages at the nursery, however. Since the lime is more concentrated in the soil solution, you should only use about three-quarters as much.

Thin soon after seedlings emerge because beets are produced from a cluster of several seeds that often come up too densely. An initial thinning to 1 inch should suffice until you can harvest baby beets, allowing the rest to mature until they're 2 to 3 inches in diameter.

(See photo on page 188.)

Tips for Growing Beets

- Keep the seed bed evenly moist. Use fiber row cover or burlap if necessary. Drying out during germination is a common cause of poor stands.
- Thin! Remember, most varieties have seed clusters that look like individual seed, so even if you don't plant too thickly, you will still have too many plants. Beets are actually not too hard to transplant. If you've got the time, start a new row or fill in vacant spots.
- Don't forget to eat the tops. Beet greens are just shorter versions of Swiss chard.

CARROTS Carrots are a challenge to most beginning gardeners, especially if they are gardening in a heavy, clay soil. Working lots of organic matter into the soil helps, but it is also a good idea to work the soil up into ridges 8 to 12 inches high and plant on the ridges. Growing the shorter varieties is another good idea. Long, skinny Imperators don't do well in heavy soils, so remember raised beds are another alternative.

Carrot seed germinates slowly. Sometimes it requires 2 to 3 weeks, so covering the bed with fiber row cover or even burlap will keep the soil evenly moist until the seed begin to come up. Check often, especially when using a burlap row cover, to ensure that you don't damage the tiny seedlings. The reason for keeping the soil evenly moist is that carrots, like most small-seeded vegetables, should be planted shallowly—or just scratched into the soil. Early growth is slow. Apply fertilizer often but judiciously at first, and the carrots will really take off as the temperatures and day lengths increase. Weekly applications of soluble fertilizer with a hose-on fertilizer sprayer should do the job, or use an organic material like fish emulsion.

The various types: Nantes are slender with rounded ends, Imperators are long and skinny, and Chantenays are broad at the top and taper to a rounded end.

(See photo on page 188.)

BASIC PLANTING INFORMATION FOR CARROTS

Space Between Rows (Inches)	Seed Spacing (Inches)	Thin to (Inches)	Seed Depth (Inches)	Days to Reach Maturity	Comments/Planting Dates/Intensive Gardening (I.G.) Spacing
14–24	¼–½	1–2	Rake lightly into surface	70–80	Selecting varieties for good flavor means you'll end up with ones that are high in sugar and vitamin A. Some carrots grow well and are heavily productive but they taste little better than what's available in the store. Common mistakes are planting too deep and not thinning. In spring: plant 6 weeks before to 2 weeks after last freeze. In fall: plant 10 to 14 weeks before first frost. I.G. spacing: 1 × 1 inch to 2 × 2 inches.

CARROT VARIETIES

Name (Source)	Color	Disease Resistance	Days to Reach Maturity	Comments
A-Plus (19)	Orange		70	One average-size carrot supplies more than the minimum daily allowance of vitamin A, and the flavor is good, too. Carrots are large—up to 8 inches long—so you will need a deep, loose soil or a raised bed for this one.
Baby Spike (8, 19)	Orange		52	Miniature carrots that have high sugar and good color.
Bolero (12, 35)	Orange	A	70	One of the new French hybrid Nantes varieties. Roots are medium long, thick, and blunt.
Chantenay (Royal, Imperial, Red Core) (WA)	Orange to Orange-Red		60–70	Typically produces tapered, stocky roots that are good in tight soils. There is still no variety that will perform without good soil preparation.
Danvers 126 (Half Long) (WA)	Orange		70–80	Short, stocky roots usually less than 6 inches in length are good in tight soils.
Gold King (Northrup King seed racks)	Orange-Red		70	Tapered, stump-rooted variety with good orange-red color.
Imperator 58 (1)	Orange		70	A long variety that needs a deep, loose soil.

Key to Disease and Pest Abbreviations
A = alternaria

CARROT VARIETIES (CONT.)

Name (Source)	Color	Disease Resistance	Days to Reach Maturity	Comments
Ingot (29)	Dark Orange		65	Another one of the high vitamin-A varieties with excellent flavor. This one is a Nantes type.
Juwarot (33)	Orange		70	(When you figure out how to pronounce this one, call us.) It produces small to medium-size roots that are delicious and have double the vitamin A.
Mokum (3)	Orange		65	One of the really sweet varieties that develops early so it can be harvested as a "baby" carrot or left to mature.
Nandor hybrid (19)	Orange-Red		66	A new hybrid that seems to have it all—it's sweet, coreless, tender, and a good producer.
Nantes (Scarlet, Coreless, Baby) (WA)	Orange to Orange-Red		65–70	There are many variations of this variety and most have done well in Southern soils. Scarlet Nantes is almost coreless, tasty, and bright orange-red. Roots are typically cylindrical and stump-rooted.
Nelson (12)	Dark Orange		60	This variety has been recommended to replace Clarion, which was one of the best-tasting carrots in our trials. Clarion didn't have good vigor; perhaps Nelson (being an F1 hybrid) will. Nantes type with 6-inch-long cylindrical, blunt-shaped roots.
Orange Sherbert (31)	Orange		60	Hybrid Nantes × Imperator type with excellent flavor. Cylindrical roots can develop up to 10 inches in length or they can be harvested when medium size.
Orlando Gold (5)	Orange		65	Good commercial variety for deep, muck soils of Florida. Probably best grown in raised beds where tight soils are a problem. Also has 30% more carotene.
Sweetness (hybrid) (5)	Orange		65	Very sweet, 6-inch-long, cylindrical Nantes type. All-America Selection.
Texas Gold Spike (1)	Orange		70	Cylindrical, 8 to 10 inches long, with short foliage.
Thumbelina (WA)	Orange		50	These carrots develop more like radishes—1 to 1½ inches in diameter, sweet, and extra early. Another All-America Selection.

Tips for Growing Carrots

- Don't plant too deep. Scratching in with a rake should suffice. Add 1/3 radish seed to the planting. It will come up rapidly and mark the rows.
- Thin for "baby" carrots so that full-size carrots will have 1 to 2 inches of space to mature.
- Rich, organic soil, even raised beds may be necessary for good production. Excellent drainage is a must for quality carrots.
- Fiber row cover can be used to keep the soil moist until seed germinate. It can also provide several degrees of frost protection. Use old boards to hold down the edges and lay the material loosely over the row and allow it to float. After seed germinate, remove the cover during warm, sunny periods but keep it handy in case of an untimely frost.
- Carrots are heavy feeders. Use a hose-on fertilizer sprayer weekly or carefully side dress with granular or organic fertilizers weekly.

CELERY   Most gardeners don't bother to grow celery because it is generally available at the store and the quality is good. But it's easy to grow when planted in the fall, and you can harvest a few stalks as you need them. Celery relatives like lovage (WA), with strong, celery-flavored leaves and petioles; smallage (11, 17, 27), which is primarily grown for seeds; and Par-Cel (3), a hybrid with characteristics of parsley and celery, require similar

CELERY VARIETIES

Name (Source)	Color	Disease Resistance	Days to Reach Maturity	Comments
Florida strains (like 683) (WA)	Green		100	Bushy with more stalks than Utah strains.
Golden Self-blanching (WA)	Yellow-Green		90	Natural yellow-green color makes it appear to have been blanched. Stokes Golden Plume (31) is an improved variety.
Utah strains (WA)	Green	Some Fusarium Wilt	90–120	Utah 52–70 is one of the most common varieties offered. Stalks are tall and plants are vigorous. Ventura (31), Starlet (35), and 52–70 (31) are improved varieties.

BASIC PLANTING INFORMATION FOR CELERY

Space Between Rows (Inches)	Seed Spacing (Inches)	Thin to (Inches)	Seed Depth (Inches)	Days to Reach Maturity	Comments/Planting Dates/Intensive Gardening (I.G.) Spacing
24–36	Transplants	6–10	¼	80–105	This vegetable is often neglected in the home garden because it is available in good quality at the grocery market. It's really not hard to grow. Use lots of fertilizer, especially with nitrate nitrogen, and cover before a severe freeze. Six- to 8-inch PVC can be used to blanch the stalks. In spring: plant 4 weeks before or up until day of last freeze. In fall: plant 6 to 10 weeks before first frost. I.G. spacing: 10 × 10 inches to 12 × 12 inches.

cultivation. There's also a more diminutive Chinese Celery (4, 14, 32) available from catalogs specializing in Asian vegetables.

Turn several inches of organic matter into the soil and don't spare the fertilizer. Work 2 to 4 pounds of 15-5-10 or a similar analysis into the soil at planting, and side dress every 3 to 4 weeks with a tablespoon of 15-5-10 per foot of row or foliar feed weekly with a hose-on fertilizer sprayer. Use 18-inch sections of 8-inch PVC to blanch the stalks for a milder celery.

(See photo on page 189.)

Tips for Growing Celery

- Home gardeners should start with transplants.
- Fertilize heavily. Try using one of the hose-on fertilizer sprayers weekly through the mild growing periods of the cool season.
- Protect from freezing temperatures below 30° F.
- Use 12- to 18-inch sections of 8-inch PVC pipe or 1-gallon nursery pots with the bottoms removed to blanch your celery. But don't put the pipes around the plants until they have grown tall enough for the foliage to stick out.
- Celery is commercially grown on highly organic, muck soils so heap on the compost.
- Harvest a few stalks at a time to prolong the season.

CHARD

CHARD This leafy vegetable is simply a beet that doesn't form a large, attractive root. It grows best in cool weather, will stand a mild frost of 28° F or so if conditioned to cold, and yet it grows well into the summer. Most gardeners will find they can grow a lot more chard than they can eat. In recent years a number of new varieties of chard have surfaced. Red-leaf (actually the petiole is the really red part) varieties have been around for a while, but now we have multicolor blends to choose from and fancy European varieties with large, white petioles. This is an easy vegetable to grow. It's one that is pretty enough for the flower bed and sure to elicit lots of oohs and ahs from your friends.

Grow just as you would beets but allow for wider spacing.
(See photos on page 189.)

CHARD VARIETIES

Name (Source)	Color	Days to Reach Maturity	Comments
Lucullus (WA)	Yellow–Green	60	Standard green variety with white stems. Still very good and popular.
Paros (28)	Dark Green	65	One of the new French varieties with darker green leaves and striking white petiole and mid-rib. Distinctively mild and sweet.
Rhubarb (WA)	Red–Green	65	This was one of the first red varieties. Charlotte (3) is very similar. Vulcan (19) is one of the newest improvements on this color theme.
Swiss Chard of Geneva (19)	Medium Green	60	Another improved variety. Similar to Paros but the mid-ribs aren't quite as prominent.

Tips for Growing Swiss Chard

- Like beets, this vegetable will thrive in a neutral to alkaline soil pH. If you have a sandy, acid soil you may need 5 pounds of lime per 100 square feet. Work into the soil prior to planting. It is, however, always best to apply lime based on a soil test from the state agricultural extension service.
- Begin to harvest the outer leaves when they are about 12 inches tall. By just taking a few at a time, you can extend the harvest over a long season.
- This is a relatively pest-free vegetable, but slugs and snails may be a problem. Lure them into grapefruit-half rinds and destroy them.

BASIC PLANTING INFORMATION FOR CHARD

Space Between Rows (Inches)	Seed Spacing (Inches)	Thin to (Inches)	Seed Depth (Inches)	Days to Reach Maturity	Comments/Planting Dates/Intensive Gardening (I.G.) Spacing
18–30	2–3	6–8	½	50–60	Don't overplant chard. Leaves can be harvested a few at a time so the production can be high. Also consider the red-leaf varieties in the flower beds. In spring: plant 2 to 4 weeks before last freeze. In fall: plant 12 to 16 weeks before first frost. I.G. spacing: 6 × 6 inches to 8 × 8 inches.

CRUCIFERS (CABBAGE, CAULIFLOWER, BROCCOLI, BRUSSELS SPROUTS, KOHLRABI, COLLARDS, KALE, MUSTARD, TURNIPS, AND RADISHES)

The crucifer, or mustard family, is a large group of leafy vegetables prized for their leaves, modified buds, flower buds, roots, and enlarged stems. They are cool-weather crops that are grown primarily in the fall, winter, and early spring in the South.

These close relatives share similar cultural requirements, growing best in rich, fertile, sandy, acid soils that are high in nitrogen. Their close genetic ties also means they share the same insect and disease problems.

When growing members of the mustard family it's critical to remove old and dead plants, keep the garden clean, and rotate crops so that members of their closely related family will not follow each other in the garden beds.

The crucifer family has received considerable attention in the last few years due to their ability to lessen the risk of certain cancers. More specifically, numerous medical studies have indicated that eating broccoli, cabbage, brussels sprouts, and others may have a substantial health benefit.

CABBAGE

CABBAGE Cabbage is found in its wild state in various locations throughout the world, from Greece to Great Britain. It's probably been cultivated and used since 2000 to 2500 B.C.

Cabbage thrives in a cool, moist climate. It tolerates considerable cold with no damage and is said to develop better quality and sweetness after receiving a frost. Cabbage can easily handle temperatures as low as 15° to 18° F, and has been known to survive when temperatures drop into the single digits.

BASIC PLANTING INFORMATION FOR CABBAGE

Space Between Rows (Inches)	Seed Spacing (Inches)	Thin to (Inches)	Seed Depth (Inches)	Days to Reach Maturity	Comments/Planting Dates/Intensive Gardening (I.G.) Spacing
24–48	3–4 or set transplants	18–24	¼–½	60–120	Plant cabbage 4 to 8 weeks before fall freeze and 2 to 4 weeks before last spring freeze. I.G. spacing: 12 to 15 × 24 to 36 inches.

Plan to plant your cabbage plants in the fall or early spring. Cabbage is a large plant that requires lots of room. Spacing plants as much as 24 to 36 inches apart is common when growing larger varieties.

Cabbage plants grow best in rich, fertile soils with a pH of 5.5 to 6.5. But they're not overly particular about the soil texture. They perform well in sands, clay, or muck soils, as long as the drainage is adequate.

Care should be taken when cultivating around cabbage plants. They are extremely shallow rooted, and deep cultivation can stunt vigorous healthy plants. Your best quality cabbage will develop when plants are grown fast, and without checking (slow down of growth). This means you should plant vigorous, young plants and regularly give them small doses of fertilizers, mostly nitrogen, until the tender, sweet heads are ready for harvest.

When selecting a variety, you'll find the plant breeders have been busy. There are red, green, greenish blue, savoy (crinkled leaves), flat-head, and pointed-head types, as well as many other kinds. Regardless of the type, always select early maturing varieties. The South is blessed with mild winters, but the weather warms up rapidly in the spring, and hot fall weather greatly limits the prime cabbage-growing weather.

(See photo on page 196.)

Tips for Growing Cabbage

- Cabbage plants get large, so provide them with enough space.
- For peak quality, plants should be grown quickly without stress. Plant stress produces a strong flavor.
- Cabbage is a heavy nitrogen feeder. Provide your plants with small amounts of nitrogen, often.
- Avoid deep cultivation around the plants; they are very shallow rooted.
- Cabbage grows best in cool, mild weather.

CABBAGE VARIETIES

Name (Source)	Size in Pounds	Days to Reach Maturity	Comments
Bravo Hybrid (1, 9)	3–6	85	Resistant to fusarium yellows and black rot. Large globe-shaped, blue-green heads.
Early Jersey Wakefield (WA)	2½–3	65	An old, but good variety with solid pointed heads. Compact plants are excellent for small gardens.
Golden Acre (8, 37)	3	64	Tight, well-formed heads with excellent quality.
Gourmet Hybrid (1, 31)	3–5	68	A round to slightly flattened head with ruffled wrapper leaves.
Late Flat Dutch (1, 5, 8, 29, 37)	25–30	105	An extra large, flattened head with excellent quality. This is an old, but good variety.
Market Prize Hybrid (9)	3–4	76	Vigorous, uniform, high-quality heads with a deep blue-green color. Resistant to fusarium yellows and downy mildew.
Red Rookie Hybrid (19, 35)	3–6	75	Nice large plants with firm, deep purple-red, globe-shaped heads.
Red Acre (5, 8, 24, 29)	2–3	76	A compact plant that produces nice, small red heads.
Rio Verde Hybrid (1, 35)	3–6	85	Slightly flattened heads with a deep blue-green color.
Roundup Hybrid (31)	3–10	86	A late to mid-season variety with large, firm, round heads.
Ruby Ball Hybrid (3, 17, 22, 24, 33, 35)	3	65	Deep red heads on small, compact plants. Good heat and cold tolerance.
Savoy King Hybrid (1, 17, 33, 35)	4	90	Excellent, highly productive, savoy heads on vigorous plants.
Savoy Ace Hybrid (WA)	3–4	80	A high-quality, blue-green, savoy-type cabbage; very uniform, round heads with good fusarium yellow resistance.
Solid Blue #780 Hybrid (35)	3–4	78	Good blue-green color with large wrapper leaves; uniform and good flavor. Resistant to black root, black speck, fusarium yellow, and tip burn.
Solid Red #841 Hybrid (35)	3–4	84	Widely adapted, dark red, round heads on vigorous uniform plants.
Stonehead Hybrid (WA)	4–7	67	All-America winner. Large, tight heads on compact plants to help save space. Good flavor, and resistant to fusarium yellows and black rot.

Other cabbage varieties worth trying include: Emerald Cross, Blueboy, Savoy Princess, Jet Pack, Express, Market Topper, Red Head, Showboat, and Prime Time.

CAULIFLOWER

The caulifower is grown for its large white head or curd. The curd is nothing more than the short flower parts before they open. Its culture is very similar to cabbage's. They are large plants, like cabbage plants, that require plenty of room, abundant amounts of nitrogen, and cool temperatures.

Cauliflower is the most demanding member of the family. It is primarily grown in the fall when conditions are favorable for a longer period of time than in spring. The plants are very cold tolerant, but once their heads begin to develop, they must be protected from a hard freeze, which can damage the tender curd.

Healthy, vigorous transplants should be put out as soon as the cooler fall temperatures begin to show up, or about 6 to 8 weeks before the first fall freeze. It's important to get healthy plants. Stressed plants can result in buttoning (formation of a small, poorly developed curd). Like cabbage, cauliflower is a heavy feeder requiring frequent, but light applications of nitrogen.

The cauliflower curd responds to sunlight by developing a creamy, yellow-to-purple color. This off-color doesn't change the quality of the curd. For pure white heads, you should blanch the heads by pulling the outer leaves up over the head when the curd is about the size of a silver dollar, and tying the leaves in place with twine or a rubber band. Several varieties of cauliflower are self-blanching, or at least semiself-blanching. They have large leaves that curl in and cover the developing head, protecting it from the sun. (See photos on page 190.) Cauliflower should be harvested when the head is large and solid, but before the curd begins to separate.

Cauliflower is sensitive to boron deficiency, which causes a hollow, water-soaked stem, and browning of the curd. This also causes the head to become bitter. This problem can easily be corrected by applying a couple of ounces of borax dissolved in water per 100 square feet.

BASIC PLANTING INFORMATION
FOR CAULIFLOWER

Space Between Rows (Inches)	Seed Spacing (Inches)	Thin to (Inches)	Seed Depth (Inches)	Days to Reach Maturity	Comments/Planting Dates/Intensive Gardening (I.G.) Spacing
24–48	Transplant	24	1/4–1/2	50–75	Cauliflower is best planted in the fall 6 to 8 weeks before the first freeze. I.G. spacing: 24 × 24 inches.

Tips for Growing Cauliflower

- Plant in a well-drained, slightly acid soil.
- Allow plenty of room for plants to grow.
- Provide the plants with generous amounts of nitrogen.
- For sparkling white heads, pull the wrapped leaves up over the head and tie with twine or rubber bands.
- Each cauliflower plant produces one head, so plants should be removed after harvest.

CAULIFLOWER VARIETIES

Name (Source)	Days to Reach Maturity	Comments
Candid Charm Hybrid (1, 35)	75	Has very large 7- to 9 inch heads on large, vigorous plants. Leaves cover head well.
Early White Hybrid (2, 22)	52	A very early, large cauliflower with tight, pure white heads.
Majestic Hybrid (35)	66	Compact plants with large 7- to 8-inch, pure white heads; plants show good tolerance to downy mildew and black rot.
Milkyway Hybrid (19)	45	Extra early variety with 8-inch, pure white head. Worth trying in the spring.
Snow Crown Hybrid (WA)	68	All-America winner. Early, uniform, large white heads on vigorous plants.
Snow King Hybrid (5)	50	All-America winner. Large heads on vigorous, disease-resistant plants. Worth trying in the spring.
Snowball Y (1, 37)	68	Six- to 7-inch heads protected by heavy leaf growth on vigorous plants.
Snowball A (35)	60	An old, open-pollinated variety that is still good. Early, large, uniform heads.
Violet Queen Hybrid (3, 12, 17, 31)	55	The best of the purple cauliflowers. Tastes like white types, but brightens up any dip tray. Turns green when cooked.
White Rock Hybrid (31, 35)	68	A self-blanching cauliflower with both excellent taste and vigor.

Other cauliflower varieties worth trying are: Montano, Serrano, Cashmere, Glacier, and White Sails.

BROCCOLI
Broccoli may be the wonder vegetable for the nineties. It's high in vitamin A, ascorbic acid, thiamine, riboflavin, niacin, calcium, and iron. Broccoli is also one of the most productive crucifers. After harvesting the large central head, you can look forward to several weeks of cutting the smaller side shoots. Side shoot production, however, only occurs with some varieties.

Broccoli is easy to grow. It can handle the adversities of the Southern climate much better than cauliflower or cabbage. Like all the members of the crucifer family, broccoli performs best in well-drained, sandy to sandy loam, slightly acid, fertile soils that are also high in organic matter. It tolerates a wide range of soils as long as drainage is good.

For the best quality, the plants must be grown fast and without checking. Any slow down in growth will reduce yield and quality. Plant spacing plays a major role in head size. Wide spacing, like one plant per 24- × 36-inch area, will yield large heads. Closer spacing (such as 18- × 18-inch distancing) will increase the overall yield of the planting, but individual head size will not be as large.

Broccoli should be harvested when the heads are fully developed, but before they begin to separate. Watch the heads closely, especially in the

BASIC PLANTING INFORMATION FOR BROCCOLI

Space Between Rows (Inches)	Seed Spacing (Inches)	Thin to (Inches)	Seed Depth (Inches)	Days to Reach Maturity	Comments/Planting Dates/Intensive Gardening (I.G.) Spacing
24–36	4–6 or transplant	Transplant 18 inches apart	1/4–1/2	55–80	Broccoli should be planted 2 to 4 weeks before last spring freeze and 6 to 8 weeks before first fall freeze. I.G. spacing: 12 × 18 inches or 18 × 18 inches

Tips for Growing Broccoli

- Always start by planting healthy, vigorous transplants.
- Fertilize regularly with small amounts of a high-nitrogen fertilizer.
- For spring planting, always select fast-maturing varieties so that the heads can be harvested before hot weather sets in.
- Once you've harvested the large central head, watch for the development of side shoots.
- Harvest before the heads begin to separate.

spring, because they quickly change from just right to full bloom.

Broccoli, along with many other members of this family, are allelopathic (suppression of growth of one plant by another due to the release of certain toxins), which may cause the crops grown after them to grow poorly.

(See photos on page 191.)

BROCCOLI VARIETIES

Name (Source)	Days to Reach Maturity	Comments
Brigadier Hybrid (35)	69	A high-quality, large-headed variety for fall planting.
Emperor Hybrid (12, 19, 31)	64	A widely adapted broccoli, with large 7-inch head.
Galaxy Hybrid (37)	55	Compact plants with medium to large, well-formed heads. Early heads are formed well above the foliage.
Green Valiant Hybrid (8, 12, 35, 31)	83	An excellent late maturing variety for the upper South.
Green Goliath Hybrid (2, 31)	55	Good for home gardens because of extended harvest period. Produces lots of side shoots.
Greek Duke Hybrid (1, 37)	54	Early, 7- to 8-inch heads on compact plants. Good for spring gardens.
Green Comet Hybrid (WA)	55	All-America winner. Very early, large heads with excellent quality.
Packman Hybrid (WA)	57	An early, large, good-quality variety; well adapted to spring and fall production. Produces abundant side shoots.
Premium Crop (WA)	62	A widely adapted, good-flavored variety. It produces lots of side shoots after harvesting the main head.

Other broccoli varieties worth trying include: Mercedes, Italian Green Sprouting, Citation, Bonanza, Love Me Tender, Symphony, Baccus, Embassy, and Early Dawn.

*B*RUSSELS SPROUTS Growing brussels sprouts is a little more challenging than growing most of the members of this family. They are extremely cold tolerant, which is good because fall-planted plants rarely produce until spring.

BASIC PLANTING INFORMATION
FOR BRUSSELS SPROUTS

Space Between Rows (Inches)	Seed Spacing (Inches)	Thin to (Inches)	Seed Depth (Inches)	Days to Reach Maturity	Comments/Planting Dates/Intensive Gardening (I.G.) Spacing
24–36	Transplants	12–18	¼–½	85–110	Because of its long production season, brussels sprouts are only recommended for fall planting. Plant them 6 to 8 weeks before the first fall freeze. I.G. spacing: 12 × 12 inches or 18 × 18 inches.

For years, Jade Cross was the only variety of brussels sprouts available for Southern gardeners. It is a 100-day crop, requiring almost 4 months from planting to harvest. But in the past few years, we've seen some earlier-maturing varieties appear on the market.

Brussels sprouts can only be grown as a fall and winter vegetable. It requires months of cool weather for successful production, and the spring season just doesn't stay cool long enough. The growing instructions for brussels sprouts are the same as the ones for growing cauliflowers.

The buds at the base of each leaf enlarge to 1 to 2 inches in diameter, then the sprouts are harvested by twisting them off the main stalk. Many gardeners believe you must remove the lower leaves if the sprouts are to enlarge.

BRUSSELS SPROUTS VARIETIES

Name (Source)	Days to Reach Maturity	Comments
Jade Cross Hybrid (WA)	97	A vigorous hybrid with good-size sprouts. One of the best varieties for the Southern gardener.
Long Island Improved (1, 37)	108	An old variety, adapted to the upper South.
Oliver Hybrid (31, 33)	90	A very vigorous variety with large, smooth sprouts.
Prince Marvel Hybrid (9, 31)	97	Firm, smooth sprouts on tall, vigorous plants.
Royal Marvel Hybrid (24, 35)	85	A very early Jade-Cross type with tight, well-formed sprouts.
Rubine (3, 19, 22)	105	A novelty. These purple-red sprouts really liven up the garden!

Tips for Growing Brussels Sprouts

- Brussels sprouts require 4 months of mild, cool weather.
- Fall is the best time to plant brussels sprouts.
- Brussels sprouts are very cold tolerant, surviving temperatures that drop into the low teens.
- Rich, fertile soils are required for rapid, vigorous growth.
- Buds are harvested when they are 1 to 2 inches in diameter.

This is not really true, but the removal of the lower leaves will make harvesting much easier.

One thing that does help speed up the production of the sprouts is the removal of the tip of the plant. By removing the terminal bud, you stimulate the development of the side buds. If you'll remove the terminal bud on every other plant, you'll harvest early sprouts while leaving enough plants for a later harvest.

Brussels sprouts are very nutritious, being rich in vitamin A and ascorbic acid, as well as riboflavin, niacin, calcium, and iron.

(See photo on page 196.)

KALE, COLLARDS, AND KOHLRABI Collards are a traditional Southern green widely grown and enjoyed by the region's gardeners. The care and culture instructions for collards are the same as those for kale and kohlrabi.

Collards and kale are grown for their tender leaves while kohlrabi is grown for its leaves and tender, enlarged stem. All of these can be easily established either from seed or transplants. They are best suited to the spring,

BASIC PLANTING INFORMATION FOR COLLARDS, KALE, AND KOHLRABI

Space Between Rows (Inches)	Seed Spacing (Inches)	Thin to (Inches)	Seed Depth (Inches)	Days to Reach Maturity	Comments/Planting Dates/Intensive Gardening (I.G.) Spacing
18–36	3–4	8–12	$1/4$–$1/2$	50–75	Plant 4 to 6 weeks before fall freeze, or until 4 weeks after last spring freeze. I.G. spacing: 6 × 6 inches to 12 × 12 inches.

fall, and winter; and their quick growth allows for several plantings each season.

You should begin planting each fall as soon as you feel a little coldness in the air. Continue planting as often as every week or so, until the first freeze of winter. Kale, collards, and kohlrabi are very cold tolerant, surviving temperatures into the low teens. They even seem to develop a slight sweetness when exposed to a frost or light freeze.

When planting seed, it's important to prepare the soil well, raking out the clods. The seed are small, so care must be taken not to plant them too deep. Lightly scatter the seed over the bed, rake lightly, and water in. Newly planted seed should be kept moist until they begin to sprout.

Once the plants are up and growing, you should begin thinning. The plants you remove can be used in the kitchen, or if they are small, transplanted to another spot.

Because this group of plants is fast growing, maturing in less than 2 months, you will have very little time for fertilizing. A well-prepared soil, with good fertility, will solve this problem while producing high-quality, vigorous plants.

Kale and collard leaves are harvested when they are fully developed but still tender. Plants can be allowed to regrow, so you may harvest over and over again. Kohlrabi should be harvested when the swollen stem is 2 to 3 inches in diameter.

(See photos on pages 193 and 196.)

KOHLRABI VARIETIES

Name (Source)	Days to Reach Maturity	Comments
Early Purple Vienna (WA)	60	Similar to Early White Vienna with purple leaves and skin.
Early White Vienna (WA)	55	Enlarged, edible stem; is tender, high-quality, with a mild turnip flavor.
Grand Duke Hybrid (WA)	50	All-America winner. An early, mild Kohlrabi; good for eating raw or cooked. Good disease tolerance.
Purple Danube Hybrid (1, 19)	40	Deep purple, slightly flattened; very early variety.

Other varieties worthy of trying, include: Waldemar, Kolpak, and Express Forcer.

KALE VARIETIES

Name (Source)	Days to Reach Maturity	Comments
Red Russian (12, 17, 28, 29)	50	A tender, mild, very large variety with purple stems and veins and blue-green leaves.
Siberian Improved (WA)	60–65	Dwarf 12- to 15-inch-high plants with thick, blue-green, frilled leaves.
Vates (also called Dwarf Blue Curled, or Dwarf Blue Scotch) (WA)	55	A well-known variety with attractive, curled, blue-green leaves.

Other notable varieties include: Blue Knight Hybrid, Blue Armor Hybrid, and Verdura.

Tips for Growing Collards, Kale, and Kohlrabi

- When direct seeding, barely cover these small seed to ensure good germination.
- Nitrogen is the main nutrient needed for fast, tender growth.
- Plants grow best during cool, moist weather. Hot weather will produce strong-flavored leaves and stems.
- Their flavor is sweetest after a light frost.

COLLARD VARIETIES

Name (Source)	Days to Reach Maturity	Comments
Blue Max Hybrid (35)	68	An excellent hybrid variety with attractive blue-green, slightly savoyed leaves.
Champion Hybrid (WA)	78	A Vates type that resists bolting better; vigorous plants.
Georgia (2, 19, 29, 30, 35, 37)	75	An old favorite that does well throughout the South.
Vates (WA)	75	Compact plants with thick, broad leaves. An old favorite.

Other varieties worth trying include: Top Bunch Hybrid, Hicrop Hybrid, and Morris Heading.

Tips for Growing Mustard and Turnips

- Fast, unchecked growth produces tender greens and sweet turnip roots.
- The small seed should be planted shallow to ensure good germination.
- Prepare a well-drained, fertile soil for top quality.
- When thinning your plants to the final spacing, remember that the young plants are great when eaten fresh or cooked.

MUSTARD AND TURNIPS
Mustard and turnips are fast-growing members of the cabbage family grown for their delicate, leafy greens, and, in the case of turnips, for their roots as well. Because of their short growing season, the soil must be well prepared and fertile at planting time.

These two vegetables have small seed that should be lightly raked in and watered well. These cool-season greens are best suited for fall and spring planting, when they can grow fast, so the greens will be tender and the turnip roots sweet and crisp.

Once the plants are about 6 inches tall, they should be thinned to 3 to 4 inches apart. This will allow the remaining plants to grow unchecked, and the thinned plants can be used in the kitchen. When the plants are thinned, they should be lightly side dressed with a nitrogen fertilizer.

The turnip and mustard greens can be harvested a leaf at a time to spread out the harvest. The turnip roots should be harvested when they are young and tender, about 2 to 3 inches in diameter.

(See photos on pages 195 and 198.)

BASIC PLANTING INFORMATION
FOR MUSTARD AND TURNIPS

Space Between Rows (Inches)	Seed Spacing (Inches)	Thin to (Inches)	Seed Depth (Inches)	Days to Reach Maturity	Comments/Planting Dates/Intensive Gardening (I.G.) Spacing
18–24	1	3–4	$1/4$–$1/2$	30–55	Begin planting every week or so, starting 8 to 12 weeks before the first freeze, and 6 weeks before the last spring freeze. I.G. spacing: 3 × 3 inches to 3 × 6 inches.

MUSTARD VARIETIES

Name (Source)	Days to Reach Maturity	Comments
Florida Broad Leaf (WA)	50	An old standard, large, broad-leaf, with distinct white mid-ribs. Vigorous.
Savanna Hybrid (19, 35)	35	Very early, productive plants with smooth, thick, tangy-flavored leaves.
Southern Giant Curled (WA)	45	Popular curled or frilled-leaf variety. Popular for blanching.
Tendergreen Hybrid (WA)	40	Large, fast-growing plants with smooth, dark green leaves. Mustard-spinach flavor.

Other varieties worth growing include: Red Giant Mustard, Muzana, and Purple Osaka.

TURNIP VARIETIES

Name (Source)	Days to Reach Maturity	Comments
All Top Hybrid (1, 35)	50	Grown for its greens only; it does not produce an enlarged root. Very uniform, smooth, green leaves.
Just Right Hybrid (24, 35)	28 greens 60 roots	All America winner A good dual-purpose turnip with glossy foliage and large snow white root.
Market Express (28)	30–40	Very early Japanese variety, grown for its outstanding quality; harvested when roots are about 1 inch in diameter.
Purple Top White Globe (WA)	57	An old standard that remains popular with many gardeners. A large turnip root with a bright purple top.
Royal Globe II Hybrid (24)	45–50	An excellent hybrid; Purple Top Globe-type with good uniformity and vigor.
Royal Crown Hybrid (1, 22, 35)	52	A hybrid, Purple Top Globe-type with excellent uniformity. Very good quality roots and tops.
Seven Top (29, 30, 31, 35, 37)	40–50	A high-quality variety grown just for greens. Harvest while young and tender.
Shogoin (24, 37)	42	Grown primarily for its tender, mild-flavored greens. White, globe-shaped root should be used when young.
Tokyo Cross Hybrid (WA)	35	All-America winner. Very uniform, pure white roots with high-quality foliage. Very early, but plants hold quality well.
White Lady Hybrid (24, 31, 35)	35–45	Very high-quality turnips with excellent quality tops and pure white, sweet roots. Roots are best when harvested young and tender.

Novelty turnips worth trying: Scarlet Ball and Golden Ball.

RADISHES Radishes can be a lot of fun to grow, and they are great vegetables for young children to grow. Their ease of culture and quick growth make them a perfect choice for the youngest gardeners in the family.

A good, rich soil will produce 1- to 1½-inch roots in less than a month. The key to high-quality radishes is spacing and stress-free growing conditions. Thin your radish plants just days after they emerge to a spacing of 1 to 1½ inches. For large-rooted varieties, more space will be needed.

The pungent flavor often encountered with radishes is due to plant stress, which can occur in the form of heat, drought, excess moisture, insects, or disease—anything that can slow down growth.

By planting during the mild weather of spring and fall, preparing your soil well, and providing an abundance of nitrogen and plenty of space for bulb development, you can produce multiple crops of delicious radishes. Be sure to harvest the roots when they are still young and tender.

(See photo on page 198.)

RADISH VARIETIES

Name (Source)	Days to Reach Maturity	Comments
Champion (WA)	28	A round, scarlet red, very fine-textured root. Very uniform, and good quality.
Cherry Belle (WA)	26	A well-known, old variety that is still reliable and good. All-America Selection.
Early Scarlet Globe (5, 31, 37)	23	A very crisp, globe-shaped, red radish with mild white flesh.
Easter Egg II (WA)	25	A mix of lavender, red, pink, and white round roots. Lots of fun for kids to grow!
Flamboyant (28)	28	A 3-inch-long, cylindrical, red radish with a white tip; a gourmet French radish.
Fluo Hybrid (3, 22)	24	The first hybrid French breakfast radish. Elongated red root with a white tip.
French Breakfast (WA)	23	An oblong, scarlet root with white tips. Good flavor, mildly pungent.
Fuego (31)	22	A bright red, round root with very short tops. Disease resistant and heat tolerant.
Snow Belle (5, 9, 19, 31, 35)	28	A white, round, fine-textured, high-quality radish.
Sparkler (1, 5, 17, 24, 31, 37)	25	Half scarlet, half white round root with crisp white flesh.
White Icicle (WA)	27	A good, old, icicle-shaped variety.

BASIC PLANTING INFORMATION FOR RADISHES

Space Between Rows (Inches)	Seed Spacing (Inches)	Thin to (Inches)	Seed Depth (Inches)	Days to Reach Maturity	Comments/Planting Dates/Intensive Gardening (I.G.) Spacing
18–24	½ inch	1–2	¼–½	25–30	Start planting 3 months before first fall freeze. Start spring planting about 6 weeks before last spring freeze. I.G. spacing: 2 × 2 inches to 2 × 4 inches.

Tips for Growing Radishes

- Plant seed shallow, and thin as soon as the plants come up.
- Prepare your soil well because there's no time to fertilize before harvest.
- Plant in the spring and fall when the weather is mild and the plants can grow rapidly.
- Harvest when the roots are small and tender for best quality.
- Do several plantings. 7 to 10 days apart to extend harvest time.

GARLIC   Is it an herb or a vegetable? Herb growers probably consider it one of theirs, but it is so important in our kitchens and there are now so many varieties, it deserves full treatment.

Garlic is planted in the fall. The softneck varieties (artichoke and silverskin categories) are typically best for Southern gardens. The hardneck vari-

BASIC PLANTING INFORMATION FOR GARLIC

Space Between Rows (Inches)	Seed Spacing (Inches)	Thin to (Inches)	Seed Depth (Inches)	Days to Reach Maturity	Comments/Planting Dates/Intensive Gardening (I.G.) Spacing
12–24	Cloves 2 inches apart	4–6	Cover tip ½ inch	120–160	Garlic is often touted as a companion crop to repel insect pests. Unfortunately it has a few of its own—notably thrips—and it is a cool-season crop, so it won't be around to benefit tomatoes, etc. In fall: start planting 12 weeks before first frost. I.G. spacing: 4 × 4 inches to 6 × 6 inches.

GARLIC VARIETIES

Name (Source)	Color	Days to Reach Maturity	Comments
California Early (Late) (6, 24)	White	150–200	Silverskin or softneck varieties are the most commonly planted. Rarely produces seed stalk.
Creole (6)	Pink	150–200	Elongated, pink bulbs have a slightly sweet flavor.
Elephant Garlic (WA)	White	150–200	Not really a garlic; it's a leek with garliclike buds. This is a very popular vegetable and impressive, too—the buds can be the size of softballs. The flavor is good and it's garlicky but not quite the same as good garlic.
Mexican Red or Spanish Rojo (6)	Pink-Red	150–200	Another of the Creole group. Considered pungent, but much preferred by many cooks.

eties (rocambole, porcelains) will do well in some areas of the upper South.

Garlic cloves are sometimes presprouted prior to planting to ensure a uniform stand in the garden, but they are normally planted ½ inch deep and spaced about 2 inches apart at planting.

Like all members of the onion family, they are heavy feeders that like lots of organic matter. The stems don't need to be broken over in the spring (neither do onions) to promote bulb formation.

(See photo on page 192.)

Tips for Growing Garlic

- Presprout cloves to ensure a uniform planting.
- Fertilize heavily. Use soluble fertilizers regularly, or at least be sure to use a fertilizer for side dressing with nitrate nitrogen (i.e., ammonium nitrate or potassium nitrate).
- You may have to spray for thrips in the spring. These rasping insects will make the leaves look silvery, eventually brown, from the damage they do when feeding.
- For long-term storage, especially in the humid South, try freezing individual garlic cloves after harvest. Use freezer jars because the garlic flavor will likely flavor the entire contents of the freezer even when enclosed in the best plastic bags.

---

*L*ETTUCES   This vegetable is the highlight of the cool-season garden in the South. In fact, lettuce has been popular for a long time—it was used by the Romans and Egyptians. It's a plant that needs rapid growth to be sweet and free from bitterness. That's one reason it doesn't grow well in the heat of summer. It's also sensitive to long days and usually bolts (goes to seed) beginning in late spring. (See photo on page 194.) If the lettuce is bitter when harvested, try a few days of refrigeration to allow for breakdown of the bitter, milky sap.

Leaf lettuces, bibb or butterhead types, and romaine or cos varieties are the best for most Southern gardens. Crisphead (head or iceberg) lettuce often suffers freeze damage just as it is maturing. Not only is it difficult to grow (a long, mild winter helps) but, when you do succeed, it matures all at once. The other types can be harvested a few leaves at a time throughout the winter, and that's a big advantage.

Lettuce seed (like most small seed) need light to germinate. Beginning gardeners often are disappointed in their first planting because few, if any, seedlings emerge. Lettuce seed should be lightly raked into the soil's surface and kept constantly moist until it germinates; planting lettuce seed too deep is a common mistake. Also, lettuce seed doesn't store well, so it is best to buy new seed every year. Fortunately, lettuce transplants easily, so you can also buy plants at the nursery or start your own in flats.

Lettuce is usually pretty hardy (can stand temperatures as low as 28° F or so), but a lot depends on conditioning. Going from 70° F during the day to 28° F that night spells disaster. However, lettuce seed doesn't like hot soil. It

BASIC PLANTING INFORMATION FOR LETTUCE

Space Between Rows (Inches)	Seed Spacing (Inches)	Thin to (Inches)	Seed Depth (Inches)	Days to Reach Maturity	Comments/Planting Dates/Intensive Gardening (I.G.) Spacing
12–24	½–1	8–12	Lightly cover	40–90	The days it takes to reach maturity can vary considerably depending on whether you start from seed or transplants. The heading varieties take longer. If planting from seed, be sure to thin and thin early. Crowded plants, even the leaf lettuce types, may look good in the row, but when harvested they will be spindly. In spring: plant 6 weeks before to 2 weeks after last freeze. In fall: plant 12 to 14 weeks before first frost from seed, 8 to 12 weeks before first frost from transplants. I.G. spacing: 6 × 6 inches to 8 × 8 inches.

HEADING LETTUCE VARIETIES

Name (Source)	Color	Disease Resistance	Days to Reach Maturity	Comments
Great Lakes varieties (WA)	Light Green	TB	90	Good commercial varieties like Great Lakes 659 are best for the home-owner. Adapted to heavy soils.
659 MT (1, 37)	Light Green		85	New variety for trial in the South.
Ithaca (WA)	Light Green	TB, BR	85	Medium-size heads develop best in highly organic, muck-type soils.
Mission (19)	Light Green		75	Good variety that's well adapted to gardens, even in the lower South. Though still a fall-planted crop.
Summertime (2, 9, 17)	Light Green	TB, BR	75	Resistant (not immune) to bolting to seed. Low growing and compact.

SEMIHEADING LETTUCE VARIETIES

Name (Source)	Color	Disease Resistance	Days to Reach Maturity	Comments
Akcel (3)	Light Green		60–75	French greenhouse butterhead, which should also do well outside during mild winters. Excellent quality.
Anuenue (12, 30)	Light Green	Heat	50–60	Semi-iceberg type with a small, crisp heart. Developed by the University of Hawaii for good heat resistance.
Bibb(s) (WA)	Light Green	Some to viruses	60	Leaves in the loosely folded heads are delicious, if somewhat limp.
Buttercrunch (WA)	Dark Green	Heat	65	This All-America Selection is what most bibb varieties would like to be—semiheading with crisp, deli-cious leaves. This is the one lettuce to grow if you grow no others.
Floricos (Ferry Morse seed racks)	Yellow-Green	Heat, LMV, TB	70	Good commercial variety, slightly smaller than Valmaine. Growth habit is upright and slightly spreading.
Ostinata (31)	Light Green	TB	80	Good greenhouse bibb-type variety. Resistant to bolting, so also good in the garden for late winter/spring use.
Paris Island Cos (WA)	Medium Green		75	Standard Cos (romaine) variety. Heads are silver green and medium tall.
Valmaine (1, 18, 27)	Medium Green		75	This is a commercial variety of ro-maine in many areas of the South. Heads are more open than those of Paris Island Cos. Guzmaine (13, 31), from Florida, is similar.

Key to Disease and Pest Abbreviations
BR = mid-rib browning   LMV = lettuce mosaic burn   TB = tip burn

will go dormant if planted in soil that is warmer than 80° to 92° or so. This is one reason early fall plantings often fail.

(See photos on pages 194 and 195.)

LEAF LETTUCE VARIETIES

Name (Source)	Color	Disease Resistance	Days to Reach Maturity	Comments
Black–seeded Simpson (WA)	Light Green		50	An old standard leaf lettuce variety with less quality compared with newer varieties. Improved forms like Simpson Elite (Parks) have less tendency to become bitter. Bitterness can be a factor when any variety is grown under stress (i.e., when dry or too hot).
Deer Tongue (Matchless) (3)	Light Green		50	This variety produces narrow, triangular leaves with thick midribs. It is often used in mesclun mixes (see cool-season gourmet selections).
Grand Rapids (WA)	Light Green	TB	60	Another old leaf lettuce variety with heavily curled and frilly leaves.
Green Ice (19)	Medium Green		45	The leaves of this vigorous variety are deeply savoyed and the plant is resistant to spring bolting.
Lollo Rosso (WA)	Green, Pink		45	Italian variety with striking pink-tinged leaves. An improved, more vigorous form is Selma Lollo (19).
Oak Leaf (Red, Royal) (WA)	Light Green or Red Tinged		50	Leaves are elongated, oak-shaped, and have thick midribs. Resistant to becoming bitter in late spring.
Prizehead (8, Northrup King seed racks)	Green, Brown with Red Edges		50	Not really a heading variety in the iceberg sense, but it does form a loose head of frilly multicolored leaves.
Red Sails (WA)	Green, Red		45	This high-vitamin variety is often more bronze than red, but the color intensifies during cooler weather. Vigorous, easy-to-grow variety.
Ruby (22, 31)	Red		45	Ruby is a good description for this one. It is one of the most highly colored leaf lettuces. Red Fire is similar but the color is more of a bright red than a dark red.
Salad Bowl (3, 19)	Light Green		50	This All-America Selection is still a good, slow-bolting leaf lettuce variety.
Vulcan (12, 18, 31)	Red		45	This variety is one of the more striking red-leaf lettuces. It is slow bolting and produces heavy heads.

Tips for Growing Lettuce

- Don't cover lettuce seed. It needs light to germinate. Just scratch it into the soil with a rake and water it in. Better yet, cover with fiber row cover and sprinkle with water daily until germination is complete. This is particularly helpful in the heat of late summer or early fall.

- Lettuce also transplants easily. Start plants in a greenhouse or coldframe and move them out when the weather improves.

- This is another crop that demands heavy fertilization. Since it also grows in cool weather, fertilizers with the nitrate (NO3) form of nitrogen will be most readily available. Most commercial soluble fertilizers (RaPidGro, Miracle Grow, etc.) contain some nitrates, or if you can find it, use salt peter (KNO3)—it's a great source of nitrogen and potassium (potash). Organic gardeners should get good results with fish or seaweed fertilizers—though you may want to hold the anchovies on your favorite Caesar salad if you fertilize too close to harvest.

- If your lettuce is slightly bitter, try storing it in the refrigerator for a few days. This lessens the bitter flavor often associated with fresh (especially leaf) lettuce.

- The major pest of lettuce is the cabbage looper, and biological sprays containing *Bacillus thuringiensis* (Bt) or its toxic derivative are a nontoxic (to all but caterpillars with an alkaline gut) blessing. Be sure to spray in the evening because the product is sensitive to UV light and will break down during the day. Caterpillars eat this product, get sick, stop feeding almost immediately, and then die within a week or less.

GARDEN (ENGLISH) AND EDIBLE PODDED PEAS

This is a very challenging vegetable to grow in most areas of the South. The edible podded or Snow pea probably offers the most potential. During the limited production time, you can eat virtually everything you harvest—not just the shelled-out seeds. Fresh peas are so superior to the canned product it's a wonder any kid served the canned variety ever gives the fresh vegetable a try. Memories of shelling fresh peas in Grandma's garden and eating them as fast as they could be picked is what keeps many gardeners trying to succeed with this vegetable.

BASIC PLANTING INFORMATION FOR GARDEN (ENGLISH) PEAS AND EDIBLE PODDED PEAS

Space Between Rows (Inches)	Seed Spacing (Inches)	Thin to (Inches)	Seed Depth (Inches)	Days to Reach Maturity	Comments/Planting Dates/Intensive Gardening (I.G.) Spacing
24–36	1–2	2–3	1	50–70	The key to producing this crop is early planting. In the fall this means planting in the heat of August. Seedlings can tolerate the high temperatures, hopefully coming into production well before a hard freeze. The spring crop may be planted in January when young seedlings will be at risk from a late freeze but hopefully will come into production before it gets too hot. In spring: plant 4 weeks before to 1 week after last freeze. In fall: plant 12 to 14 weeks before first frost. I.G. spacing: 2 × 2 inches.

This is one of our oldest cultivated vegetables. It was enjoyed by the Romans, Greeks, and Egyptians. Peas can be grown most successfully in the fall by planting earlier than you would think advisable. The seedlings might not appreciate August weather, but they can tolerate it, and they will come into production as temperatures cool off in the fall. The hardest part may be getting the seed to germinate. Cover the seed with compost or a loose potting soil and keep the bed covered with fiber row cover sprinkled daily to cool the soil and promote a better stand.

Spring planting is equally tricky. You need to plant in January or February, taking a chance that the tender seedlings might get frozen out, but hoping that they will survive to produce before the heat of summer and powdery mildew end the harvest.

Tips for Growing Garden (English) and Edible Podded Peas

- Treat seed with a garden inoculant before planting.
- Plant early, even if growing conditions aren't ideal. You've got to beat the heat. This usually means August for a fall crop, January for a spring crop.
- Most of the productive varieties like Sugar Snap are strong vining types, so plan to construct a trellis.

The most productive varieties are the climbing types, especially if we have a mild winter. In areas where these windows of planting opportunity are short, they may be the only ones worth trying, however.

(See photo on page 188.)

GARDEN (ENGLISH) PEA AND EDIBLE PODDED PEA VARIETIES

Name (Source)	English (EP) or Edible Podded (EdP)	Disease Resistance	Days to Reach Maturity	Comments
Alaska (WA)	EP	FW	50–60	This English pea variety is worth trying just because it is so early. In fact, when trying new varieties, look for the earliest ones.
Daybreak (12, 19)	EP		56	This very early, vigorous variety should be just the ticket for Southern gardeners.
Giroy (19)	EP (Petit Pois)	FW, TY	65	This type of baby French pea may be the ultimate challenge, but, no doubt, your dinner guests will rave about the results.
Green Arrow (WA)	EP	DM, FW, LCV	65–70	High-quality variety with excellent disease resistance.
Laxton's Progress (5, 8)	EP	FW	60	This is an old variety and there are several improved forms. It is comparatively early and forms large pods.
Maestro (2, 12)	EP	PM, PEM, BYM, CW	60	Sometimes referred to as an improved Alaska, this is another early one with good disease resistance.
Oregon Sugar Pod 2 (5, 9, 35)	EdP	PM, FW, PEMV	65	One of the old standard Snow peas. It is still a good one and a strong grower. You'll need a 5- to 6-foot high trellis for this one. Harvest while the pods are still flat.
Snappy, Super (2)	EdP	PM	65	Not quite as sweet as Sugar Snap but still very good quality. It is also a strong, vigorous vining type. Harvest when peas are full size but still tender.
Spring (31)	EP	ASG	57	This strong growing variety tops out at 18 to 22 inches. Pods are medium size and the peas are excellent for freezing.

Key to Disease and Pest Abbreviations
ASG = alternaria stem canker   BYMV = bean yellows mosaic virus   CW = common wilt
DM = downy mildew   FW = fusarium wilt   LCV = leaf curl virus   PM = powdery mildew
PEM = pea enation mosaic   TY = top yellows

PEA VARIETIES (CONT.)

Name (Source)	English (EP) or Edible Podded (EdP)	Disease Resistance	Days to Reach Maturity	Comments
Sugar Snap (WA)	EdP	PW	72	This is the variety that got Southern gardeners thinking about peas again. It is a strong vining variety and very productive. The pods should be harvested when the peas are full size. At this stage they are tender, but the pods have to be strung—break and pull down both ends to remove the fibers. A number of new varieties have spun off from the original All-America Selection Sugar Snap including Early Snap, Sugar Pop, Sugar Bon, Super SugarMel, and Sugar Daddy. Sugar Snap is still a hard one to top.
Wando (2, 9)	EP	Heat Resistant	65–70	Developed for resistance to heat, this is the one to try for spring production.

SPINACH   Spinach isn't the easiest vegetable to grow, but it is one of the real treats of the home garden because it is rarely available fresh and of good quality at the produce market. Southern gardeners will mostly be limited to the fall and winter season for this one; it rapidly bolts to seed in the spring and summer, primarily due to longer days. Although this vegetable will tolerate freezing conditions, it needs to be acclimated to them gradually. Temperatures that drop from 70° F one day to the teens that night will be disastrous.

Spinach really is nutritious. It is especially rich in vitamin A and iron. Though many a youngster has shuddered at the thought of having to eat

BASIC PLANTING INFORMATION FOR SPINACH

Space Between Rows (Inches)	Seed Spacing (Inches)	Thin to (Inches)	Seed Depth (Inches)	Days to Reach Maturity	Comments/Planting Dates/Intensive Gardening (I.G.) Spacing
14–18	1	3–5	1/2–3/4	45–60	One of the few vegetables that prefers a neutral to alkaline soil pH (7.0 to 7.5). In spring: plant any time from 8 weeks before or up to day of last freeze. In fall: plant 2 to 16 weeks before first frost. I.G. spacing: 5 × 5 inches.

SPINACH VARIETIES

Name (Source)	Color	Disease Resistance	Days to Reach Maturity	Comments
Bloomsdales (WA)	Green		45	An old standard variety of which there are many variations. Lacks the hybrid vigor that often spells success for the home gardener.
Coho (1, 24)	Green	BM, WR	40	Hybrid variety with good disease resistance.
Fall Green (Improved Green Valley, AR 82-5) (1, 24)	Green	WR	40	Excellent resistance to the fungus white rust.
Hybrid 7 (WA)	Green		45	One of the early hybrids and still popular.
Italian Summer (28)	Green		40	A warm-weather-tolerant hybrid, it still isn't adapted to summer conditions in the lower South. Plants are upright and only slightly savoyed (crinkled).
Melody (WA)	Green	DM	45	This All-America Selection hybrid is a great one for the home gardener. Leaves are thick, rounded, and semi-savoyed with excellent quality.
Nordic (19, 28)	Green	DM	40	Leaves of this variety are large and smooth, making it easy to clean. If you garden in sandy soil, this is the variety for you. It also is tasty, productive, and slow to bolt.
Olympia (31)	Green	DM	45	This is another of the flat-leaved, slow-to-bolt varieties.
Ozarka II (1, 24)	Green	WR	45	Popular home variety with white rust resistance. If you grow spinach year after year, you will eventually need this resistance.
Skookum (1, 35)	Dark Green	DM	45	One of the many new disease-resistant hybrids. Leaves are semi-savoyed and the plants are resistant to bolting.
Tyee (WA)	Dark Green	DM, BM tolerant	55	Fall variety with large, heavily savoyed leaves.
Vienna (19, 31)	Green	DM, SB	40	Hybrid variety with heavily savoyed, erect leaves. Resistant to bolting.

Key to Disease and Pest Abbreviations
BM = blue mold   DM = downy mildew   SB = spinach blight   WR = white rust

cooked spinach from a can, the fresh product is much better when cooked, and fresh spinach in a salad is a wonderful change of pace.

This is one of the few vegetables (beets and chard included) that likes a neutral to alkaline soil pH. Thus, liming will be necessary if you have an acid soil or if you're growing in raised beds with a prepared soil. Even in areas with heavy clay "gumbo" soils that tend to be slightly alkaline, liming may be necessary if you've added lots of organic matter.

Spinach needs to be started in the early fall when it's still hot. So plan to use fiber row cover for shade and wind protection. It can also be started in late winter, but spring production will be cut short by flower stalk development as the days get longer and the temperatures hotter.

(See photo on page 199.)

Tips for Growing Spinach

- This is one of the few vegetables that prefers a neutral to alkaline soil (pH 7.0 to 7.5). Most vegetables like a slightly acid soil (pH 6.5), so you may want to mix 5 pounds of agricultural lime (or 3 pounds of hydrated lime) per 100 square feet of spinach bed area before planting. Have a soil test done first, unless you are confident that you know the soil pH in your garden.
- Fall spinach is by far the easiest to grow, especially in the lower South. During a mild winter you may be able to plant almost anytime—even during December and January—and seed is cheap, so don't hesitate to experiment.
- Fiber row cover floated over the row helps a lot when trying to get small seedlings started in September and October.
- Spinach also works quite well when transplanted. In fact, that's probably the best way to go for a spring planting in a small garden. Start plants in a greenhouse or cold frame during the worst of the winter and get a jump on early production.

ONIONS   Home gardeners in the South are beginning to realize that they can grow the best bulb onions in the country if they plant short-day varieties. In the past, nurseries offered plants of varieties like Sweet Spanish (okay in the upper South) or onion sets. For most of the South, these onions will produce scallions at best because they are intermediate or long-day varieties. So what? Well, along the Gulf Coast, for instance, the longest day of

BASIC PLANTING INFORMATION FOR ONIONS

Space Between Rows (Inches)	Seed Spacing (Inches)	Thin to (Inches)	Seed Depth (Inches)	Days to Reach Maturity	Comments/Planting Dates/Intensive Gardening (I.G.) Spacing
12–24	½	4–6	¼–½	95–160	Onions are really easy from seed. For most of the lower South you will want short-day varieties seeded in October/November and transplanted in January. Don't set out transplants in the fall—chances are they will bolt to seed rather than form nice bulbs. In spring: plant 4 to 6 weeks before last freeze (transplants or seeded bunching varieties). In fall: plant 4 to 6 weeks before first frost (seed or short-day bulb onions). I.G. spacing: 4 × 4 inches to 6 × 6 inches.

Tips for Growing Onions

- Plant short-day varieties like Texas Supersweet (1015), Grano, or Granex.
- Use plenty of nitrogen fertilizer through the growing season but avoid formulations containing sulfur, especially ammonium sulfate (21-0-0). High-sulfur content in the soil can make the onions hotter.
- Don't set out transplants in the fall—that's the time for seeding. Remember pencil-size or larger seedlings in January at thinning/transplanting might as well be harvested. Don't cut the tops off of the seedlings. The big growers just do that to make them fit in the crates.
- Expect thrip damage in the spring as temperatures warm up and the onions really start to grow. This rasping insect loves onions, garlic, etc. Whether you use an organic spray or a labeled chemical pesticide, controlling thrips can make a big difference in the quality of your onion crop.
- Pink root is the major disease problem. It usually comes in on commercial transplants, so this is just one more reason to grow your own from seed. The disease usually doesn't kill the plant, but the roots will be stunted.

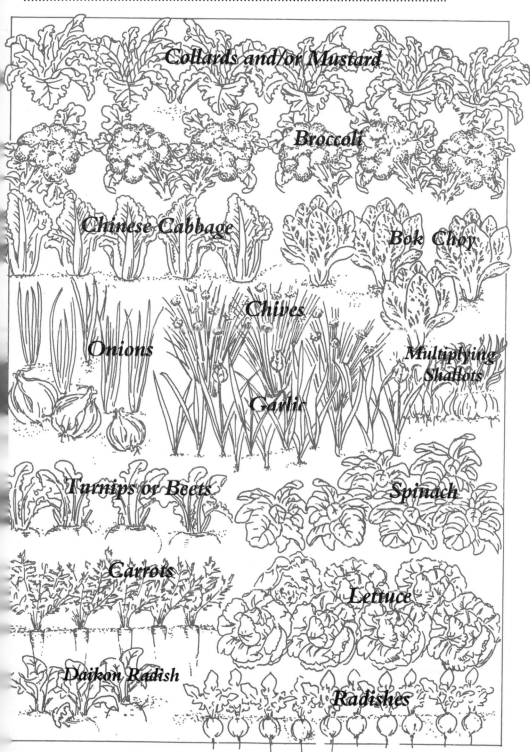

Collards and/or Mustard

Broccoli

Chinese Cabbage

Bok Choy

Chives

Onions

Multiplying Shallots

Garlic

Turnips or Beets

Spinach

Carrots

Lettuce

Daikon Radish

Radishes

Cool-Season Garden Plan.

Oregon Sugar Pod garden peas.

Scarlet Nantes carrots.

Detroit dark red beets.

Paros Swiss chard.

Rhubarb Swiss chard.

Celery.

Above: Cauliflower, tied so it will blanch.
Right: Alverda cauliflower.

Above: Violet Queen broccoli.
Left: Snow Crown cauliflower, blanched (front) and unblanched (rear).

Green Comet broccoli.

Packman broccoli.

Supersweet Texas 1015 onions.

Mexican garlic.

Kohlrabi.

Mission (head) lettuce.

Lettuce bolting (to seed).

Bibb (semi-heading) lettuce.

Royal Oak Leaf lettuce.

Purple Osaka mustard greens.

Tendergreen mustard.

Red Sails (leaf) lettuce.

Jersey Wakefield cabbage.

Jade Cross brussels sprouts.

Blue Max collards.

Kale.

Michili Chinese cabbage.

Radicchio.

Wong Bok Chinese cabbage.

Bok Choy.

Cherrie Belle radishes.

Arugula.

Tokyo Market Express turnips.

Misato rose flesh radish.

Daikon.

Tyee spinach.

Mesclun.

Dandelions.

Chives.

Italian basil.

Cilantro.

Mint.

Dill.

Parsley.

Winter savory.

Rosemary.

French thyme.

the year is around 14½ hours; these varieties require a day length of 15 hours or more to initiate bulbing. Theoretically you could string light bulbs over the onion row, set them on a timer to come on from 10:00 p.m. to 2:00 a.m. each night in March, and get a long-day effect, but short-day onions are better anyway. Their big failing is that they don't store well.

Most gardeners like to start with transplants. However, in the lower South bulbing onions are best planted from seed in the fall—October or November. The seedlings can be transplanted or thinned for green onions in January, and big, sweet onions can be harvested in April or May. Any seedlings that are larger than a pencil at transplanting time are usually best harvested for green onions because these jumbos often bolt to seed before producing a large bulb.

Onions should be fertilized close to the plant because they have a limited root system. Don't leave fertilizer right next to the stem, and thoroughly water each time. Sulfur tends to increase the pungency of onions, so avoid using sulfur-containing fertilizers like ammonium sulfate. Instead, use ammonium or potassium nitrate and side dress every 3 to 4 weeks if you want big onions.

(See photo on page 192.)

ONION VARIETIES

Name (Source)	Color	Disease Resistance	Days to Reach Maturity	Comments
Burgundy (1, 8, 24, 30, 37)	Red	PR	95–165	The variety's dark red, flattened bulbs are 4 to 5 inches in diameter. Mild, sweet short-day variety with poor storage potential typical of short-day varieties.
Creole C 5 (8)	Red		110–140	Bulbs of this variety are large and semi-globe shaped. Developed in Louisiana for hot, humid conditions.
Evergreen White Bunching (WA)	White	PR, T	60–120	This variety produces 4 to 9 scallions per plant. There are a number of other bunching onions including Red Welsh and yellow/brown varieties.
Excel 986 (13)	Yellow	PR	120–160	Flattened, Bermuda-type short-day onion. Sweet with average keeping potential.
Granex (Yellow, White, Red) (WA)	Yellow, White, Red		110–140	Vigorous, hybrid short-day varieties. Typical of these varieties, the bulbs are sweet but don't store well.

Key to Disease and Pest Abbreviations
PR = pink root   T = thrips

ONION VARIETIES (CONT.)

Name (Source)	Color	Disease Resistance	Days to Reach Maturity	Comments
Grano, TX 502 (Yellow, White, Red) (WA)	Yellow, White, Red		120–160	Another multicolor series. The yellow 502 is the best known. Vidalia onions are grown from this variety—or they have been. Because Texas Supersweet (1015y) is so much sweeter genetically, they are now growing it. Apparently around Vidalia, GA, they have low-sulfur soils, which tend to produce sweeter onions. Grano onions are large and shaped like tops.
Louisiana Multiplying Shallots (24) (Area Nurseries)	White		120–240	These onion sets are usually available at the local feed store or nursery in the South. They may be planted as early as September and often remain in the ground until April. Because they multiply, it is easy to pull a few off the side of clumps without harvesting the entire bunch. Eventually they will form a white shallot-like bulb. These shallots are very spicy compared to French shallots (brown, frog leg, etc. [15]) but, at least in the lower South, they are your best chance for success.
Ringer (1)	Yellow	PR	110–160	A short-day variety developed for onion rings. Why not grow your own, then bread and freeze a few?
Supersweet, TX (1015y) (WA)	Yellow		110–160	This wonderful onion was developed by Dr. Pike of the Texas Agricultural Experiment Station. Onion lovers are said to eat them like apples because they're so sweet. Bulbs are very large, globe-shaped, and store better than the average short-day onion.

Growers in the upper South can also plant intermediate to long-day onions like Vega, Sweet Spanish, Yula, Ebenezer, Mustang, Bermuda, Sweet Sandwich, Benny's Red, and Ruby.

COOL-SEASON GOURMET SELECTIONS

Asian vegetables like Pak Choi (also called Bak Choy) and Chinese cabbage are becoming commonplace. For the average home gardener, these and many other vegetables that flourish during our Southern fall and winter weather are still a bit exotic. Before we get into the really exotic cool-season vegetables, let's discuss some of the more common ones in unusual colors.

Variations on a Color Theme

*B*EETS.   This vegetable isn't high on everyone's list, and chances are finding them in white, yellow, or white/red striped (Chioggia [12, 18]) won't do much for their popularity. Burpee's Golden beets (2) actually do sound more appetizing than the standard red sort. When steamed with a little butter (no, make that a lot of butter), salt, and pepper, they start to sound edible. Albina Vereduna white beets (3, 18) are super sweet and won't bleed red into salads.

*B*ROCCOLI.   Not all broccolis are dark green. The odd-looking Romanesco (18) is lime green. It's also a late-season variety that won't mature in most Southern gardens outside of a greenhouse. The really unusual broccolis are the purple ones. Until the variety Violet Queen (18) came along (see photo on page 190), these types also were late-maturing sorts that just wouldn't make it before the first hard freeze in the fall. Purple Cape (33—listed as a cauliflower) has also been grown with some success, but it is even later to mature than Violet Queen. They all turn green when cooked, but the purple ones look spectacular on a fresh veggie tray.

*B*RUSSELS SPROUTS.   What about purple brussels sprouts? You bet. The variety Rubine (19) is the color of a purple cabbage—actually, they are all closely related. This variety is less vigorous than the hybrid green varieties, but it can still be grown with regular applications of fertilizer and a mild winter.

*C*ABBAGE.   This won't come as big news, but, of course, there are red cabbages. One of the better ones is Rio Grande Red (1, 31).

*C*ARROTS.   White is the main color variation here in the South. White carrots were apparently grown for stock feed at one time, especially on the West Coast. Now they are mostly seen as a plant variation to weed out of new breeding lines. Belgium White (17), however, is still available.

CAULIFLOWER.   Lime green varieties like Alverda (18, 31) (see photo on page 190) and Chartreuse II (18) are the new rage. They even show up at the grocery store occasionally. They taste great and they are probably more nutritious than the blanched white ones. An even newer color variation is Orange Bouquet (18)—probably looks like it's covered with butter when cooked.

CELERY.   Pink- and red-stemmed celeries (27) are supposed to be hardier than regular celery, so they should be super for our fall gardens. They will also look great on the relish tray.

LETTUCES.   Some vegetables just naturally come in a variety of colors. In this instance, a number of red-leaf lettuces are already included in the section on lettuce.

MUSTARD GREENS.   Purple and red are the noteworthy variations. Purple Osaka (4, 14, 18, 25, 27, 32) (see photo on page 195) was one of the first we tried. It not only tasted good, perhaps a bit more pungent than other varieties, but it looked pretty enough to plant in the flower beds. Red-leaf mustards (similar to Osaka) are really reddish purple and don't have the attractive green-leaf petioles of Purple Osaka.

ONIONS.   We expect to see bulb onions in reds, purples, yellows, and whites, but bunching onions are typically white or sometimes yellow. Red bunching onions are a bit more unusual. Red Beard (31, 32) is a red-stalked variety that should really get the attention of your dinner guests.

RADISHES.   You expect this vegetable to come in a variety of colors, but some are really exotic, such as Easter Egg II (WA), with roots that may be lavender, red, or white. One of the Asian varieties, Misato Rose Flesh (14, 17, 32), takes this variation on a color theme to the core (see photo on page 198). The turnip-shaped roots are white with a tinge of green, but the interior is bright pink.

TURNIPS.   It used to be that you could expect a turnip to be purple on top of white. Then the hybrid Asian varieties like Tokyo Market (WA) and Tokyo Express (WA) started showing up in catalogs and folks realized that small, white turnips, only slightly bigger than radishes, were sweet and ready to harvest in about a month. Well, get ready. Turnips also come in red, and they, too, are good. Harvest them at the baby stage (about 3/4 inch in diameter) and cook up the tops as well. In fact, turnip greens may be the best part. Scarlet Red Ball (17, 18) and Sweet Scarlet (17, 18) are the ones to look for, and if that's not enough variation for you, there is also a Golden Ball variety (17).

More Cool-Season Specialty Selections

*A*RUGULA *(Rocket)* (WA) is a mustardy green very popular these days in salads and salad mixes like mesclun (see mesclun section below). (See photo on page 198.) It should be planted and used sparingly. Three to five feet of row should be sufficient with plants thinned 4 to 6 inches apart.

*B*OK CHOY *(Spoon cabbage, Pak Choi)* is closely related to Chinese cabbage even though it looks quite different. (See photo on page 197.) It's the beautiful white-leaf petioles that we are primarily interested in with this vegetable. There are some varieties (Choy Sum, Yu Choy [4, 14, 32]) that are grown for the young flowering shoots. This is another easy one to grow, especially in the fall. Choy Sum may actually be better in late winter or early spring because we want it to flower.

*B*ROCCOLI RAAB (WA) looks like mustard or turnip greens, but it is harvested for the young flowering shoots. It's much more popular in the Northeast but it can certainly be grown with ease in the South, especially in late winter or early spring.

*C*ELERIAC (WA) is a form of celery that develops a swollen root at ground level. It can be grated for salads, cooked, or just stared at. This is one strange-looking vegetable. The roots are sometimes discolored or hollow, so it's important to plant a good variety and push it with plenty of fertilizer. Mentor (28) and Diamant (3) are new varieties that are much improved compared to older varieties.

*C*ELTUCE (WA) is quite lettuce-like; in fact, the young leaves are often used instead of lettuce. The tender stems are the main prize, however. Steamed or stir-fried, they are reportedly delicious.

*C*HICORY is typically a bitter salad vegetable. The trick seems to be growing it so that it is slightly bitter but good, especially when mixed with other salad greens. **Witloof Chicory** (WA) is the really challenging member of this group. It's certainly not impossible for Southern gardeners to grow it, however. Plant seed or transplants in late summer or early fall. Dig up the roots with the leaves cut off, but the crown (growing point) intact, just before the first hard freeze and grow the torpedo-shaped vegetable in a dark, cool place. You can pack the roots in wooden crates or old 5-gallon nursery pots with a bit of potting soil or peat moss to stimulate this vigorous, blanched (blanching apparently reduces the bitterness), and very expensive salad green for your table. It's a wonder that someone isn't growing this one commercially (at $5 to $7 per pound).

CHINESE CABBAGE (and Friends).   (See photos on page 197.) Different countries in Asia refer to the same vegetable by different names. In fact, different names may be used in different regions of the same country. It all adds up to a lot of confusion. To simplify things a bit, let's first look at Chinese cabbage. There are two basic forms. The short, stocky heads are known as napa, wong bok, or che foo. The first two are essentially the same, while the che foo varieties have bright green, less hairy leaves. Then there are the michili (also called chihili) types, which are taller with loose outer leaves and a head that's smaller in diameter—like a rolled newspaper. These are all quite easy to grow in the fall garden; however, most will bolt to seed quickly in the spring. Some varieties like Spring Triumph (32) are better in the late winter or spring garden, but the urge to produce seed is strong in this vegetable with longer days and warmer weather.

In the fall garden it is easy to set out transplants about the same time you would set out broccoli and harvest a big crop before the first hard freeze. These vegetables will stand temperatures down to 28° F or so if they have been conditioned to colder weather. Unfortunately, we can go from 70° to 28° F in the span of a few hours. If temperatures are predicted in the mid-20s and your crop is near maturity, it's probably best to harvest and see how many Chinese cabbage-eating friends you can find. Rows should be 24 to 36 inches apart with plants 8 to 12 inches apart in the row.

CHINESE KALE (Chinese broccoli, Gai lon) (WA) is closely related to common broccoli, but it is grown for its small flowering shoots. Compared to regular broccoli, the heads seem kind of puny—smaller even than most broccoli side shoots. Fortunately the plant produces lots of them and 4 to 6 inches of the stem is tender as well.

CORN SALAD (mache) (3, 7, 15, 17, 18, 27, 28, 33) is a mild, spatulate-leaved green that has a hint of rose flavor. Though it grows well, the plant is not overly vigorous—a spacing of 4 to 6 inches should be about right. For salads, individual leaves can be harvested as needed.

CRESS (WA) is a sprightly vegetable used in salads and on sandwiches. It comes in three forms—four, if you count nasturtiums. **Garden Cress**

(Curled cress, *Lapidium sativum*) (WA) likes cool weather (really, all the cresses do). It's also good in the winter greenhouse. The leaves of this vegetable are more curled than than those of Upland cress and it is often harvested when barely more than a sprout—at 2 to 3 inches. **Upland Cress (Land Cress, *Barbarea verna*)** (WA) grows about 6 to 8 inches in height and will spread a foot or so. This is a good one to use in mesclun mixes (3, 15, 18, 22, 27) or in place of watercress. It is planted on dry land though it will need good moisture. **Watercress** (4, 14, 17, 27, 32) is the most difficult to grow of the cresses. It needs a shallow slow-moving stream for best growth. You could create one with a recirculating pump, but the other cresses are similar and much easier to grow. Actually, nasturtiums (WA) are so close to watercress in flavor and texture that you should at least give them a try before you dig up the backyard. Both the leaves and the flowers are delicious. Nasturtiums aren't without problems however. They don't like our summers and they won't stand a freeze. Try them in hanging baskets, brought in when it is going to freeze; or better yet, they get absolutely weedy in a cool, winter greenhouse.

*D*AIKON (WA) looks like a White Icicle radish on steroids. (See photo on page 199.) Some varieties of this vegetable can grow to 18 inches in length and 2 to 3 inches in diameter and still be edible. There are many different kinds of Asian radish. The Korean sorts (4, 14, 32) are shorter and stockier, as are the Chinese varieties (4, 14, 32). One Japanese radish, Sakurijima (5, 17), is turnip-shaped and can weigh 10 pounds or more. That's a lot of heartburn. Really, these radishes are very mild and they seem to keep forever. Cut off a chunk for a salad, wrap plastic wrap around the end, and put it back in the fridge. Months later, it will still be good. Long Black Spanish (15, 17) and the German beer radish, Munich Bier (3), are a couple of other strange radishes. Both are fairly strong. The Munich Bier is a white radish that is sliced thin and served with salt and beer.

All of these exotic radishes will need extra growing room. Space the smaller ones 3 to 4 inches apart, the daikon types 6 to 8 inches apart.

*D*ANDELIONS (WA) aren't the serious weed in the South that they often become in Northern gardens, so planting some on purpose isn't quite as crazy as it may sound. (See photo on page 199.) We do have a dandelion-like weed here in the South, but it is actually false dandelion. If you like a sprinkle of bitter greens in your salad, give the cultivated variety a try.

*F*ENNELS (WA), popular as garnishes, include the common variety grown for the anise-flavored foliage and seeds and sweet fennel grown primarily for the celery-like (though anise-flavored) stem bases. Bronze fennel

(25, 27) is really more purple than bronze, but otherwise it is similar to the common fennel. For those folks more interested in attracting butterflies than in eating fennel, black swallowtail butterfly larvae love all three fennels.

*F*ENUGREEK (17) sprouts are becoming very popular as cool-season salad fodder. These are typically produced indoors, but Fenugreek can also be grown outside by sowing the seed thickly in raised beds or in containers where they are harvested at the mesclun stage (1 to 2 inches of the 3 to 4 inches growth).

*G*ARLIC (WA) is easy to grow as a fall-planted crop. To ensure a uniform stand, you might want to presprout the individual cloves in a bed of loose potting soil by planting them with one-third of the tip out of the soil, but that's about as tricky as it gets. What has really gotten complicated in recent years is the availability of so many varieties. It used to be that you planted white cloves or the strong pink ones (often referred to as Mexican or Italian garlic). Now Filaree Farm (6) has an entire catalog devoted to garlic. They list wild forms, rocamboles (strong flavor and coiled flower stalks), continentals, Asiatics, Southern continentals, artichoke, and silverskin varieties. They also include a discussion of elephant garlic (WA), which is actually a strong-flavored leek (which is why Filaree Farms doesn't sell it). Elephant garlic is a very popular garlic substitute in the South. It grows very well here and the flavor is comparatively mild. The Filaree Farm catalog makes for great reading, and it is a "must" if you're a garlic lover. Southern Exposure Seeds also lists a number of garlics.

One sad note: garlic is often touted as a good companion plant to repel insects that might attack your other crops, such as tomatoes. Unfortunately, garlic doesn't grow during the same season as the tomato and thrips love garlic. The best way to store garlic in our humid, Southern climate is to clean the buds down to individual cloves and then freeze them in freezer jars.

*G*LOBE ARTICHOKES (WA) and *CARDOON* (3, 28) are lumped together because neither have much potential for most areas of the South, and they are both members of the thistle family. If one could be sure of a mild winter, they could be planted from seed or divisions in the fall. By spring, the artichokes would produce a few chokes and the cardoon could be blanched and the petioles harvested for pickling or frying. Large divisions of the globe artichoke are sometimes available in late winter, and with luck, plus an early spring, you might succeed with planting at this time. Both of these plants really struggle through our summers, but if you are lucky enough to get them through to cooler weather, once again, you at least have a chance. As you harvest your three artichokes the next spring, they will probably be in season and on special at the grocery store.

LEEKS (WA) are often neglected by Southern gardeners and yet the onion family thrives in our mild winters. This will be a long season crop—planted from seed in October or November and harvested before summer heat in April or May. The edible portion of this vegetable is the enlarged stem, which is very mild. It is usually harvested when 1 to 2 inches in diameter, but it can also be used scallion size for a real treat. Extras can be chopped up and frozen to ensure a year-round supply of leek soup. A new early maturing variety, Otina (28), should be a good one to try.

MESCLUN (3, 15, 18, 22, 27, 28) isn't really a vegetable, it is a mix of greens used young and fresh for salads. (See photo on page 199.) Typically the mix includes: a lettuce like Oakleaf, possibly endive, chervil, arugula, cress, chickory, and even dandelion. Several catalogs offer seed mixes and they work okay, but if you want to grow this popular and expensive blend on a larger scale, plant the ingredients separately and mix them at harvest time. The problem with the seed mixes is that some ingredients like arugula grow fast enough to be weedy, and your mesclun may end up tasting strongly of arugula and completely absent of chervil, for example.

MUSTARDS. We tend to think of mustard as a Southern soul food, but the leafy mustards we consume as greens originated in the Orient. Consequently there are many varieties beyond the green and curled green types that we usually see in Southern gardens. Purple and red mustards have been covered earlier under "Variations on a Color Theme." Others include: Chinese Heading Mustard (4, 14, 32) and Mustard-Spinach (Komatsuna, WA). **Mizuna** (WA) is a shiny-leaved, mustard-like vegetable popular in Japan. Its deeply serrated leaves are used for stir-fry or in pickling.

OTHER ONIONS, including top onions, various multipliers, and shallots, love our winters, too. All grow very well, especially the Louisiana multiplying shallots. The biggest disappointment has been with the mild French shallots (15). They grow pretty well during the winter, but then fizzle before making nice bulbs in the late spring. Perhaps it is the combination of wet weather and heat, but it may also be related to daylength. Many onions require a longer daylength to initiate bulbing than most Southern gardeners ever get.

PARSNIP (WA) is an often neglected vegetable. It grows well in the cool-season garden, but two favorite gourmet seed companies don't even list it. Maybe there's good reason that folks don't grow parsnips. You have to hide it in a pretty good stew to make it edible. Hollow Crown (WA)—even the name sounds bad—is the most common variety. Grow parsnips the same way you would carrots, except thin to 3 inches apart and plant in the fall only; this crop takes 100–plus days to mature.

RADICCHIO is similar to leaf lettuce but more challenging to grow. (See photo on page 197.) The key is to plant new varieties like Carmen (31), Guilio (3, 12, 19, 28), Fireball (18), or Rossana (28) that have a genetic tendency to form heads. Old varieties like Rosa de Verona (WA) are easy to grow but they rarely form heads, so there's little blanching and the end product is more bitter. Plants also seem to head better when direct seeded rather than set out as transplants. In recent years we have experimented with small plants of these modern hybrids carefully planted from 4–packs with an undisturbed 1- × 2-inch block of soil. We've been getting 50% or better heading and a much more uniform crop. If direct seeding, barely scratch the tiny seed into the soil surface and cover with fiber row cover to ensure a good, uniform stand. Then don't be afraid to thin. Plants need to be 8 to 12 inches apart for good head development. At $5 to $6 per pound in the store, this is a tempting vegetable to find a place for in the cool-season garden. Pan Di Zucchero (28) is a green-leaf variety that is milder and much easier to grow. However, it's unlikely that it will sell as well as the red varieties.

RHUBARB (WA) is a perennial for our Northern gardening friends, but for us it is impossible to grow successfully or, at best, maybe worth a try as a fall-planted annual. Buy new divisions each fall, grow them through the winter, harvest in the spring, and expect the plants to die in the summer.

RUTABAGA (WA) could be described as a yellow-fleshed turnip, but that description isn't entirely adequate. Rutabagas tend to have a smoother, waxier flesh. The outside is often waxed to prolong storage potential, though this isn't what causes the smooth texture of the interior. Rutabagas are most often cooked, and they are really quite good. The roots are large, 4 to 6 inches in diameter, and most varieties will need fall planting because maturity can take 90 to 120 days. Be sure to thin to 4 to 6 inches apart to allow for full development.

SALSIFY AND SCORZONERA (3, 8, 27) are root crops that have limited appeal. Both grow quite well during the cool season with essentially the same growing procedure as carrots, but the end product is so-so. Salsify forms a white, carrot-like root that when cooked is supposed to have an oyster-like flavor. The main root often has numerous side roots, which, after trimming, doesn't leave a whole lot to eat. Scorzonera is similar but the skin is black.

The Vegetable Lover's Herb Garden

HERBS (YOU WILL REALLY USE)

Herbs are a natural addition to the vegetable garden. They can be somewhat daunting to the beginning gardener, however. What to grow, how much to grow, and how to use them are typical questions. There have been some excellent books written on the subject for Southern gardeners, including: *Southern Herb Growing* by Madalene Hill and Gwen Barclay with Jean Hardy and *Herb Growing in the South* by Sol Meltzer. These books are required reading for the advanced herb enthusiast.

Most herbs need good drainage (vigorous mints like spearmint excepted). This means planting them in raised beds or containers for most of us. Hanging baskets can be especially useful because you can hang them right outside the kitchen door. Though many herbs originated along the dry, infertile Mediterranean coast, most will do best with at least moderate fertilization. This can be particularly important when growing herbs in containers like hanging baskets. Use slow-release or organic fertilizers as a reservoir when initially planting the container and supplement with soluble fertilizers or a liquid organic like fish emulsion to keep them healthy.

Herbs are generally pest free, though you may get an occasional spider mite on the rosemary, thrips on the garlic, and so on. Chances are you will never have to spray the herb bed with pesticides. That's fortunate because there aren't many pesticides you can use on minor crops like herbs. Insecticidal soaps and organic sprays should control the occasional intruder.

The average gardener won't have room for a formal herb bed, so, besides using containers, herbs can also be worked into the flower bed, and annuals like basil can simply be planted in the garden row. Most herbs will grow best in full sun, but because they are mostly leafy plants, many will tolerate some shade. A few, like the mints, will even thrive in it.

Herbs are propagated both by seed and from cuttings. Some herbs work well either way. Basil is usually grown from seed, just because it's so easy to grow this way, but it will also root from cuttings. Rosemary can be propagated from seed but germination is often poor and the resulting quality of plants is more variable. Since there are rosemary varieties that are prostrate or that have better cold resistance, it is best to clone them by taking cuttings, thus ensuring plants with identical characteristics.

The Ones You'll Really Use

ARUGULA (WA) is a leafy herb that we have discussed more thoroughly under "More Cool-Season Specialty Sections." It is often used sparingly in salad mixes like mesclun. Its strong flavor qualifies it as an herb in many references.

Herb	Grown From	Season	Spacing	Height	Harvest Within	Harvest Until
Arugula (Roquette)	Seed	Cool	6–8 inches in row, rows—12–24 inches	4–6 inches	45–60 days	April/May, bolts in spring

BASIL (WA) is one of the easiest herbs to cultivate. (See photo on page 200.) It is indispensable in Italian dishes from pasta to pizza to pesto. It's also easy to grow, as long as the temperature is warm. This makes it especially prized in the winter. If you have a greenhouse, consider this a crop to grow along with the greenhouse tomatoes, cukes, and lettuces. You'll be the envy of your friends when you serve fresh pesto at Christmas dinner, and if you grow extra, local restaurants should welcome you with open arms. In addition to regular basil, there are cinnamon-, clove-, lemon-, and licorice-flavored basils. Of these, the lemon-flavored one will probably find the most favor. It can be used for teas, or its mild lemon flavor can add a delicate touch to sauces.

Herb	Grown From	Season	Spacing	Height	Harvest Within	Harvest Until
Basil	Seed	Warm	4–6 inches in row, rows—8–24 inches	8–24 inches	30–45 days	Frost

CHIVES (WA) come in several forms. The traditional sort has round leaves, pink flowers, and a mild onion flavor. (See photo on page 200.) This is the herb so often listed as a topping for your baked potato, but it is rarely delivered. Chopped green onions are the best most restaurants can do. True chives would be too expensive, but you can have them on your baked potatoes at home for at least seven months of the year. Seedlings started in September should be ready to harvest by November, and the harvest should last into June, when temperatures get too hot. Then struggling plants should be left alone in hopes they will survive and grow again in the fall.

GARLIC CHIVES (4, 14, 32) have flat leaves, white flowers, and you guessed it—a garlicky flavor. They also like cool weather, but they will grow almost year round with weedlike vigor. Garlic chives are stronger than traditional chives, almost bitter if overused, so go easy.

Herb	Grown From	Season	Spacing	Height	Harvest Within	Harvest Until
Chives	Seed, divisions	Cool (8–12 weeks before average frost)	4–6 inches in row, rows—12–18 inches	8–10 inches	60–90 days	Early summer for garlic chives, year round for garlic

CILANTRO (WA) is an ancient herb that is becoming a staple in many Southern kitchens. (See photo on page 200.) An eighteenth-century vegetable book from France referred to its now-popular flavor as woodbug-like (stinkbug-like). However, a small amount in Mexican and, for that matter, many Asian dishes is indispensable. Usually it's the leaves we think of using, but the seeds are spicy, aromatic, and completely different in flavor. The seeds go more with fruit, desserts, pastries, and the like.

This is an easy plant to grow as long as you plant it in the fall. It quickly bolts to seed in the spring. This means that when you need it for salsas in the summer, it's gone. Fortunately, it can be frozen in an oil mix or purchased at the market for use in summer.

Herb	Grown From	Season	Spacing	Height	Harvest Within	Harvest Until
Cilantro	Seed	Fall (8–12 weeks before first frost)	6–10 inches in row, rows—18–24 inches	8–12 inches, at flowering 18–24 inches	45–60 days	It bolts to seed in spring

DILL (WA) is another easy one as long as it is planted in the fall. (See photo on page 201.) It can be grown in late winter or early spring but it quickly goes to seed. The trick is to coordinate it with your pickle crop. Even though it bolts to seed, it is still possible to plant successive crops every couple of weeks through the spring and early summer to ensure that you have dill for pickles, etc.

Dill really is a weed. It can grow 3½ feet tall and reseed for eternity. A new variety, Bouquet, stays under 2 feet until it begins to bloom. The main pest of dill are hornworms. They can strip the leaves down to bare stems in no time. Fortunately BT (*Bacillus thuringiensis*) is nontoxic and effective if you catch them when they are small. Hand removal works, too: hold both ends of a 1-inch caterpillar and stretch it to 2 inches.

Herb	Grown From	Season	Spacing	Height	Harvest Within	Harvest Until
Dill	Seed	Fall–early summer	8–12 inches in the row, rows—18–24 inches	24–42	45 days	Seed formation

GARLIC (WA) is so important that we've included a more thorough discussion of it under cool-season crops. It's often considered an herb, though, and we didn't want to appear remiss by omitting it from this section.

MEXICAN MARIGOLD (11, 17, 25) is really a marigold, but it is a different species from the flower-garden sort. This one is *Tagetes lucida,* and not only does it not look like the standard marigold, it certainly doesn't smell like it either. It is often recommended as a substitute for the true tarragon, which is difficult to grow in the South because it likes San Francisco-like weather. In addition, it can be used for teas or in salads. It is delightful just to pinch a few leaves and enjoy the anise-, rootbeer-like fragrance.

The small yellow flowers won't show up until late summer. Like many subtropical plants, this one won't bloom until the days shorten to about 12 hours. Plants aren't reliably hardy except in the lower South. Even along the Gulf Coast they will freeze out in a hard winter.

Herb	Grown From	Season	Spacing	Height	Harvest Within	Harvest Until
Mexican Marigold (Sometimes Called Mint)	Cuttings, or seed is possible	Warm	12–18 inches in row, rows—18–24 inches	24–30 inches	30–45 days	Hard freeze

MINTS (WA) include some Southern favorites. (See photo on page 201.) What would tea or mint juleps be without spearmint? Then there's peppermint, orange mint, applemint, etc. This is one group that will tolerate excess moisture and shade. Most, however, will grow best with morning sun and good soil rich in organic matter. Many a patch of spearmint flourishes under the dripping faucet of the typical Southern home.

Herb	Grown From	Season	Spacing	Height	Harvest Within	Harvest Until
Mints	Cuttings, seed	Warm (perennial)	12–18 inches in row, rows—18–24 inches	8–12 inches	30–45 days	Cool weather reduces growth

OREGANO (WA) is the pizza/spaghetti herb. Actually, it can be widely used in a number of dishes and there are many forms of oregano. Sweet marjoram is a slightly milder relative; Greek and Spanish oregano are the ones most commonly used in Italian dishes. The oregano oil is common in a number of plants. Two that are adapted to Southern gardens are: Mexican Oregano (*Poliomintha longiflora*), a shrubby plant with pink flowers that draws hummingbirds, and Mexican Oregano (*Lippia graveolens*), which grows along the Texas-Mexico border. These plants are sometimes propagated locally and available at nurseries.

Herb	Grown From	Season	Spacing	Height	Harvest Within	Harvest Until
Oregano	Cuttings, seed	All	12–18 inches in row, rows—18–24 inches	12–18 inches	60 days	Year round, except after a hard freeze or during summer stress

PARSLEY (WA) is easy to grow during fall and winter. (See photo on page 201.) For some reason, the curly-leafed forms will continue into the summer while the plain-leafed Italian types (considered primo for culinary use) bolt to seed quickly in late spring. Parsley is much more than a garnish to counteract the effects of garlic. It is a mainstay in a good cook's arsenal, and we can grow it 8 to 9 months of the year. It's even pretty, so it can go in the flower bed as a border for cool-season annuals if you don't have an herb garden.

Herb	Grown From	Season	Spacing	Height	Harvest Within	Harvest Until
Parsley	Seed	Cool, seed 16 weeks before first frost; transplants 10–12 weeks before first frost	8–12 inches in row, rows—18–24 inches	6–24 inches	90 days after seeding, 60 days after transplanting	Late spring, early summer

RED BAY (*Persea borbonia*) is a native southern tree. It makes a good substitute for the **Sweet Bay,** or **True Bay** (*Laurus nobilis*) (17), of the Mediterranean. Unfortunately this latter plant is not reliably hardy north of the Gulf

Coast. Even though Red Bay doesn't have as strong a flavor, it works fine—just use twice as much. The Red Bay is a small tree that you should be able to fit into the landscape. Its one problem is the gall insect, which causes bumps all over the leaves. Even if we could spray for it, it would be difficult to time the spray correctly. The adult insect that causes the plant gall to form is only present for a short period of time. The best approach is to ignore it and use the healthy leaves for cooking. Check local nurseries specializing in native plants to obtain Red Bay.

If you opt to grow the True Bay, consider growing it in a large whiskey barrel or a similar-size ceramic container. This way you can protect it when temperatures are predicted to drop below 28° F.

ROSEMARY (WA) isn't reliably hardy from the Gulf Coast north, but if planted along a south-facing wall, it will be somewhat protected. (See photo on page 202.) Grow the prostrate forms (17) and cover them with an old blanket or a similar type of good insulation when temperatures are predicted to fall below 30° F. This plant demands good drainage, so raised beds are appropriate.

Herb	Grown From	Season	Spacing	Height	Harvest Within	Harvest Until
Rosemary	Cuttings preferably, seed also possible	Warm, perennial if protected	18–24 inches in row, rows— 24–36 inches	Prostrate varieties 12–18 inches, uprights 30–36 inches	4 weeks after setting transplants	Continuous

SAVORY (WA), in both its winter (perennial) and summer (annual) forms, is especially good with vegetables and, most traditionally, with beans. (See photo on page 202.) The plants are creeping in habit and fairly easy to grow. Though considered warm-season plants, they thrive in early spring and in the fall.

Herb	Grown From	Season	Spacing	Height	Harvest Within	Harvest Until
Savory (Winter and Summer)	Seed or cuttings	Warm to year round (winter savory)	6–8 inches in the row, rows— 12–18 inches apart	2–4 inches	45–60 days	Hard freeze or summer heat stress

THYMES (WA) are available in many forms—lemon, creeping, True French, wooley, caraway, nutmeg, common, and others. (See photo on page

202.) In addition to creeping forms, there are upright thymes. Usually, they all suffer in the summer and may freeze in the winter. Fortunately, there are varieties that grow quite well and have a number of culinary uses. In the kitchen, common thyme and lemon thyme will be most appreciated.

Herb	Grown From	Season	Spacing	Height	Harvest Within	Harvest Until
Thyme	Cuttings, seed	When warm (65°–70° F)	4–6 inches in the row, rows—8–18 inches	2–8 inches	4 weeks after setting transplants, 10 weeks from seed	Hard freeze or heat stress

Other Specialty Herbs

A dedicated herbalist would be lost with only the herbs we've covered so far. Once you've learned to grow and use many of the ones already mentioned, you will probably want to grow others, including the following. **ANISE HYSSOP** (17) is an easy-to-grow perennial that makes a delicious, anise-flavored tea. **BORAGE** (WA) is an attractive warm-season plant with hairy, blue-green leaves and lavender-blue flowers. Its tender new leaves can be chopped up to add a mild cucumber flavor to salads, but it is mostly pretty to look at. **SALAD BURNET** (WA) thrives in cool weather. Its tender leaves also give salads a cucumber flavor. **CATNIP** (WA) really does turn cats on, so you will probably have to grow this perennial member of the mint family in a pot or basket that can be hung out of kitty's way. **CHERVIL** (WA) is a cool-season annual with a mild anise flavor that looks like a delicate parsley. **COSTMARY** (17) is a perennial with lance-shaped leaves that have a wintergreen flavor and are used to make teas. **EPAZOTE** (10, 16, 17, 23, 27) is a popular dried bean herb and a potential weed. **FENNEL** (WA) comes in two basic forms—common, grown for its anise-flavored seeds (makes an excellent tea) and leaves; and sweet fennel, grown for its swollen, celery-like (anise-flavored) leaf stalks. **SCENTED GERANIUMS** (17) are tough plants that will survive all but the hardest winters (from the Gulf Coast and South) and most of our summers. Varieties include: rose, peppermint, lemon, and nutmeg. **LEMON BALM** (WA) is a sprawling, perennial shrub with lance-shaped leaves that have a strong lemon flavor. **LEMONGRASS** (17, 32) is a tender perennial that looks like a small clump of Johnsongrass but with mild lemon-flavored leaves. **SAGE** (WA) is a popular herb, but one that suffers in the excessive rainfall we often have in the South. Pineapple sage is easier to grow, but it wouldn't be a good substitute because it tastes different.

Using Herbs

Herbs make an attractive addition to the garden or flower bed, but don't stop there. Put them to use. Fresh herbs are different, usually much better than their dried counterparts on the grocery shelf. Though drying your own is an option, there are better ways to preserve the herbs not used fresh in cooking. Freezing in olive oil is one of the best ways. Chop up the herb by hand or in a food processor and then add just enough oil to make a thick paste. Freeze in small portions and use year round, virtually as you would use it fresh.

Herb butters are great, too. To a pound of softened butter or margarine, add 6 to 8 tablespoons of freshly chopped herbs like parsley, chives, oregano, or thyme, and blend well. Allow the flavors to marry for at least a few hours while you whip up a batch of caraway/rye bread and prepare to swoon.

Drying is probably the least desirable way of preserving excess herbs from the garden, and in our humid, Southern climate you will likely need some help if you decide to do so. You can put the herbs in the oven with the heat on low (or pilot light only if using a gas oven) and leave the door open a crack. There are food dehydrators that are inexpensive and will work well, and some people have used the microwave on low power with success.

Herbal vinegars are yet another option. In addition to your favorite herbs, you may want to add hot peppers or spices. Warm the mixture (don't boil), then store in a nonmetallic, covered container for several days before bottling, with or without herbs, peppers, etc. Herbal vinegars are great on salads and cooked greens. Whatever you do, use the herbs you grow!

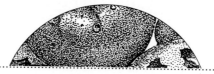

Pest and Disease Control in the Vegetable Garden

PEST AND DISEASE CONTROL FOR TROUBLESHOOTERS

Pest control in the Southern garden is especially challenging. The seasons are long, the alternate weed hosts numerous, and the rainfall is often abundant. Insects typically overwinter with no problem, they raise several generations of offspring during the extended seasons, and some build up on weed hosts. Viruses, which seem to get worse all the time, can be transmitted by certain insects from some of these weeds to many vegetable crops. Other diseases caused by fungi and bacteria flourish during periods of high rainfall. Weeds, too, love our rainy climate.

While the pests seem to be getting worse, the willingness to use chemical pesticides is waning. Many gardeners believe that if they are going to grow their own vegetables they surely can do it with fewer pesticides. To a great extent, this is true. Using certain cultural techniques will help. Trapping and/or hand picking insects is often sufficient in the small garden. The use of low-toxicity, organic sprays is often practical in the small garden when hand picking isn't adequate or practical. If this approach works, that's great, but don't underestimate the disease, insect, and weed pressure of our climate.

Many gardeners take the organic approach because the media has made them chemophobic with sensational reports of pollution, poisons, and toxins. Sure, chemical-related medical problems occur, but rarely. This is still the greatest agricultural nation the world has ever known, thanks to the hard-working, rarely appreciated farmers of this country and to advancements in agricultural science—including the development of chemical pesticides.

Our gardening philosophy is strictly middle of the road; we use the best of organic doctrines and common sense when it comes to pest control. Certainly, you should search high and wide for all the organic matter you can find for your soil, use mulches (plant adapted, disease–resistant varieties), and use low-toxicity controls when practical, but don't avoid the use of the more economical chemical fertilizers or pesticides when necessary.

For example, look at the life cycle of a tomato plant. When first planted, it needs a rich loose soil with soluble fertilizer elements close to the root system. It needs to be protected from the damaging effects of wind, early insect attack that could spread a virus disease at the very beginning of its development, and perhaps from frost. Frequent spring rains increase the disease pressure, and before you know it, early blight fungus can turn the leaves—first yellow then brown from the bottom up. Later, as the fruit starts to develop, stinkbugs begin to feed, causing the fruit to develop yellow patches with a corky layer of tissue underneath. Sounds discouraging, but you can succeed with the commonsense approach.

1. Before planting, work 4 to 6 inches of rich compost into the soil. Also include 2 to 3 pounds of a complete fertilizer like 13–13–13 (or an organic like cotton seed meal) per 100 square feet.

2. Work the soil up into ridges 12 to 18 inches in height for good drainage.

3. Use a starter solution made up of a $\frac{1}{3}$-strength soluble fertilizer—one pint per plant. A slow-release fertilizer can also be put 1 inch under the plant roots as it is being set out.

4. Use fiber row cover around wire tomato cages to keep out insects, reduce wind damage, and give a few degrees of frost protection.

5. Spray a preventative fungicide like chlorothalonil early in the season to prevent the development of fungal diseases like early blight. Be sure to spray the underside of leaves as well as the top sides. As fruit begins to mature, preventative sprays probably won't be needed any longer.

6. Watch for spider mites, stinkbugs, and hornworms, but spray chemical pesticides only when populations can't be controlled with hand removal or the use of insecticidal soaps, wettable sulfur, BT, or other low-toxicity sprays.

7. Enjoy your healthy garden and sleep easy!

A number of techniques can be used to control pests beyond the use of chemical or even organic pesticides.

Solarization is a simple but effective way to reduce the population of weeds, insects, nematodes, and diseases in the soil. (See photo on page 251.) The soil is first worked up and leveled. It should be free of weeds, debris, and large clods. Clear, UV-resistant polyethylene film 4 to 6 mils thick is used to cover the prepared soil with the edges tucked into a trench around the area, which is then covered to hold the plastic in place. The soil needs to be moist under the plastic. Small areas can be watered prior to covering; large areas are usually fitted with irrigation lines (i.e., bi-wall or hose fittings are pushed under) to water the soil after the cover is in place. Timing is critical, too. July and August are the best months, but June and September will often work as well. It takes 4 to 6 weeks to effectively solarize the soil. Remember, this isn't a sterilization process. Some weeds, like Purple Nutsedge, will only be partially controlled and nematode populations will only be reduced. An additional benefit is that crops planted in a solarized area often grow faster and produce more. No doubt, freedom from weed competition and pathogens is a factor in this growth response, but soluble nitrogen may also be increased and beneficial microorganisms like Trichoderma and Actinomycete may survive the solarization process and recolonize the soil more quickly than pathogens do.

Dry tilling is somewhat the opposite of solarization. It's a technique used primarily for nematode reduction. Because the microscopic roundworms that attack the roots of so many of our garden vegetables need moisture to survive, dry tilling is used during the heat of summer to deprive them of moisture and reduce their numbers. As you've probably surmised, this isn't a pleasant time to be in the garden operating a tiller, but it is nontoxic and fairly effective.

Cereal rye, such as the Elbon variety, can be grown through the winter to reduce nematode populations. The bad part is that this is a great time to be growing cool-season crops like broccoli and you'll hate to give up the space. It's also a chore to mow and dig under in the spring, though you are also getting a green manure crop. After all, who said gardening was easy?

Marigolds can be planted in the summer to reduce nematode populations. It is important to plant them in a solid block. Sorry, you can't get by with interplanting them in the okra patch, and you need to plant the small-flowered wild types to get the fullest effect. The plants should be plowed under and allowed to rot. Oh, and you will probably have to fight the spider mites they attract, too.

Fiber row cover is one of the greatest garden accessories yet devised. We use it to cover tomato cages, to cover raised beds (tack it to one side and float it over the row, holding it loosely with 2 × 2s on the other side), and we've even used it around clusters of tomatoes to keep the birds and bugs off so that the fruit can develop to a delicious redness before we photograph them.

(See photo on page 251.) Row cover not only excludes insects that might damage vegetables or transmit viruses, it also protects young plants from the damaging effects of wind and can give a few degrees of frost protection. It is typically left on during the early part of the season and removed as plants need insects for pollination or as the plants grow too large. It only reduces the sun's intensity about 10%, so plants don't stretch out and productivity isn't reduced. By carefully removing it and storing it in a dry place, we are able to use it for several years.

Trap crops and traps can also be used to reduce your dependence on pesticides. For example, the leaf-footed bug that likes to suck out the juices from tomato fruits, etc., likes sunflower seeds even better. Plant a row away from the garden and stop them there, if necessary. Aphids usually prefer radishes over lettuce—though for some gardeners it may be a toss-up which to save. Slugs and snails can be trapped under grapefruit halves or lured into spray can lids imbedded at soil level and filled with beer. Yellow and white sticky traps are readily available from organic product suppliers and no doubt the list of these nontoxic alternatives will increase.

Cultural techniques, such as using wider spacing for increased air circulation can also help reduce diseases. Snapping 3 to 4 bottom leaves off of the tomato plants after they are 18 to 24 inches tall will improve air movement around the base of the plants and reduce fungal infections. Cleaning up debris that can serve as a source of future infections is also helpful. Staking, caging, or training plants on a trellis are techniques that improve air circulation and get the fruit off the ground so it is less likely to rot.

Rogue's Gallery of Common Garden Pests

Varmints are a bigger problem than the beginning gardener might think. They can be especially troublesome in the country, but armadillos, rabbits, raccoons, and birds often wreak havoc even in the city.

Armadillos are after white grubs and other soil delicacies. Even though they don't eat the garden plants, they often damage them while digging for the grubs. Treating the garden soil with a recommended insecticide in early July (when the grubs are small) should help to discourage the armadillos by reducing their food source. They can also be trapped. Use live traps and locate the traps along trails coming from ground burrows, if possible, because putting bait in the trap isn't effective. A couple of 2 × 6s funneling into the entrance of the trap will help keep them on course.

Birds are mostly a problem with fruit crops, but they will peck holes in ripening tomatoes. Crows particularly love to dig at a fresh planting of corn. Noise-making devices can help in the country. Rubber snakes, owls, and beach ball "scare eyes" will work for a while, especially if you move them occasionally, but birds are persistent. Red Christmas balls hung in the tomato plants just before the fruit begins to ripen seems to create a bad enough experience for mockingbirds that they may stay out of the tomato patch for a while. Plan to repaint the balls, however, because the first rain will wash off the red coating. Bird netting can be pulled over the plants close to harvest time, but it makes harvesting a hassle. We sometimes cover tomato clusters with patches of fiber row cover to allow full ripening for pictures, but stapling little diapers of row cover around each tomato cluster is a genuine hassle. Small receptacles of water placed in and around the plants are supposed to satisfy the birds' need for water and keep them out of the tomatoes.

Rabbits don't seem to be very intimidated by blood meal, as has been suggested. Human hair or predator scents (manures) may repel them for a while, but you'll need to cultivate a friendship with your local barber and/or zoo keeper. Actually, fox scents have been sold commercially and the circus usually comes to town once a year. Large dogs, short electric fences, and hardware cloth fences are other possibilities. If you decide to use a fence, for most of these pests you will need to extend it into the soil a foot or two to keep them from digging under.

Raccoons love sweet corn, melons, and other garden delicacies. They are also extremely intelligent and brazen. Some folks have been known to feed them dog food on the back porch because they're cute. (No wonder they think we grow our gardens for them.) Live traps and relocation are a possibility, but be careful, these cute animals will bite. Leaving a radio on in the garden tuned to an all night talk station may scare them off, at least during the corn harvest season, and sprinkling the blackberry prunings down the row during harvest time is another possible deterrent.

Gophers are often a problem in sandy soils. Baits and traps are the most commonly used controls, but they are not always effective. Check with your local county extension agent for the best control technique in your area.

Rats and mice can also damage fruit, especially melons. Use traps baited with peanut butter.

Insects that attack our crops usually get our attention immediately, whereas diseases often go unchecked until it is too late. (See pages 252–258 for photos of the insects and diseases discussed in the following pages.) Early in the development of insecticides, most gardeners figured any bug was a bad bug and, at the first sign of infestation, out came the sprayer. Now we're more aware that there are good bugs as well as bad ones, and are using sprays only when it's necessary. The scientists have dubbed this technique Integrated Pest Management (IPM). It involves careful monitoring and pesticide use only when damaging thresholds of the pest have been reached. We might have also called this commonsense pest management. Increasingly, the use of predators, parasites, and low-toxicity pesticides are being incorporated into the scheme of pest control.

True bugs include the stinkbugs and beneficials like the wheel bug and assassin bug. The stinkbugs are most common, especially the green stinkbug and the leaf-footed bug. Squash bugs also build up on cucurbits. These pests suck the juices out of the plant or developing fruit and may cause the plant to wilt or the fruit to develop yellow spots with white corky areas under the skin where the cells have been damaged. Pesticides are often necessary, though hand removal (wear gloves) particularly early in the season will reduce their numbers.

Never as numerous, the beneficial bug's proboscis (snout) is more prominent. Apparently blood is thicker than sap. They aren't a real threat to gardeners, but they can bite if provoked.

Aphids are small (about the size of a pinhead), pear-shaped insects that can build up in tremendous numbers before you know it. Most are fertile females that hit the ground ready to procreate. As they feed on the plant juices they excrete a honeydew that ants, including our imported fire ant, feed on. In fact, the fire ants farm them for this purpose—they carry them around and even protect them. Aphids not only damage the plants by sucking out the juices, they may transmit viruses, too. If enough of the honeydew collects, a black sooty mold will grow on it. While not a pathogen, it does shade the leaf somewhat.

Beetles that are garden pests include the spotted cucumber beetle, striped cucumber beetle, flea beetle, potato beetle, and bean beetle. All of these rogues can riddle leaves with holes, and the larval stage is often as damaging as a root worm. The sneakiest of the bunch is the flea beetle. Chances are you won't even catch this one in the act unless you find some of the larvae. The adults are very active, and before you know it your mustard greens (they love bok choy and mizuna, too) are riddled with small holes. Lady beetles are, of course, good guys and should be encouraged. If you have good populations of lady beetles working on aphids in the garden, try a high-pressure water spray to reduce the number of aphids and let the lady beetles clean them up.

Caterpillars often chew up plants in the garden before we can catch them. For one thing, they are difficult to see when they're small, and by the time they've become 3-inch tomato hornworms it's too late to spray. Fortunately, most of these caterpillars can be controlled with a nontoxic biological spray called *Bacillus thuringiensis* (Bt). They eat the spray preparation, become sick almost immediately, and stop feeding. Within a week they're dead. This isn't the quick response we have come to expect from pesticides, but it is often more effective. Since these biological preparations are sensitive to UV light, it is important to spray them in late afternoon or evening. While this spray is effective for most caterpillars like hornworms, cabbage loopers, fruit worms, and others, it won't do the job on cutworms. Sure, it will kill them—but not before they have already done their damage the first night after transplanting. Physical barriers are the key here. Wax paper or aluminum foil collars that extend several inches up the stem and an inch or so into the soil will keep them away from tender transplants until they become too tough to cut off. Milk cartons, etc., have also done the job.

Leaf miners are often more unsightly than damaging, but they do build up on tomato leaves to the point that the leaf is barely able to function. The leaf miner is the larva of a small fly and the key to control is killing the adult. Once the larva is safely between the cell layers of the leaf, it is well protected. If you just have a few squiggly lines on the lower leaves, pick them off and then begin a spray program. Even insecticidal soaps should work if you are persistent. This may involve spraying twice a week for several weeks.

Pill bugs, slugs, and snails are often devastating to young plants, and even more mature plants are sometimes damaged. Be sure if you use a slug and snail bait that it is labeled for the vegetable garden. Some are for use around ornamentals only. Traps may be your best bet. These pests really are attracted to beer and grapefruit halves. They will also hide under a board placed in the garden. Pluck them from under the board, drop them into a can of chemical fertilizer, and watch them dissolve. A dusting of wood ashes seems to get in the gears of pill bugs and the ashes provide some potash fertilizer at the same time.

Whiteflies weren't even a garden nuisance 10 years ago, and they are still not a major pest for most home gardeners. The virulent sweet potato or poinsettia whitefly gives us reason to be concerned. This pest has been devastating to commercial lettuce, cucurbits, tomatoes, etc. It is hard to control with chemical pesticides and rapidly develops resistance to even the most toxic of these chemicals. Beneficials offer some promise, at least in the greenhouse, but even the encarsia parasite doesn't reproduce on this variation of the whitefly. Early detection and spraying with a recommended insecticide (including insecticidal soaps, sabadilla, or permethrin) should keep them from reaching damaging population levels in the home garden.

Diseases, Too

Fungal leaf spots including early blight, septoria leaf spot, downy, and powdery mildew are common in the garden. Early blight can be one of the most devastating. After tomato plants have been in the ground a month or so, you'll begin to notice a few yellow leaves near the bottom of the plants, then suddenly the foliage quickly turns from yellow to brown and the disease rapidly moves up the plant. By the time you notice the problem, find out what's happening, and decide to spray, you may not have much left to save. That's the trouble with most diseases. It's best to prevent them rather than to try to cure the infection once it's marching through your garden.

If you'll spray fungicides early in the season, from the time you first set out transplants, making sure to cover the underside of the leaves as well as the tops, chances are as the fruit begins to size up you can stop spraying as you approach harvest time.

Fruit rots include those caused by fungal and bacterial diseases, plus a common malady known as blossom end rot, which isn't caused by a disease organism at all. Most fruit rots can be eliminated by growing the plants in cages, up on trellises, or by using mulches. Wider spacing, in the case of Choanephora Fruit Rot on squash, is often adequate, though a preventative fungicide spray may be necessary to prevent this disease in wet years. It starts as a black whiskery growth on the decaying petals after bloom, and if you only have a few plants, careful removal of the shriveled petals after the flowers close will also reduce infection.

Blossom end rot appears as a black sunken area at the bottom, or blossom end, of the fruit. It is caused by uneven water availability and is a particular problem with tomatoes. Plant your tomatoes high on ridges or in raised beds, and mulch to conserve water during dry periods. Container-grown plants are especially susceptible because they can dry out so rapidly. Adequate calcium nutrition seems to reduce the problem. Calcium nitrate fertilizer can be used to side dress plants (try a tablespoon per foot of row) and CaCl solutions are sometimes sold for use as a foliar spray.

Viral diseases seem to be getting worse. Plants appear stunted, sometimes curled, twisted, or with shoestring-like growths at the end of leaves. They may also be a mottled yellow, and the fruit is typically distorted or off-color. Once the virus is in the plant, either transmitted by insect vectors or mechanically (by working with an infected plant followed by a healthy one), it is there for good and it's best to remove the plant as soon as you suspect the virus has infected it. Covering the plant or the entire row with fiber row cover early in the season can help exclude insects that transmit viruses, and insecticidal sprays will reduce insect populations that can spread the disease. There is also some resistance in tomatoes and most recently in squash, but this is only resistance, not immunity. The resistance also is limited to one or a few virus diseases (i.e., tobacco mosaic virus, or TMV), and thus another virus like the tomato spotted wilt virus could still ruin your crop.

Wilt diseases are especially frustrating because they don't show up until late in the season and are terminal. Sometimes the organism plugs up the vascular tissue, as with fusarium wilt, or the stem may be girdled at the soil line with the Southern blight fungus. In the case of fusarium there is widespread resistance in tomatoes and to a limited degree in other crops. Southern blight is particularly bad because it is also successful at decaying organic matter. Deep plowing helps in the field; crop rotation and soil fungicides are your best bet in the home garden.

Weeds

Nutsedge, in particular the purple variety, is a common thorn in the Southern gardener's side. Weed control chemicals won't work in the small garden, so hand pulling, hoeing, and mulching are the answers. Mulching is the best of the three. Try putting down a layer of newspapers 8 to 10 sheets thick between the rows and then covering this layer with old hay or grass clippings to keep the newspapers from drying out and blowing into the neighbors' yards. Also, if you will soak the papers in water before trying to lay them out they will stay put better. Sprinkle a liberal amount of nitrogen fertilizer over the paper before you cover it so that it will rot by the end of the season. You'll be adding more organic matter each season. The nutsedge, nutgrass, will get through this mulch eventually, but your crops will be up and producing first. Solarization will also help, but the nutlets of purple nutsedge are tough.

Bermuda grass can be almost as bad as nutsedge, but you can get a better kill with solarization or by pretreating with glyphosate the season before you plant. If your soil is loose and organic, all these weeds are comparatively easy to pull out. Once again, the newspaper mulch helps (and it is a great way to get rid of newspapers!).

Biological Control of Garden Pests

It's often true that the vegetable patch is full of pests constantly trying to destroy the garden you've created. Fortunately, nature has provided us with all sorts of checks and balances to help keep the pests under control.

Most notably, there are beneficial insects that spend the day destroying and eating many garden pests. Beneficial insects can be ordered from many sources and released in your garden. Don't forget, though, that they are also present naturally. By allowing your naturally occurring beneficials to thrive, you'll greatly reduce the need for pesticides (whether chemical or organic).

This can be accomplished by the carefully planned use of pesticides (again, used only when absolutely necessary) that don't impact the beneficials you're trying to protect. You can also plant trap crops to attract the food needed for the good guys. For example, curly mustard, a favorite of aphids, can be used to build up lady beetles or the lacewing population; then it can be destroyed, mowed, or hoed so that the beneficials can move into the rest of your garden.

Remember, most beneficial insects are mobile and, short of screening your garden, there's not much you can do to keep the good guys from moving on.

Knowing Your Garden Good Guys

Trichogramma Wasp is a very tiny 1/25-inch insect that attacks more than 200 different pests. This tiny wasp will never be noticed in the garden, but it's out there working. Avoid sprays containing pyrethrum and using bug zappers. They are both death to the tiny wasp.

Praying Mantids are only a minor benefit to the gardener. They are cannibalistic, feeding heavily on their own kind even as the egg mass begins to hatch, so very few survive. Those that do survive prefer large, slow prey like crickets, bees, and grasshoppers, which are only minor garden problems, or are beneficial.

Lady beetles are brightly colored and queens of the garden, spending their time devouring aphids, scale, and insect eggs. If you decide to purchase a few lady beetles, wait until aphids are around and then release the lady beetles into cages placed over aphid–infested plants. Otherwise, most will fly off before you get the benefit.

Assassin bugs and Wheel bugs are large, ferocious-looking insects with long beaks that are used to spear caterpillars and other soft-bodied insects to suck the juice out. The assassin bug has been known to give gardeners a nasty bite, so leave this one alone.

Parasitic Nematodes are microscopic roundworms and a lot like the bad nematodes, except that they feed on insect larva, soft-bodied insects, and almost any living thing found in the soil. This is one insect that might be good to introduce into your garden. They are purchased by the millions. You'll need about 5 million per 300 square feet of garden.

Bacillus thuringiensis is a natural bacteria that, when ingested by most caterpillars, causes them to stop feeding and die. The San Diego strain of Bt will also control very young Colorado potato beetle larvae. Bt is sold under a number of product names (Bio Worm Killer, Thuricide, Dipel, and others) and is very safe.

Botanical Sprays

These are plant-derived extracts that have proven to have insecticidal properties. Some are very safe, while others should not be used even though they are considered organic.

Pyrethrum is derived from the flowers of several chrysanthemum species. It causes rapid paralysis of most insects and when used in combination with other products can be an excellent, safe, insecticide. **Caution:** some people have allergic reactions to this material.

Nicotine sulfate is a highly toxic extract from tobacco, used to control sucking insects. Most chemical insecticides are less toxic than this one.

Sabadilla is obtained from the seed of a lily-like plant that works as both a contact and stomach poison for a wide variety of insects. Not particularly toxic to mammals, but the dust can irritate the eyes and respiratory tract. A mask should be worn when using this insecticide.

Rotenone is derived from the roots of derris plants from Asia, and cube plants from South America. Highly toxic to fish and insects. Wear a mask because dust can irritate the respiratory system.

Ryania comes from the stems of a woody South American shrub. It is a stomach poison that is moderately toxic and controls a wide range of insects.

Chemical Conversions

When using a pesticide (whether organic or chemical), it's important to read the label and follow it to the letter. It's often difficult to calculate the proper rates to use. The following tables will help you with this task.

CONVERSION EQUATIONS

LIQUID	1 level tablespoon = 3 level teaspoons
	1 fluid ounce = 2 tablespoons, or 29.57 milliliters
	1 cup = 8 fluid ounces
	1 pint = 2 cups = 16 fluid ounces
	1 quart = 2 pints = 32 fluid ounces
	1 gallon = 4 quarts = 128 fluid ounces
WEIGHT	1 ounce = 28.3 grams
	1 pound = 16 ounces = 454 grams

WETTABLE POWDERS

(Number of ounces of wettable powder to use in small sprayers when amount per 100 gallons is known. A small postal scale can be used to weigh out wettable powders.)

100 Gallons	10 Gallons	5 Gallons	2 Gallons	1 Gallon
4 ounces	0.4 ounce	0.2 ounce	0.1 ounce	—
8 ounces	0.8 ounce	0.4 ounce	0.2 ounce	0.1 ounce
1 pound	1.6 ounces	0.8 ounce	0.3 ounce	0.2 ounce
2 pounds	3.2 ounces	1.6 ounces	0.6 ounce	0.3 ounce
3 pounds	4.8 ounces	2.4 ounces	1 ounce	0.5 ounce
4 pounds	6.4 ounces	3.2 ounces	1.3 ounces	0.6 ounce
5 pounds	8 ounces	4 ounces	1.6 ounces	0.8 ounce

LIQUID CONCENTRATES

(Number of fluid ounces of liquid concentrates to use in small sprayers when amount per 100 gallons is known.)

100 Gallons	10 Gallons	5 Gallons	2 Gallons	1 Gallons
1 pint	1.6 fluid ounces	0.8 fluid ounce	0.3 fluid ounce	0.2 fluid ounce
1 quart	3.2 fluid ounces	1.6 fluid ounces	0.7 fluid ounce	0.3 fluid ounce
2 quarts	6.4 fluid ounces	3.2 fluid ounces	1.3 fluid ounces	0.6 fluid ounce
1 gallon	12.8 fluid ounces	6.4 fluid ounces	2.6 fluid ounces	1.3 fluid ounces

VEGETABLE DISEASE CONTROL GUIDE

Vegetable / Disease Problem	Chemical and Organic Fungicides (See Key for Names of Applications)											
	1	2	3	4	5	6	7	8	9	10	11	12
Asparagus												
Crown Rot				•								
Leaf Spot				•								
Rust				•								
Beans (All types)												
Anthracnose		•		•								•
Bacterial Blight			•						•			
Damping Off						•						
Fungal Blight		•		•								
Mildews		•		•					•			
Molds	•						•			•		
Rust		•										
Beets												
Downy Mildew			•								•	
Carrots												
Leaf Spots		•	•	•						•		
Mildews								•				
Celery												
Blights	•	•	•	•						•		
Corn												
Leaf Blights		•		•	•							
Rust		•										
Crucifers: Broccoli, Brussels Sprouts, Cabbage, Cauliflower, Collards, Turnips, Mustard, Kohlrabi, Etc.												
Black Rot		•										
Club Root						•						
Leaf Spot		•	•	•								
Mildews		•	•	•				•		•		
Cucurbits: Cantaloupes, Cucumbers, Melons, Pumpkins, Squashes												
Anthracnose	•	•	•	•								•
Downy Mildew		•	•	•						•	•	

Vegetable / Disease Problem	Chemical and Organic Fungicides (See Key for Names of Applications)											
	1	2	3	4	5	6	7	8	9	10	11	12
Leaf Spot		•	•	•								•
Powdery Mildew									•	•	•	
Eggplant												
Anthracnose			•	•						•		
Fruit Rot			•	•						•		
Leaf Spot			•	•						•		
Lettuce and Endive												
Anthracnose				•								
Downy Mildew			•	•								
Leaf Spot				•								
Onions (Garlic, Shallots, Leeks)												
Downy Mildew		•	•		•							
Gray Mold		•										
Purple Blotch		•	•		•							
Peas (Southern)												
Anthracnose		•										
Downy Mildew		•										
Leaf Spot		•										
Powdery Mildew			•					•				
Rust		•										
Peppers												
Anthracnose				•								
Bacterial Leaf Spot			•	•						•		
Fungal Leaf Spot				•								
Southern Blight							•					
Potato (Irish)												
Blights		•	•	•	•	•				•		
Stem Rot							•					
Spinach												
Anthracnose				•						•		
Downy Mildew				•						•		
Leaf Spot				•						•		
Rust				•						•		
Tomato												
Anthracnose		•		•	•							•
Bacterial Spot			•							•		
Blights		•	•	•	•					•		•
Fruit Rots		•										
Gray Mold	•	•		•						•		•
Leaf Spots	•	•		•	•							•
Southern Blight							•					

Key

1 = Benomyl (Benlate)
2 = Chlorothalonil (Daconil, Bravo)
3 = Copper Hydroxide (Kocide 101, Champion)
4 = Copper Sulfate (Basicop)
5 = Mancozeb (Dithane, Manzate 200)
6 = Maneb (Maneb 80)
7 = PCNB (Terraclor)
8 = Sulfur (several formulations)
9 = Triadimefon (Bayleton)
10 = Tribasic Copper Sulfate + Sulfur (Topcop)
11 = Triophanate Methyl (Topsin M)
12 = Ziram (Ziram)

Whenever selecting a pesticide for controlling a disease or insect problem, always read and follow the label directions completely.

VEGETABLE INSECT CONTROL GUIDE

Chemical and Organic Insecticides
(See Key for Insecticide Names)

Vegetable / Insect Problem	1	2	3	4	5	6	7	8	9	10	11	12	13	14	15	16	17	18	19	20	21
Asparagus																					
Aphids		•			•							•	•	•				•	•	•	•
Beetles		•								•			•	•	•			•	•	•	•
Caterpillars, Worms	•	•											•	•	•			•	•		•
Slugs, Snails											•										
Beans (All Types)																					
Aphids		•		•	•			•	•	•		•	•	•	•	•		•	•	•	•
Beetles, Weevils		•		•				•	•				•	•	•	•		•	•	•	•
Caterpillars, Worms	•	•		•				•		•			•	•	•	•		•	•	•	•
Slugs, Snails											•										
Spider Mites				•	•	•		•	•	•		•	•	•	•	•		•	•	•	•
Stinkbugs		•		•				•					•	•	•	•		•			
Beets																					
Beetles	•									•			•		•						
Caterpillars, Worms		•								•			•	•	•						
Slugs, Snails																		•			
Carrots																					
Beetles				•						•					•						
Caterpillars, Worms	•	•		•						•			•		•						
Leafhoppers		•								•			•								
Slugs, Snails		•								•			•			•		•			
Celery																					
Aphids										•			•								
Beetles										•			•								
Caterpillars, Worms										•			•								
Slugs, Snails											•										

	1	2	3	4	5	6	7	8	9	10	11	12	13	14	15	16	17	18	19	20	21
Corn																					
Aphids		•		•	•		•	•	•	•		•	•	•							
Caterpillars, Worms	•	•		•									•	•							
Slugs, Snails					•						•							•			
Crucifers: Broccoli, Brussels Sprouts, Cabbage, Cauliflower, Collards, Turnips, Mustard, Kohlrabi, Etc.																					
Aphids		•		•	•		•	•	•	•		•	•	•					•		•
Caterpillars, Worms	•	•	•	•									•	•	•						
Slugs, Snails		•		•	•						•							•			
Stinkbugs													•			•					
Cucumbers, Pumpkins, Squashes																					
Aphids		•		•	•		•	•	•	•		•	•	•	•						
Beetles		•	•	•					•	•			•	•	•					•	
Slugs, Snails					•						•							•			
Spider Mites				•	•	•	•			•				•			•				
Stinkbugs		•		•					•	•			•	•	•						
Vine Borers	•			•									•								
Eggplant																					
Aphids		•		•	•		•	•	•	•		•	•	•	•						
Beetles		•	•	•					•	•			•	•	•					•	
Spider Mites				•	•	•	•			•				•			•				
Stinkbugs		•		•					•	•			•	•	•						

Key to insecticide numbers

1 = Bt (Dipel, Bio worm Killer, Thuricide, Biobit)
2 = Carbaryl (Sevin)
3 = Chlorpyrifos (Lorsban)
4 = Diazinon
5 = Insecticidal soap
6 = Dicofol (Kelthane)
7 = Dimethoate (Cygon)
8 = Disulfoton (Disyston)
9 = Endosulfan (Thiodan)
10 = Malathion (Cython)
11 = Metaldehyde
12 = Nicotinsulfate (Black Leaf 40)
13 = Permethrin (Ambush, Pounce)
14 = Pyrethrins (Pyrenone, Pyrelin)
15 = Rotenone
16 = Sabadilla
17 = Sulfur
18 = Carbaryl + Metaldehyde
19 = Pyrethrins + Insecticidal soap
20 = Methoxychlor + Rotenone
21 = Rotenone + Pyrethrins

VEGETABLE INSECT CONTROL GUIDE (CONT.)

Chemical and Organic Insecticides
(See Key for Insecticide Names)

Vegetable / Insect Problem	1	2	3	4	5	6	7	8	9	10	11	12	13	14	15	16	17	18	19	20	21
Lettuces and Endive																					
Aphids		●		●	●		●		●	●			●		●	●		●			●
Beetles		●		●	●				●	●			●		●	●					●
Caterpillars, Worms	●			●	●				●						●	●		●			●
Slugs, Snails																					
Spider Mites				●	●		●		●	●			●		●	●		●			
Onions (Garlic, Shallots, Leeks)																					
Caterpillars, Worms	●			●					●	●			●	●	●			●	●		●
Root Maggots				●									●	●	●						●
Slugs, Snails				●							●										
Thrips				●									●	●							
Peas (Southern)																					
Aphids		●			●		●		●	●		●	●		●						
Beetles, Weevils		●			●		●		●	●		●	●		●		●				
Caterpillars					●		●		●			●	●								
Spider Mites				●	●		●		●	●		●									
Peppers																					
Aphids		●		●	●		●					●	●	●				●	●	●	
Beetles		●		●	●		●	●		●		●	●	●				●	●	●	
Caterpillars, Worms	●	●			●		●					●	●					●	●	●	
Spider Mites					●		●					●		●				●	●	●	
Thrips						●	●						●					●			
Potatoes (Irish)																					
Aphids		●		●					●	●			●	●	●	●		●		●	
Beetles		●		●			●		●				●	●		●	●	●		●	

Caterpillars, Worms
Spider Mites
Wireworms

Spinach
Aphids
Beetles
Caterpillars, Worms
Slugs, Snails
Spider Mites

Tomato
Aphids
Beetles
Caterpillars, Worms
Spider Mites
Stinkbugs
Whitefly

Watermelon, Cantaloupe
Aphids
Beetles
Spider Mites
Stinkbugs
Vine Borers

Key to insecticide numbers

1 = Bt (Dipel, Bio worm Killer, Thurcide, Biobit)
2 = Carbaryl (Sevin)
3 = Chlorpyrifos (Lorsban)
4 = Diazinon
5 = Insecticidal soap
6 = Dicofol (Kelthane)
7 = Dimethoate (Cygon)
8 = Disulfoton (Disyston)

9 = Endosulfan (Thiodan)
10 = Malathion (Cython)
11 = Metaldehyde
12 = Nicotine sulfate (Black Leaf 40)

13 = Permethrin (Ambush, Pounce)
14 = Pyrethrins (Pyrenone, Pyrelin)
15 = Rotenone
16 = Sabadilla

17 = Sulfur
18 = Carbaryl + Metaldaldehyde
19 = Pyrethrins + Insecticidal soap
20 = Methoxychlor + Rotenone
21 = Rotenone + Pyrethrins

Remember, pesticide labeling changes frequently. This table is to be used as a guide. Always read and follow all label instructions.

GARDEN PROBLEMS COMMON TO MANY VEGETABLES

Symptoms	Possible Causes	Controls & Comments
Poor fruit yield; fruit may be small and have poor taste.	• Uneven moisture	• Supply water during dry periods. Use a mulch.
	• Poor soil fertility	• Do a soil test. Increase fertility foliar feed.
	• Improper temperature	• Plant at right time. Check soil temperature.
Plants grow slowly; leaves are light green.	• Insufficient light	• Thin plants; do not plant in shade.
	• Cool weather	
	• Poor soil fertility	• Do a soil test.
	• Improper pH	• Do a soil test.
	• Excess water	• Do not overwater; improve drainage.
Seedlings don't emerge.	• Dry soil	• Supply water. Use row cover.
	• Seeds washed away	
	• Damping off (fungal problem)	• Do not overwater; treat seed with registered fungicide. Allow soil to warm before planting.
	• Incorrect planting depth	
	• Slow germination due to weather	
	• Root maggots	• Use registered soil insecticide.
	• Old seed	• Store seed in a dry, cool place. Use current season's seed.
	• Birds/rodents	• Cover seed bed with row cover or bird net.
Wilted seedlings; seedlings fall over.	• Dry soil	• Supply water.
	• Damping off (fungal disease)	• Do not overwater; treat seed with registered fungicide.
	• Cutworms	• Use registered soil insecticide. Make foil or wax paper collars for young plants.
	• Root maggots	• Use registered soil insecticide.
Chewed seedlings' bottom leaves may turn yellow.	• Rodents, rabbits, or birds	• Fence or cover with bird netting.
	• Various insects	• Use registered insecticide.
	• Dry soil	• Water.
	• Root rot (fungal disease)	• Do not overwater; remove old plant debris; rotate crops.
	• Vascular wilt (fungal disease) mainly affecting: tomatoes, potatoes, eggplant, peppers	• Plant resistant varieties; rotate plant families.
	• Root knot (nematode problem)	• Dry tilling. Plant resistant varieties; rotate; soil solarization.

Symptoms	Possible Causes	Controls & Comments
	• Various root-feeding nematodes	• Dry tilling. Submit soil sample for nematode analysis; soil solarization.
	• Waterlogged soil	• Improve drainage.
General leaf yellowing; no wilting.	• Nutrient or mineral deficiency	• Do a soil test. Foliar application of soluble fertilizer with micronutrients.
	• Insufficient light	• Thin plants; move garden location.
Leaves stippled with tiny white spots.	• Spider mites	• Treat with registered miticide, soap, or water spray.
	• Air pollution (ozone)	
Leaf margins turn brown and shrivel.	• Dry soil	• Supply water.
	• Salt damage	• Do not place garden where de-icing salt may have been applied on nearby concrete.
	• Fertilizer burn	• Do a soil test for soluble salts level; do not over-apply fertilizer; flush soil with water (leach).
	• Potassium deficiency	• Do a soil test; add potassium fertilizer like Kmag or KNO3.
	• Cold injury	• Provide plant protection.
Discrete brown spots on leaves; some spots may coalesce.	• Fungal or bacterial leaf spot disease	• See control under specific disease.
	• Chemical injury	• Do not apply chemicals that are not registered for use on the plant; apply chemicals at registered rates; some chemical injury occurs from drift.
Brown spots at leaf margin.	• Chemical injury	• Don't apply chemicals in the heat of the day or when plants are dry.
White powdery growth on upper leaf surface.	• Powdery mildew (fungal disease)	• Use registered fungicide; plant resistant varieties; increase spacing for better air circulation.
Leaves shredded or stripped.	• Hail damage	
	• Rodents	• Place fence around garden.
	• Slugs	• Use slug bait or commercial bait. Beer traps.
	• Dead tissue dropping out after fungal infection	• Use registered fungicide before problem reaches this stage.
	• Various insects	• Identify insect, then use appropriate insecticide. Wash off insects or remove insects by hand.

continued

Symptoms	Possible Causes	Controls & Comments
Leaves with yellow and green mosaic or mottle pattern; leaves may be puckered and plants stunted.	• Virus disease	• Plant resistant varieties if available; control weeds and insects; remove affected plants; remove old plant debris. Cover plants with row cover to eliminate insect vector.
Leaves curled, puckered, or distorted.	• Herbicide injury (common on tomatoes, cucumbers) • Virus disease • Aphids (insects)	• If lawn herbicides are used, apply after wind has died down. Do not apply in heat of day. • Same controls as above. • Treat plants with registered insecticides; wash off with water; spray with soap.

GARDEN PROBLEMS COMMON TO ASPARAGUS

Tops turn yellow, brown, and die back; reddish brown, orange, or black pustules on stems and leaves.	• Rust (fungal disease)	• Cut tops close to ground in fall and destroy; plant resistant varieties.
Shoots wilt, turn yellow, then brown; roots are reddish color.	• Fusarium wilt (fungal disease) • Root rot (fungal disease)	• Destroy infected plants. Move planting area. • Rotate; remove old plant debris; plant in well-drained area; use registered fungicides.
Small spears.	• Immature plants • Over-harvested plants • Poor fertility • Insufficient dormancy • Poor drainage	• Asparagus produces small spears for the first 2 to 3 years after planting. • Do not harvest late into the season; plants cannot store enough food for the following season. • Do a soil test. Increase nitrogen level. • Use the garden area for something more productive. • Do not overwater; plant in a well-drained area.
Spears crooked.	• Mechanical injury from windblown sand or mishandling • Insect injury	• Use windbreaks. • Minor damage doesn't need control. Control insects with registered insecticide.
Spears turn brown and soft.	• Frost injury • Root rot (fungal disease)	• Protect spears with mulch on nights when cold temperatures are expected. • Remove old plant debris; rotate; plant in well-drained area.

Symptoms	Possible Causes	Controls & Comments
Leaves chewed; slime may be present on leaves; no evidence of insects.	• Slugs (emerge at night and hide during day)	• Use commercial slug bait. Use beer trap.
Spears and leaves chewed or scarred.	• Insects	• Use registered insecticide; minor damage doesn't need control.

GARDEN PROBLEMS COMMON TO BEANS AND SOUTHERN PEAS

Symptoms	Possible Causes	Controls & Comments
Plants wilt or are stunted; leaves may turn yellow.	• Wet soil	• Provide good drainage; do not overwater.
	• Dry soil	• Supply water.
	• Root rot (fungal disease)	• Remove old plant debris; rotate; plant in well-drained area.
	• Knots on roots (nematode problem)	• Rotate; dry tilling; solarization.
	• Poor fertility	• Build up your soil.
Failure to set pods.	• High temperatures, causing blossoms to drop	• Time planting better.
	• Dry soil	• Supply water.
	• Wet soil, causing lack of oxygen to roots	• Do not overwater; plant in well-drained soil.
	• Mature pods left on vines, causing seed production rather than pod set	• Pick pods regularly.
	• Excessive fertilizer and rank growth	• Do not over-fertilize.
Rust-colored powdery spots surrounded by yellow halos on leaves, stems, and pods.	• Rust (fungal disease)	• Plant resistant varieties; remove old plant debris.
Soft, watery spots on leaves, stems, and pods; white moldy growth on these plant parts; plants wilt and die; wilted, water-soaked leaves.	• White mold (fungal disease)	• Use registered fungicide; rotate; remove old plant debris; improve air circulation.
Thin, white, powdery growth on leaves and pods.	• Powdery mildew (fungal disease)	• Plant resistant varieties; rotate; remove old plant debris.
Small, brown spots surrounded by yellow halos on leaves; leaves wither.	• Bacterial blight	• Avoid overhead watering, which spreads the disease; use registered copper bactericide/fungicide.
Brown spots without yellow halos appear on leaves and pods; leaves wither.	• Fungal disease (any of several)	• Submit sample for laboratory diagnosis at state agricultural university.

Symptoms	Possible Causes	Controls & Comments
Leaves chewed.	• Beetles	• Use registered insecticide or remove by hand.
Leaves with shiny white spots.	• Spider mites	• Use registered miticide; high-pressure water sprayer.
Young leaves curled, distorted, and yellow clusters of tiny insects on leaves and stems.	• Aphids	• Use registered insecticide, beneficial insects, or soap.
	• Thrips • Stinkbugs	• Use registered insecticide, remove by hand, or plant trap crop.
Young leaves mottled.	• Viruses	• Plant resistant varieties; remove diseased plants; insect control using row cover.

GARDEN PROBLEMS COMMON TO BEETS

Small, circular spots with light centers and dark borders on leaves.	• Cercospora leaf spot (fungal disease)	• Pick off and destroy affected leaves.
Roots cracked; black areas on surface and inside root; plant stunted.	• Boron deficiency	• Do a soil test; maintain pH between 6 and 7; apply solution of household borax if necessary (1 tablespoon household borax per 12 gallons of water per 100 foot row).
Leaf margins rolled upward; leaves brittle and puckered along veins; plants stunted.	• Virus disease	• Control leafhoppers that spread the disease; weed control. Remove and destroy affected plant.
Misshapen roots.	• Overcrowding	• Thin beets early.
Cracked roots.	• Improper watering	• Maintain even soil moisture and use mulches.
Leaves with many small holes.	• Flea beetles	• Treat early with registered insecticide.
Root scarred or tunneled.	• Root maggots, weevils	• Destroy infected plants; next year, work in registered soil insecticide when preparing soil. Practice crop rotation.
Beets hard.	• Over-mature	• Harvest at proper time.

GARDEN PROBLEMS COMMON TO CARROTS

Brown spots on leaves; spots may also appear on roots.	• Leaf blight	• Apply registered fungicide; practice crop rotation.
Inner leaves yellowed; outer leaves reddish purple; roots stunted and bitter.	• Aster yellows (mycoplasma disease)	• Remove affected plants; weed control; leafhopper control with registered insecticide. Use resistant varieties.
Root tops green.	• Root tops exposed to sunlight	• Cover exposed roots with soil or mulch.

Symptoms	Possible Causes	Controls & Comments
Roots misshapen; split tunneled.	• Overcrowding • Root knot (nematode problem) • Wireworms	• Thin carrots early. • Rotate; plant Elbon rye. • Dry tilling; solarization.
Plants stunted and yellowed; roots misshapen; small knots on fibrous roots.	• Root knot (nematode problem)	• See control above.
Tiny holes on leaves.	• Flea beetles	• Use registered insecticide.
Yellowing of leaves, curling, and stunting.	• Leafhoppers	• Use registered insecticide.

GARDEN PROBLEMS COMMON TO CELERY

Poor growth; stunted plants.		• Not adapted to many areas in the South. Not enough nitrogen; side dress or foliar feed.
Stalks tough and bitter.	• High temperatures • Dry soil • Poor fertility • Over-maturity	• Plant at proper time. • Celery requires high moisture; use mulch. • Increase nitrogen. • Harvest when tender.
Plants stunted and yellowed; stalks twisted and brittle.	• Aster yellows (mycoplasma disease)	• See control under carrots.
Plants wilted; soft, watery rot on leaves and stalks; heart of plant may be black.	• Fungal crown rot • Black heart (due to calcium deficiency)	• Apply registered fungicide; rotate and remove old plant debris. • Calcium deficiency results from uneven water supply or improper pH; water during dry periods; soil test; maintain soil pH between 6.5 and 8.
Blotches or tunnels in leaves.	• Leaf miners	• Remove damaged leaves.
Brown or gray spots on leaves and stalks.	• Fungal leaf spot	• Apply registered fungicide.
Seed stem (bolting).	• Physiological disorder	• Plant in fall.

GARDEN PROBLEMS COMMON TO COLE CROPS: CABBAGE, BROCCOLI, TURNIPS, CAULIFLOWER, BRUSSELS SPROUTS, COLLARDS, KALE AND MUSTARD

Cracking of cabbage heads.	• Excess water taken up by plant causes head to burst. • Variety	• Harvest heads as soon as mature. • Avoid overwater after period of drought. • Plant recommended varieties.

continued

Symptoms	Possible Causes	Controls & Comments
Poor heading.	• Overcrowding • Dry soil • High temperatures • Poor fertility • Root knot (nematode problem) • Root rot (fungal disease)	• Thin plants early. • Supply water. • Plant at proper time. • Increase nitrogen. • Check roots for knots; rotate; solarization. • Rotate; remove old plant debris; plant in well-drained soil.
Discolored cauliflower head.	• Exposure to sun • Boron deficiencies	• Blanch by tieing leaves over head when heads begin to form. • See control under beets.
Brown spots on leaves.	• Alternaria leaf spot (fungus)	• Apply registered fungicide.
V-shaped lesions on leaf margin.	• Blackrot (bacteria)	• Practice crop rotation; plant resistant varieties.
Plants wilt and turn yellow; roots are discolored and poorly developed; roots may be hard and brittle.	• Blackleg (fungal disease) • Wirestem (fungal disease) • Cabbage maggot	• Use western grown hot-water-treated seed; rotate crops. • Remove old plant debris. • Work in a registered soil insecticide at planting time. Rotate crops.
Gray, powdery growth on lower leaf margin.	• Downy mildew	• Use registered fungicide and resistant varieties.
Plants stunted and yellowed (especially cabbage, cabbage roots not discolored).	• Dry soil • Poor fertility • Fusarium yellows (fungal disease) • Cabbage maggot	• Supply water. • Increase fertility. • Plant resistant varieties; rotate. • Work in a soil insecticide at planting time.
Head soft and rotted.	• Soft rot of cabbage, broccoli, mustard (bacteria disease)	• Rotate; plant in well-drained soil; provide good air circulation.
Rough, brown, raised areas on under surface of leaves.	• Oedema, physiological problem due to uneven water supply	• Maintain adequate soil moisture. Use mulches.
Leaves riddled with shotholes.	• Flea beetles	• Use registered insecticide.
Leaves chewed.	• Imported cabbage worm, cabbage looper, diamondback moth	• Identify insect; use registered biological sprays with Bt.
Some leaves curled and yellowed; shriveled or deformed plants.	• Aphids • Harlequin bugs	• Use registered insecticide. Hand removal, and catch crop.
Bolting.	• Physiological disorder	• Plant at right time; plant recommended varieties.

GARDEN PROBLEMS COMMON TO CORN

Symptoms	Possible Causes	Controls & Comments
Ears not completely filled with kernels.	• Poor pollination • Birds • Low soil moisture	• Plant in blocks of at least 3 to 4 rows; hand pollinate. • Put paper bag over ear after pollination. • Uniform soil moisture.
White smooth or black powdery galls on stalk, leaves, ears, or tassels.	• Smut (fungal disease)	• Cut off galls before they turn black; remove old plant debris; plant tolerant varieties.
Brown lesions on stalks near joints; stalks rotted inside; kernels pink or moldy.	• Fungal stalk and ear rot (any of several)	• Remove old plant debris; maintain uniform soil moisture.
Yellowish or tan elliptical spots on lower leaves first and older leaves later.	• Northern and Southern corn leaf blight	• Plant resistant varieties; apply registered fungicide.
Plants stunted with yellow and green stripe or mosaic pattern; older leaves pale yellow.	• Maize dwarf mosaic (virus disease)	• Weed control, especially Johnson grass; aphid control; destroy affected plants; do not handle healthy plants after affected ones. Plant resistant varieties.
Small pustules containing rust-colored powdery substance on leaves.	• Rust (fungal disease)	• Plant resistant varieties; remove old plant debris.
Leaves reddish on margins.	• Phosphorus deficiency • Corn stunt	• Add phosphorus. • Weed control before corn emerges; aphid control; remove affected plants.
Distorted leaf of stalk: leaves may fail to unfurl or stalk may be bent.	• Herbicide injury • Cold weather • Aphids	• Plant at proper time. • Use registered insecticide. Hard-water spray and soap.
Worm(s) feed on the tip of the ear.	• Corn ear worms	• Apply registered insecticide during silking to prevent infestation. Use biological insecticide like Bt or corn oil.
Young plants may be chewed off at ground level.	• Cutworms	• Use registered insecticide.

GARDEN PROBLEMS COMMON TO CUCURBITS: CUCUMBERS, CANTALOUPES, PUMPKINS, SQUASHES, WATERMELONS, GOURDS

Poor fruit set.	• Lack of pollination	• Be patient; male and female flowers are not produced at the same time at first; bee activity may be low due to cool weather or use of insecticides; spray insecticides in late afternoon to protect bees.

Symptoms	Possible Causes	Controls & Comments
Misshapen or bitter fruit.	• Inadequate pollination • High temperatures • Dry soil • Poor soil fertility • Stress due to slow growth	• See above for no fruit produced. • Supply water. • Build up soil fertility.
Water soaked, sunken, brown or black spot at blossom end of watermelon fruit.	• Uneven soil moisture • Blossom-end rot	• Water during dry periods. • Mulch; remove affected fruit.
Water soaked, sunken, brown or black spot on fruit, not restricted to blossom end.	• Belly rot	• Rotate; improve drainage; mulch.
Wilted plants.	• Dry soil • Root rot (fungal disease) • Fusarium wilt (fungal disease) • Root knot (nematode problem)	• Supply water. • Improve drainage; rotate. • Plant resistant varieties; rotate. • Solarization, dry tilling, rotation.
Wilted plants; larva in stems.	• Vine borers	• Use registered insecticide; place soil over stem for more rooting; remove and kill bores.
Leaves with tiny white dots.	• Spider mites	• Use registered miticide, high-pressure water spray, or soap.
Circular or irregular brown spots on leaves and/or fruit.	• Fungal diseases (any of several)	• Apply registered fungicide; rotate crop; practice clean culture by removing debris.
White, powdery growth on leaves; may be on both leaf surfaces.	• Powdery mildew (fungal disease)	• Plant resistant varieties; use registered fungicide; remove old plant debris.
Yellow spots on upper leaf surfaces; grayish fuzzy growth on underside of spots.	• Downy mildew (fungal disease)	• Plant resistant varieties; use registered fungicide; remove old plant debris.
Yellow and green mottle pattern on leaves; leaves have strapped appearance (i.e., abnormally narrow with leaf veins stretched out at leaf margins so leaves appear feathery); Multicolored fruit.	• Virus disease (several) • Herbicide injury	• Weed control before plants emerge; aphid control; remove affected plants; use floating row cover to protect from virus-transmitting insects. • Do not spray lawn herbicides on hot days; spray after wind has died down.
Holes chewed in leaves and stalks; yellow-green beetles with black stripes or spots.	• Cucumber beetles	• Use registered insecticide. Remove and destroy by hand.

Symptoms	Possible Causes	Controls & Comments
Squash and pumpkin leaves wilt, eventually become black and crisp.	• Squash bugs • Stinkbugs	• Use registered insecticide. • Once populations get out of control, consider removing plants.
Blotches or tunnels in leaves.	• Leaf miners	• Use registered insecticide only when damage is severe.

GARDEN PROBLEMS COMMON TO EGGPLANTS

Leaves with tiny white spots.	• Spider mites	• Use registered miticide, high-pressure water spray or wettable sulfur.
Blossoms drop; no fruit develops.	• Poor pollination due to unfavorable temperatures • Low fertility	• Be patient; fruit will set when temperatures become more favorable. • Increase fertility level.
Plants wilt; bottom leaves may turn yellow.	• Dry soil • Verticillium wilt (fungal disease) • Waterlogged soil • Root knot (nematode)	• Supply water. • Rotate; remove old plant debris. • Improve drainage. • Check roots for knots; rotate; remove old plant debris; solarization and dry tilling.
Plant wilt; bottom leaves may turn yellow; brown discoloration inside stem.	• Verticillium wilt (fungal disease) • Waterlogged soil • Aphids	• Rotate; remove old plant debris. • Improve drainage. • Apply registered insecticide, soap spray, or high-pressure water spray.
Circular or irregular brown spots on leaves and/or fruit.	• Fungal disease (any of several)	• Rotate; remove old plant debris.
Leaves riddled with tiny holes.	• Beetles	• Use registered insecticide.
White fungal growth at the soil line.	• Southern blight (fungus)	• Rotate; remove old plant debris.

GARDEN PROBLEMS COMMON TO LETTUCES

Bolting; may taste bitter.	• Weather too hot	• Lettuce is a cool-season crop; plant early or late to mature during cool weather. Foliar feed for faster more tender growth.
Sunken, water-soaked spots appear on lower leaves, which turn brown and slimy; head turns brown.	• Rhizoctonia bottom rot (fungal disease) • Sclerotinia drop (fungal disease)	• Rotate; remove old plant debris; plant in well-drained area. • Same cultural control as for bottom rot; fungicides are available for Sclerotinia drop.

Symptoms	Possible Causes	Controls & Comments
Sunken, water-soaked spots appear on lower leaves, which turn brown and slimy; head turns brown and slimy; hard black, pea-sized pellets found in mold between dead leaves.	• Sclerotinia drop (fungal disease)	• See above.
Stem and lower leaves rotten; dense, fuzzy gray mold on affected areas.	• Botrytis gray mold (fungal disease)	• Rotate; remove old plant debris; plant in well-drained area. Space out plants for better air circulation.
Yellow or light green blotches on upper leaf surfaces; white, fuzzy mold on underside of blotches; spots eventually turn brown.	• Downy mildew (fungal disease)	• Rotate; use registered fungicide.
Plants stunted, yellowed; youngest leaves curled; head soft.	• Aster yellows (mycoplasma disease)	• Start plants under floating row cover to protect young plants from virus-transmitting insects. Remove affected plants; weed control; insect control.
	• Mosaic virus	• Remove affected plants; weed control; insect control.
	• Nutrient deficiency	• Do a soil test.
Leaf veins and area adjacent to veins turns light yellow causing a "big vein" effect.	• Big vein (viroid disease)	• Plant in well-drained soil: viroid (virus-like particle) is spread by a soil fungus; remove affected plants; rotate planting area.
Wilted plants.	• Aphids	• Use registered insecticide, soap, or high-pressure water spray.
Holes in leaves.	• Cabbage loopers and other caterpillars	• Use registered insecticide. Remove by hand or use biological insecticide like Bt.
	• Flea beetles	• Use registered insecticide.

GARDEN PROBLEMS COMMON TO ONIONS

Water-soaked spots appear on leaves and rapidly turn brown; spots become purplish with a dark margin and surrounded with a yellow zone; spots become covered with brown, dusty mold in moist weather.	• Purple blotch (fungal disease)	• Use registered fungicide; rotate.
Numerous small white flecks on leaves; leaves die from tips back and turn brown.	• Botrytis blast (fungal disease)	• Use registered fungicide.
	• Downy mildew (fungal disease)	• Use registered fungicide.

Symptoms	Possible Causes	Controls & Comments
White flecks form on leaves and expand onto elongated leaf leasions; white to purplish mold develops on spots during moist weather; leaves drop over and dry up.	• Downy mildew (fungal disease)	• Rotate; use registered fungicide.
Leaves yellow and die back from tips; bulbs are soft and rotted.	• Fungal or bacterial bulb rot (any of several)	• Rotate; remove old plant debris; plant in well-drained soil.
Stunted plants, pink roots.	• Pink root	• Plant resistant varieties; rotate. Start your own plants.
White streaks or blotches on leaves.	• Onion thrips	• Use registered insecticide or soap.
Failure to bulb.	• Improper day length • Weather factor caused by cold winter and large plants	• Plant at right time. • Use recommended varieties; plant at right time; don't set out plants in the fall.

GARDEN PROBLEMS COMMON TO PEAS (GREEN AND EDIBLE)

Symptoms	Possible Causes	Controls & Comments
Plants stop producing peas; leaves turn yellow, then brown, and die.	• Hot weather	• Peas are cool-season vegetables—plant early in spring or late summer; plant heat-resistant varieties.
	• Root rot (several fungi) • Fusarium wilt (fungal disease)	• Rotate; plant in well-drained soil; remove old plant debris. • Plant resistant varieties; rotate; remove old plant debris.
Plants stunted; lower leaves yellow; internal stem tissue discolored brown.	• Fusarium wilt (fungal disease) • Waterlogged soil	• Plant resistant varieties; rotate; remove old plant debris. • Improve drainage.
White, powdery mold develops on upper and lower surfaces of leaves; leaves and pods may be distorted.	• Powdery mildew (fungal disease)	• Rotate; remove old plant debris. Plant resistant varieties.
Yellow or green mottle or mosaic pattern on leaves; plants stunted.	• Virus disease (any of several)	• Plant resistant varieties; weed control; insect control.
Small chlorotic spots.	• Stinkbugs	• Use recommended insecticide. Remove by hand.
Leaves with tiny white spots.	• Spider mites	• Use recommended miticide, soap, or high-pressure water spray.

GARDEN PROBLEMS COMMON TO PEPPERS

Symptoms	Possible Causes	Controls & Comments
Plants fail to set fruit.	• Weather, variety	• Always use transplants; use recommended varieties; wait for warm temperatures.
Large, sunken, tan, water-soaked spot develops on blossom end of fruit; spot turns black and mold may grow on surface.	• Blossom-end rot	• A problem when developing fruits received uneven moisture supply; water during dry periods; mulch. Apply a source of calcium like calcium nitrate—1 tablespoon per foot of row.
Thin, wrinkled, tan areas develop on fruit and fruit becomes white and papery.	• Sunscald	• Control leaf diseases with registered pesticides to prevent leaf drop, which exposes fruit to sun. Plant vigorous varieties.
Small, tan to dark brown spots develop on leaves; small brown, dry, raised spots appear on fruit.	• Bacterial spot	• Use registered copper bactericide/fungicide.
Tiny, brown specks with pale white halos develop on fruit; fruit may be distorted around specks.	• Stinkbug injury	• Use registered insecticide.
Round, brown spots on leaves with yellow halo.	• Fungal disease (any of several)	• Use registered copper bactericide; fungicide.
Plants stunted; leaves curled with yellow and green mottle. Fruit misshapen with brown streaks; rings; or yellow, green, and red mottle.	• Virus disease (any of several)	• Plant resistant varieties; weed control; insect control; remove old plant debris.
Plants wilted; dark brown canker at base of stem.	• Phytophthora (fungus)	• Improve drainage.
Plants wilted; dark brown canker at base of stem; small, hard, brown pellets form on soil and on rotted plant tissue.	• Southern blight (fungal disease)	• Rotate; remove old plant debris.
Plants wilt; lower leaves may turn yellow.	• Fungal or bacterial vascular wilt disease • Dry soil • Waterlogged soil • Root rot (fungal disease)	• Rotate; remove old plant debris. • Irrigate. • Improve drainage. • Rotate; remove old plant debris; plant in well-drained soil.
Trails, tunnels in leaves.	• Leaf miners	• Treat with registered insecticide only if infestation is severe.

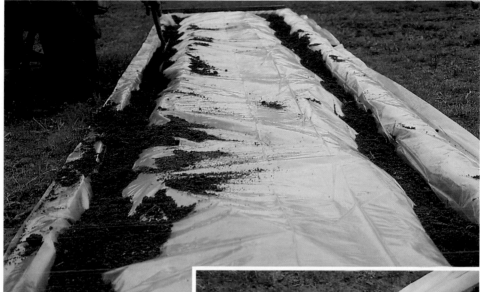

Solarization of soil.

Row cover attached to one side of bed filled with lettuce.

Leaf-footed stinkbug.

Stinkbug damage.

Wheel bug.

Tomato hornworm.

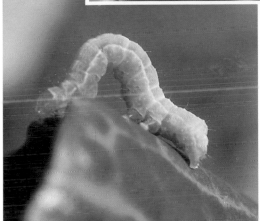

Cabbage looper.

Red aphids on a tomato leaf.

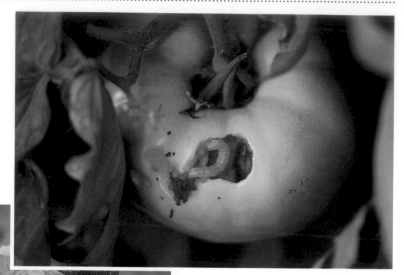

Tomato fruit worm.

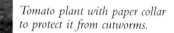

*Tomato plant with paper collar
to protect it from cutworms.*

Early tomato blight.

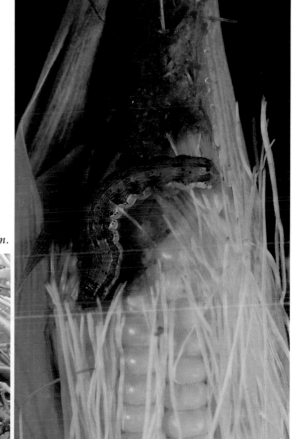

Corn ear worm.

Nematode-damaged bean roots.

Powdery mildew on cabbage leaf.

Downy mildew on sugar snap beans.

Whiteflies on eggplant foliage.

Above: Squash vine borer.
Right: Fruit rot on
untrellised cantaloupe.

Tobacco mosaic virus on squash.

Aphid.

Spotted cucumber beetle.

Flea beetle.

Tomato with fusarium wilt.

Spider mite.

Thrip.

Leaf miner.

Uncontrolled purple nutsedge.

GARDEN PROBLEMS COMMON TO POTATOES

Symptoms	Possible Causes	Controls & Comments
Potato tuber is green.	• Exposure to sun	• Mound soil up around plants; mulch; do not eat green part of potato tuber.
Brown spots on leaves and/or stem.	• Early blight	• Use registered fungicide. Start early before problem becomes severe.
Plants wilt; bottom leaves may turn yellow.	• Dry soil • Fusarium wilt (fungal disease) • Root rot (fungal disease) • Root knot (nematode problem) • Waterlogged soil	• Supply water. • Rotate; remove old plant debris. • Rotate; remove old plant debris; plant in well-drained soil. • Check roots for knots; rotate; dry till; solarization. • Improve drainage.
Plants wilt; dark brown or black canker at base of stem.	• Black leg (bacterial)	• Rotate; improve drainage.
Brown, corky scabs or pits on tubers; plants do not wilt.	• Scab (fungus)	• Do a soil test; acidify soil; maintain pH of 5.0 to 5.5; rotate out of area for 3 to 4 years; use certified seed pieces; avoid using manure.
Plants stunted; leaves turn bronze to yellow color; plants wilt; tubers have raised, knotty areas.	• Root knot (nematode problem)	• Rotate; crop solarization; dry tilling.
Shoot tips stunted, forming rosette; leaves turn yellow, then brown between veins; leaf margins curl upward; individual shoots may wilt; tubers show dark brown discolored ring internally when cut open.	• Ring rot (bacterial disease)	• Discard infected seed potatoes; plant certified disease-free seed pieces.
Tubers show irregular white or brown cavities when cut open.	• Hollow heart, caused by plants growing too rapidly	• Do not over-fertilize or plant too far apart.
Irregular brown discoloration inside tubers.	• Early frost (fall potato) • Drought • Virus disease (any of several)	• Provide crop protection. • Supply water. • Plant tolerant varieties; weed control; insect control.
Tubers have slimy, smelly rot.	• Soft rot (bacterial disease)	• Plant in well-drained soil; hill plants to encourage water runoff; wait until vines turn yellow and die to dig; store properly.

continued

Symptoms	Possible Causes	Controls & Comments
Leaves roll upward; turn light green to yellow and leathery; plants stunted.	• Leaf roll (virus disease)	• Plant certified seed pieces; insect control; weed control.
Leaves roll upward; turn purple or yellow; plants stunted; aerial tubers form.	• Aster yellows (mycoplasma disease)	• Leafhopper control; weed control.
Tunnels bored into tubers; insects feeding on tuber.	• Wireworms • Grubworms • Slugs, pill bugs	• Rotate crop. • Baits; beer traps.
Leaves chewed.	• Colorado potato beetles • Flea beetles	• Use registered insecticide or remove by hand.
Leaves wilted; small chlorotic spots.	• Aphids • Leafhoppers	• Use registered insecticide.
Trails, tunnels in leaves.	• Leaf miners	• Use registered insecticide only where damage is severe.

GARDEN PROBLEMS COMMON TO RADISHES

Roots fail to form.	• Crowded growing conditions	• Thin early to correct spacing—1 to 2 inches.
Yellow spots develop on upper leaf surfaces and later turn brown with bluish black, lace-like markings; white mold develops on undersurface of spots; inner root tissue may be discolored.	• Downy mildew (fungal disease)	• Remove old plant debris; rotate crop.
Purple to black spots develop on root surface; black discoloration extends inward in radial streaks; roots remain firm.	• Black root (fungal disease)	• Plant in well-drained soil; rotate; remove old plant debris.
Knots on roots.	• Nematodes	• Solarization; dry tilling.
Leaves riddled with tiny holes.	• Flea beetles	• Use registered insecticide.
Wilted plants, etc.	• Aphids	• Use registered insecticide, soaps, or hard water spray.
Radishes "hot."	• Over-mature • Variety • Plant stress	• Harvest at early stage. • Some varieties are pungent. • Grow plants quickly under good conditions.

GARDEN PROBLEMS COMMON TO SPINACH

Poor germination, emergence.	• High soil temperature	• Plant at correct time; start under fiber row cover.
Bolting.	• Hot weather and long days	• Spinach is a cool-season crop; plant at right time; use recommended varieties.

Symptoms	Possible Causes	Controls & Comments
Pale yellow spots appear on upper leaf surfaces; grayish purple mold develops on underside of spots; whole leaves may wither.	• Downy mildew (fungal disease)	• Use registered fungicide.
White, blister-like spots with a yellow border appear on underside of leaves; upper surfaces are pale green to yellow.	• White rust (fungal disease)	• Use registered fungicide.
Irregular, tan blotches or tunnels appear on leaves.	• Leafminers • Aphids	• Use registered insecticide only if severe. • Use soap, high-pressure water sprays, or registered insecticide.

GARDEN PROBLEMS COMMON TO SWEET POTATOES

Large cracks in root.	• Growth cracks, caused by moisture extremes • Nematodes	• Supply water during dry period. • Solarization, or dry tilling and rotation.
Brown or black spots on potato skin; discoloration extends beneath skin.	• Black rot	• Use disease-free slips.
Brown, irregular blotches on potatoe skin; discoloration does not extend beneath surface.	• Scurf (fungal disease)	• Three to 4 year rotation; use disease-free slips.
Tunneling in roots.	• Sweet potato weevils • Wireworms	• Use weevil-free slips. • Pull mulch up around the plant.
Small whitefly on leaves.	• Whiteflies	• Use registered insecticide, soaps, or oils.
Plants fail to develop roots.	• Low/high temperatures • Thrips • Variety	• Plant at right time. • Use registered insecticide. • Use recommended varieties.

GARDEN PROBLEMS COMMON TO TOMATOES

Uniformly small (⅛-inch) chocolate brown spots or dark spots with tan centers develop on leaves from bottom of plant to top; spots sometimes form on stems, but never on fruits; leaves shriveled.	• Septoria leaf spot (fungal disease) • Bacterial spot	• Use registered fungicide; remove old plant debris. • Use copper-containing bactericide and disease-free transplants.

Symptoms	Possible Causes	Controls & Comments
Plants yellow from bottom up; dark brown irregular spots with target rings and fruit; spots on fruit are often at stem end and are sunken.	• Early blight • Phoma rot (fungal disease)	• Plant resistant varieties; use registered fungicide; remove old plant debris. • Plant resistant varieties; use registered fungicide; remove old plant debris.
Light tan spots on upper leaf surfaces; dense olive green moldy growth on undersurface of spots.	• Gray leaf mold (fungal disease)	• Mainly a greenhouse problem; provide adequate ventilation to avoid high humidity.
Small (⅛-inch) chocolate brown spots on leaves and fruit; spots on fruits are raised.	• Bacterial spot (bacterial disease)	• Avoid overhead watering; use copper containing bactericide; remove old plant debris; rotate crops.
Very tiny raised specks on fruit; no white halos around spots.	• Bacterial speck (bacterial disease)	• Same controls as for bacterial spot.
Very tiny raised specks surrounded by white halos on fruit; plants wilt; center of stem discolored brown when cut longitudinally.	• Bacterial canker	• Difficult to diagnose without fruit spots; same controls as for bacterial spot and speck.
Brown spots on leaves that do not fit above descriptions.	• Various fungal leaf spots	• Use registered fungicide; avoid overhead watering.
Dark brown, leathery spot on blossom end of fruit only; mold may grow on spot.	• Blossom-end rot	• Supply water during dry periods; maintain soil uniformly moist; mulch; apply calcium nitrate or calcium chloride spray.
Black sunken spots on fruits.	• Alternaria fruit rot (fungus)	• Use registered fungicide; plant resistant varieties.
General browning of tomato skin; brown speckling of walls between seed cavities apparent when fruit is cut open.	• Double streak virus (virus)	• Plant resistant varieties (tobacco mosaic virus); weed control; do not handle healthy plants after diseased ones; remove affected plants.
Extreme malformation and scarring of fruit.	• Catfacing, caused by cool weather during fruit formation	• Plant at proper time.
Yellow-orange blotches that do not ripen at stem end of fruit; white papery spot on side of fruit facing sun.	• Sunscald	• Prevent foliar diseases that cause leaf drop and expose fruits to sun.
Ring spots on foliage; ghost rings on fruit; terminal leaves and whole plants are stunted.	• Tomato spotted wilt	• Insect control; control weeds around garden.
Leaves roll upward, feel leathery, but remain green; plants are not stunted.	• Excess water	• Common physiological disorder after wet periods.

Symptoms	Possible Causes	Controls & Comments
Leaves distorted with "strapped" or feathery look (leaves narrower than normal, tips stretched out into thin projection, veins very close together).	• Herbicide injury	• Do not apply lawn herbicides during hot weather; spray after wind has died down in later afternoon. Check history of hay manure used for mulch.
	• Cucumber mosaic (virus disease)	• It is difficult to distinguish these two problems based on symptoms alone; however, if damage occurs, during spring, when lawn herbicides are being sprayed, strongly suspect herbicide injury; virus is controlled by removing affected plants, weed control, and aphid control; place floating row cover around cages.
Plants wilted; bottom leaves may turn yellow; brown discoloration inside stem.	• Fusarium wilt (fungus) • Waterlogged soil	• Plant resistant varieties; rotate; improve drainage.
Plants stunted, wilted, and yellow; nodules on roots.	• Root knot (nematode problem)	• Rotate; remove old plant debris; solarization; dry tilling; plant resistant varieties.
Young plants cut off at ground level.	• Cutworms	• Use cutworm collars or use registered insecticide.
Young plants with many tiny holes in leaves.	• Beetles	• Tomatoes will tolerate a lot of beetle damage if they are healthy; when necessary, use registered insecticide.
Tiny white-winged insect on undersides of leaves.	• Whiteflies	• Use registered insecticide or sun oil sprays.
Leaves curled, distorted.	• Aphids	• Use registered insecticide, soap, or sun oil sprays.
Trails, tunnels in leaves.	• Leaf miners	• Use registered insecticide only if severe.
Tiny insects on leaves and stem.	• Aphids	• Use registered insecticide, soaps, or sun oil sprays.
Leaves with tiny, white spots.	• Spider mites	• Use registered miticide, soaps, or sun oil sprays.
Leaves stripped from plant; holes in fruit.	• Hornworms	• Use registered insecticide or biological spray like Bt.
	• Fruitworms • Pinworms	• Same as above. • Same as above.
Catfacing, chlorotic spots on fruit.	• Stinkbugs	• Use registered insecticide; hand remove or plant catch crop.
Fruits cracked near stem end.	• Uneven moisture supply	• Maintain uniform moisture; mulch.

Glossary

adventitious buds Buds that arise from an inner cell layer.

agronomic Typically large acreage crops grown less intensively than horticultural crops (i.e., wheat, rice).

allelopathic The ability of one plant to inhibit the growth of other plants.

antidessicant A material sprayed on the foliage to reduce transpiration or water loss.

blanch To exclude from light and reduce the amount of chlorophyll.

blue mold Synonym for downy mildew.

bolt To go to seed.

bud A compact growth unit.

callous potatoes Cut potato surfaces that have developed a layer of protective cell growth.

checking A reduction or slowdown in growth caused by environmental conditions or lack of fertility.

cheese peppers Squashed, pimento-type peppers for fresh use.

clone An identical plant, created by rooting a cutting, grafting, etc.

clove One growth unit of a garlic bulb.

cold frame A low, greenhouse-like enclosement without bottom heating.

complete fertilizer A fertilizer containing nitrogen, phosphorus, and potassium (potash)—in that order.

compost Decomposed organic matter; it should be free from heating, smell good and "earthy," and the original ingredients should be mostly unrecognizable.

cotyledon Seed leaf, most notable as a food storage organ on bean seedlings.

cover crop A crop grown to occupy the garden space, often crowding out weeds and, in the case of legumes, helping to fix nitrogen. When turned under, it becomes "green manure."

crop rotation Not planting the same vegetable in the same place each year. Even different plants from the same family may harbor the same diseases.

crucifer A member of the cabbage/mustard family.

crusting Development of a hard layer on the soil surface.

curd The developing flower parts or head of a cauliflower plant.

damping off Disease complex attacking young seedlings usually associated with cold soils.

decomposition Breakdown of organic matter.

determinate A tomato plant that stops growing, usually at 24 to 30 inches.

full stand (complete stand) Uniform seedling germination.

fungicide A chemical which prevents a fungus from germinating or otherwise entering the host plant tissue.

furrow irrigation Watering by flooding between the garden rows.

furrow The area between the garden row.

gall Plant tissue stimulated by a specific insect attack or in some cases by bacterial or fungal agents.

germination The process of seed sprouting.

gynoecious Plants that produce mostly or only female flowers.

heirloom varieties Ol' Timey varieties often saved by a single family.

herbicide A product used to kill weeds or prevent them from germinating.

humus The liquid element of compost.

hybrid A plant produced by the crossing of two divergent plant breeding lines. For example, one line may have good fruit but lack disease resistance while the other contributes disease resistance and/or other qualities. Typically each line has very uniform genetic characteristics. Extreme vigor (heterosis) is the result. Seedlings from hybrids are extremely variable.

immune "Bullet proof"—can't be infected with the disease, rare.

indeterminate A tomato plant that continues to grow; may eventually reach 8 to 10 feet in height.

inoculate To infect with a disease.

insecticide A material that kills insects.

intensive gardening Using the maximum amount of space available, vertical gardening, close spacing, etc.

integrated pest management Called IPM for short. Long-term focus on the prevention of pests. Involves careful monitoring to determine if damaging levels of a pest are present, use of predators/parasites, resistant varieties, the judicious use of pesticides, and cultural techniques to lessen the damage to the crop.

isolate Distance to prevent cross pollination.

leach To wash out the soil. In containers, it takes about seven pot fillings to cleanse the soil to the level of the water being used for leaching.

legumes Plants in the pea/bean family.

lime Agricultural lime is calcium carbonate, magnesium carbonate, or a combination of the two (dolomitic limestone). Calcium hydroxide or hydrated lime may also be available—it only takes about three-fourths as much of this more readily available form to neutralize soil acidity.

low volume irrigation (micro-irrigation, drip irrigation) Slow release of water close to the root zone, resulting in a more efficient use of the irrigation water.

microorganisms Fungi, bacteria, actinomycetes, mycoplasma, and other microscopic organisms.

monoecious Both male and female flower parts produced on the same plant.

muck soil Highly organic soil.

oedema Small, wartlike (sometimes corky) swellings on the backside of leaves caused by excess water.

onion sets Small onion bulblets.

osmacote (and alternatives) Slow-release fertilizer, may be resin coated as in the case of Osmacote, or the fertilizer may be a slowly available form.

parthenocarpic Fruit set without pollination.

peat/lite Peat moss and perlite soil mix.

percolation Movement of water through the soil profile.

pesticide General classification, which includes: insecticides, fungicides, antibiotics, and herbicides.

petioles Leaf stems.

pink blush stage When color first begins to show in the tomato fruit.

pistil Female portion of the flower.

plant tab A slow-release fertilizer tablet.

pollination Application of pollen to the pistil of the flower.

proprietary variety A variety developed by a commercial plant breeder. Usually offered exclusively by a single seed company or it may be licensed for sale by several.

rasping insects An insect, most notably the thrip, that rasps plant tissue then laps up the plant juices.

resistant Less likely to contract a disease but not immune.

rhizobium The genus for a group of bacteria that can fix atmospheric nitrogen in association with roots of legumes. Usually marketed as a dry powder for seed treatment or as a granular material to sprinkle in the planting row.

row cover (floating row cover, fiber row cover) A gauze or diaper liner-like material used to cover plants in the field, shielding them from wind damage, insects, and frost.

savoyed Crinkled-leaved variety.

semideterminate Tomato variety that grows 3 to 4 feet before ceasing strong terminal growth.

side dress To place fertilizer along the garden row. Typically, 1 tablespoon of ammonium sulfate (21-0-0) per 2 feet of row is required. Be careful not to get the fertilizer right up against the plant and follow up with a thorough watering.

silk The female growth tube of the corn plant.

slips Adventitious shoots from sweet potatoes used to propagate the new crop.

soil pH The hydrogen ion content of the soil—7.0 is neutral, below 7 is acid (sour), above 7 is alkaline (basic or sweet).

soil solution The water held between the soil particles.

soil-less media Soil mix made up without the use of soil. Usually peat or composted bark mixed with sand, perlite, vermiculite or calcined clay, lime and fertilizer elements. It may also contain a surfactant (soap or detergent wetting agent) to make it easier to wet.

stamen The male, pollen-bearing flower part.

starter solution A dilute, liquid fertilizer. Usually a soluble formulation (i.e., 20-20-20) used at one-third strength.

stippled Tiny, sunken necrotic (dead) areas in the leaf.

strung (stringing pods) To remove the strings along the sutures of bean or pea pods.

succession planting To plant the same crop every week to 2 weeks, ensuring a long season of harvest. Often used with beans, radishes, turnips, leaf lettuce, and other crops that have a narrow window of productivity.

suckers Rapidly growing shoots that come from the leaf axils (juncture of the leaf petiole and stem).

sunscald Fruit damage from the direct exposure to the sun's rays.

tassel The male corn floral part that produces pollen.

thinning To pull up or cut off seedling plants to achieve proper spacing.

tolerant Capable of living with a pest problem. Usually refers to insect or disease pests.

treated seed Garden seed coated with fungicide/repellent to ensure a good stand.

tuber A swollen, storage root.

unchecked growth Rapid growth without stunting caused by improper temperature or pest damage.

vector Usually an insect that can transmit a disease organism like a virus or mycoplasm.

water-absorbing gels Polymer gels that hold water but are capable of releasing it to the plant. Useful in potting soils for container gardening.

waterlogged soil Soil in which all the pore spaces are filled with water for more than a few hours after a heavy rain or irrigation. Water is usually standing.

whorl Cluster of leaves around a stem.

Appendices

VEGETABLE SEED CATALOGS

This is a partial list of firms selling seeds and plants. The inclusion of a firm does not guarantee reliability and an absence does not imply disapproval. These addresses were viable at the time this book was written; the authors are not responsible for changes of address or discontinued firms or varieties.
Note: When a seed is widely available, no specific catalog's number is given and **(WA)** appears as the seed source. ★ = Catalogs you must have.

1 **Baxter Seed Co., Inc.** Free list. 416 South Missouri Ave., Weslaco, TX 78596–6018. Source for many commercial varieties recommended by agricultural extension agents. Lots of melons and onions. Small packets not generally available.

2 **Burpee (W. Atlee) & Co.** Free catalog. 300 Park Ave., Warminster, PA 18991–0001. Lots of exclusive and proprietary varieties. Many more specialty vegetables, like Charantais melons, Purple Blush eggplant and Roly Poly squash, are offered than used to be available from this quality seed company. Useful when planning your garden. ★

3 **The Cook's Garden.** Catalog: $1.00. Box 65, Londonderry, VT 05148. Great source for gourmet varieties. Variety descriptions are appetite-inspiring and so are the recipes. ★

4 **Evergreen Y.H. Enterprises.** Free catalog. P.O. Box 17538, Anaheim, CA 92817. Good selection of Asian varieties plus cookbooks, growing manuals, and Asian sauces.

5 **Field's (Henry) Seed & Nursery Co.** Free catalog. Shenandoah, IA 51602. This old standby catalog is still going strong with good seed and service. Lots of new, interesting varieties, too.

6 **Filaree Farm.** Catalog: $2.00. Route 2, Box 162, Okanogan, WA 98840–9774. Garlic, garlic, and more garlic. Also books about garlic.

7 **Fox Hollow Herb & Heirloom Seed Co.** Catalog: $1.00. P.O. Box 148, McGrann, PA 16236. If you're searching for Brown Goose beans or Howling Mob sweet corn, you will find them in this interesting catalog. Lots of ol' timey varieties, herbs, and flowers.

8 **Gurney's Seed & Nursery Co.** Free catalog. 110 Capital St., Yankton, SD 57079. Lots of unusuals and varieties recommended for the South, such as short-day onions.

9 **Harris Seeds.** Free catalog. 60 Saginaw Dr., P.O. Box 22960, Rochester NY 14692–2960. Good historical and growing tips for most vegetables. Also features "Customer Favorite" varieties, and many commercial and even specialty selections like the Mexican herb epazote.

10 **Horticultural Enterprises.** Free illustrated list. P.O. Box 810082, Dallas, TX 75381. Interesting list of mostly Mexican and South American varieties; but mostly hot peppers with outline drawings. Some Asian peppers and miscellane-

ous seeds like chia and tomatillo.

11 **Hudson (J.L.), Seedsman.** Catalog: $1.00. P.O. Box 1058, Redwood City, CA 94064. Exhaustive catalog of many plant seeds from shrubs to vegetables. Interesting section with Mexican Zapotec vegetables and medicinals. Vegetable list includes many heirlooms like the Purple Calabash tomato.

12 **Johnny's Selected Seeds.** Free catalog. Foss Hill Rd., Albion, ME 04910–9731. Many heirloom and open-pollinated varieties as well as hybrids. European varieties are available, as well as a good selection of exotics—for example, four varieties of radicchio, mesclun mixes. This is a fun catalog with good prices and service. ★

13 **Kilgore Seed Co.** Catalog: $1.00. 1400 W. First St., Sanford, FL 32771. Full of good cultural information for gardeners in the South to extreme South. Source for varieties like Dade pole bean and others recommended for Florida and also great in other areas.

14 **Kitazawa Seed Co.** Free catalog. 1111 Chapman St., San Jose, CA 95126. This company has only a small list with a few color pictures, but the selection of mostly Asian vegetables is fascinating. For instance, they offer Sooyow (also sold as Soo Yoh, Suyo) cucumber—a favorite, non-hybrid burpless variety popular in Houston-area gardens—and two hybrid, but similar varieties—Palace and GY 200. If these are any more productive than Soo Yoh there could be a shortage of pickle jars in the South once these varieties are discovered. They also have melons and eggplants, greens, herbs, etc.

15 **Le Jardin du Gourmet.** Catalog: 50¢. West Danville, VT 05873. Specializing in French seeds, shallots, and gourmet foods. ★

16 **Native Seeds/SEARCH.** Seed list: $1.00. Quarterly newsletter and seed list: $10.00. 2509 N. Campbell Ave., #325, Tucson, AZ 85719. Lots of chiles, squashes, corn, and other Southwest/Indian varieties.

17 **Nichols Garden Nursery.** Free catalog. 1190 North Pacific Hwy., Albany, OR 97321. Great source for herbs, Asian and European vegetables.

18 **Ornamental Edibles.** Free Catalog. 3622 Weedin Ct., San Jose, CA 95132. Extensive list of exotics, many of them pretty enough to grow in the flower bed.

19 **Park Seed Co.** Free catalog. Colesbury Rd., Greenwood, SC 29647–0001. Beautiful color catalog with numerous exclusive varieties. Good service and quality. ★

20 **Peaceful Valley Farm Supply.** Catalog: $2.00. P.O. Box 2209, Grass Valley, CA 95945. Source for organic gardening supplies and organically grown, open-pollinated seeds.

21 **Pickle's Seeds.** Free list. 345 Curtis, Jasper, TX 75951. Extensive list of Southern peas and other Southern favorites.

22 **Pinetree Garden Seeds.** Free catalog. Box 300, New Gloucester, ME 04260. Many gourmet and unusual varieties. Extensive selection of books, too.

23 **Plants of the Southwest.** Catalog: $1.00. 1812 Second St., Santa Fe, NM 87501. Another good source for chiles and Southwestern plants.

24 **Porter & Son, Seedsmen.** Free catalog. P.O. Box 104, Stephenville, TX 76401–0104. No fancy color photos, just great seeds recommended for the South at a fair price. Quick to respond to new recommendations. Often the only source for small packages of commercial varieties. They also have old favorites like the Por-

ter tomato. ★ (out of business)

25 **Redwood City Seed Co.** Catalog: $1.00. P.O. Box 361, Redwood City, CA 94064. Chiles and other exotics including an extensive list of Asian vegetables.

26 **Ronniger's Seed Potatoes.** Catalog: $2.00. Star Route, Moyie Springs, ID 83845. Potatoes of every size, shape, and color. Interesting catalog if you're a tater grower. The biggest problem is getting shipments in mid–February when it is too cold to ship from Idaho. Also offer sunroots. ★

27 **Seeds Blum.** Catalog: $3.00. Idaho City Stage, Boise, ID 83706. Fascinating catalog. Worth the price just for the growing instructions, recipes, gourmet stuff, and interesting reading. Lots of heirloom and exotic varieties. ★

28 **Shepherd's Garden Seeds.** Catalog: $1.00. 30 Irene St., Torrington, CT 06790. One of the first gourmet catalogs and required reading. Features Asian and European varieties, plus recipes, wonderful illustrations, and mouth-watering descriptions of the vegetable varieties. ★

29 **Southern Exposure Seed Exchange.** Catalog: $3.00. P.O. Box 170, Earlysville, VA 22936. Many unusual and hard-to-find varieties, especially tomatoes and eggplants. We first discovered the Listada de Gandia eggplant here. It makes for great eating and looks like it was made of fine marble. ★

30 **Southern Seeds.** Catalog: $2.00. P.O. Box 2091, Melbourne, FL 32902. Features tropical varieties like the Calabaza squash, Chayote, etc.

31 **Stokes Seeds, Inc.** Free catalog. Box 548, Buffalo, NY 14240–0548. Beautiful color catalog and many of the varieties are great in Southern gardens. Laparie sweet pepper was a recent find. Also one of the few sources for greenhouse varieties of lettuce, cucumbers, and tomatoes. ★

32 **Sunrise Enterprises.** Catalog: $2.00. P.O. Box 330058, West Hartford, CT 06133–0058. Source for Asian seeds, plants, and cookbooks.

33 **Thompson & Morgan, Inc.** Free catalog. P.O. Box 1308, Jackson, NJ 08527–0308. Beautiful catalog with lots of mouth-watering photos. They don't just show you the vegetables, they often show them cooked and ready to eat. This is an English Company with a U.S. distributor, so the seed is rather expensive.

34 **Tomato Growers Supply Company.** Free catalog. P.O. Box 2237, Fort Myers, FL 33902. Lots of tomato varieties and an extensive list of sweet and hot peppers. ★

35 **Twilley (Otis S.) Seed Co., Inc.** Free catalog. P.O. Box 65, Trevose, PA 19053–0065. Many commercial and proprietary varieties. Good selection and quality. ★

36 **Vermont Bean Seed Co.** Free catalog. Garden Lane, Fair Haven, VT 05743. Beans, of course, and lots of gourmet varieties.

37 **Willhite Seed Co.** Free catalog. P.O. Box 23, Poolville, TX 76487. This catalog has always been a great source for melons but now it is also a great source for gourmet varieties. French varieties from Villmorin and Asian/Indian seeds. ★

NOTE: Seed racks are a common source of seed for gardeners, and most seed rack companies don't have a general consumer catalog. Burpee is the exception. Ferry Morse and Northrup King are the two most prominent seed rack suppliers without catalogs, and they have some great varieties. Fortunately, some of their varieties are also available from mailorder sources. If you shop for seed from these racks, have full confidence in trying their proprietary varieties.

ADDITIONAL SOURCES OF GARDENING INFORMATION

Flower & Garden, 4251 Pennsylvania, Kansas City, MO 64111, is published bi-monthly. It is a nicely done general gardening magazine, covering a wide range of topics.

Gardens and More is published 10 times a year by Neil Sperry, Gardens South, 400 W. Louisiana, McKinney, TX 75069. This is a general gardening magazine written for Texas and the Southern states.

Horticulture: The Magazine of American Gardening, 20 Park Plaza, Ste. 1220, Boston, MA 02116, is published monthly. It is an excellent magazine on general gardening.

IPM Practitioner is published by the Bio-Interial Resource Center (BIRC), P.O. Box 7414, Berkeley, CA 94707. Membership dues includes a subscription to *IPM Practitioner* and *Commonsense Pest Control Quarterly.* They concentrate on new innovations in pest control.

Mississippi Gardens is published bi-monthly by Mississippi Gardens, P.O. Box 7856, Jackson, MS 39284. This is a general gardening magazine written for Mississippi residents.

National Gardening, 180 Flynn Ave., Burlington, VT 05401, is published monthly. *National Gardening* is an excellent magazine, but, remember, it is national and does not always apply to the Southern gardener.

Organic Gardening, Box 7320, Red Oak, IN 51591–0320, is published 9 times a year. This is a general gardening magazine devoted to organic practices.

Sunset Magazine, 80 Willow Rd., Menlo Park, CA 94025, is published monthly. *Sunset Magazine* is written for the Western gardener, covering topics on gardening, travel, cooking, crafts, and more, but you'll occasionally find something of value.

Texas Gardener, 1105 Wooded Acres, Ste. 201, P.O. Box 9005, Waco, TX 76714–9005, is published bi-monthly. It is an excellent general gardening magazine for Texas and much of the Southeast.

Texas Horticulturist, P.O. Drawer CC, College Station, TX 77841, is a newsletter published monthly. It is also the mouthpiece for the Texas State Horticultural Society, Texas Fruit Growers Association, and Texas Greenhouse Growers Council.

The Herb Companion, 201 East Fourth St., Loveland, CO 80537, is published bi-monthly. It concentrates on herbs, including their cultivation, traditional and contemporary uses, cooking, and crafts. It is not written for the Southern gardener, but it still has some valuable information.

GARDENING SUPPLIES AND LOW-TOXICITY PEST CONTROL SOURCES

A.M. Leonard, Inc.
6665 Spiker Road
P.O. Box 816
Piqua, OH 45356

Arico Inc.
P.O. Box 4247–CRB
Tucson, AZ 85738

Beneficial BioSystems
P.O. Box 8461
Emeryville, CA 94662

Beneficial Insects Inc.
P.O. Box 40634
Memphis, TN 38174–0634

Gardener's Supply
128 Intervale Rd.
Burlington, VT 05401

Gardens Alive
National Gardening Research Center
Highway 48
P.O. Box 149
Sunman, IN 47041

Growing Naturally
P.O. Box 54
149 Pine Ln.
Pineville, PA 18946

Mellinger's Nursery
2310 W. Southern Range Rd.
North Lima, OH 44452

Nature's Control
P.O. Box 35
Medford, OR 97501

Necessary Trading Co.
8311 Salem Ave.
P.O. Box 305
New Castle, VA 24127

Ringer
9959 Valley View Rd.
Eden Prairie, MN 55344–3585

Safer's Inc.
189 Wells Ave.
Newton, MA 02159

This is only a partial list, but these are excellent sources to start with. There are many other good companies that carry gardening supplies and low-toxicity pest control supplies.

STATE EXTENSION HORTICULTURE OFFICES

Virtually every county or parish has an extension agent that can assist you with variety selection and specific information on vegetable gardening in your area. Listed below are the addresses for the extension horticulture departments at the various land grant universities in the Southern states.

Alabama   Extension Horticulture Department
Auburn University
Auburn, AL 36849

Arkansas
Extension Horticulture
316 Plant Science Bldg.
University of Arkansas
Fayetteville, AR 72701

Florida
Vegetable Crops Department
1243 Fifield Hall
University of Florida
Gainesville, FL 32611

Georgia
Extension Horticulture
University of Georgia
P.O. Box 1209
Tifton, GA 31793

Louisiana
Extension Horticulture
Rm 155, J.C. Miller Horticulture Bldg.
Louisiana State University
Baton Rouge, LA 70803

Mississippi
Department of Horticulture
P.O. Box 5446
Mississippi, MS 39762

North Carolina
Department of Horticultural Science
North Carolina State University
Raleigh, NC 27695–7606

Oklahoma
Department of Horticulture
  and Landscape Architecture
Oklahoma State University
Stillwater, OK 74078

South Carolina
Department of Horticulture
Clemson University
172 P&AS Bldg.
Clemson, SC 29634–0375

Tennessee
Plant & Soil Science
University of Tennessee
P.O. Box 1071
Knoxville, TN 37901–1071

Texas
Department of Horticulture
225 Horticulture/Forestry Bldg.
Texas A&M University
College Station, TX 77843

ABOUT THE AUTHORS

WILLIAM D. ADAMS has been a professional horticulturist with the Texas Agricultural Extension Service for more than twenty years. An accomplished photographer, he is the author of four gardening books and numerous articles for magazines such as *Flower and Garden* and *Family Circle*. He also writes a weekly gardening column for several Houston-area newspapers. He and his wife have four children and two grandsons and live in Houston, Texas, with their cairn terrier.

THOMAS R. LEROY has served as an agent for the Texas Agricultural Extension Service for more than eighteen years. In 1988, he was selected to direct the Harris County Extension Master Gardener Program and began conducting educational seminars on commercial nursery operation and the cultivation of fruits and vegetables. As a professional horticulturist, his main interest lies in home and small-acreage fruit production, plant propagation, and vegetable gardening. He lives in Conroe, Texas with his wife. They have two daughters, Christie and Niki, son-in-law Brent, and a beautiful new grandson, Tyler.